IDIOT'S GUIDES®
AS EASY AS IT GETS!

Making Money with Rental Properties

IDIOT'S GUIDES.

AS EASY AS IT GETS!

Making Money with Rental Properties

by Kimberly Smith and Lisa Iannucci

ALPHA

A member of Penguin Group (USA) Inc.

ALPHA BOOKS

Published by Penguin Group (USA) Inc.

Penguin Group (USA) Inc., 375 Hudson Street, New York, New York 10014, USA • Penguin Group (Canada), 90 Eglinton Avenue East, Suite 700, Toronto, Ontario M4P 2Y3, Canada (a division of Pearson Penguin Canada Inc.) • Penguin Books Ltd., 80 Strand, London WC2R 0RL, England • Penguin Ireland, 25 St. Stephen's Green, Dublin 2, Ireland (a division of Penguin Books Ltd.) • Penguin Group (Australia), 250 Camberwell Road, Camberwell, Victoria 3124, Australia (a division of Pearson Australia Group Pty. Ltd.) • Penguin Books India Pvt. Ltd., 11 Community Centre, Panchsheel Park, New Delhi—110 017, India • Penguin Group (NZ), 67 Apollo Drive, Rosedale, North Shore, Auckland 1311, New Zealand (a division of Pearson New Zealand Ltd.) • Penguin Books (South Africa) (Pty.) Ltd., 24 Sturdee Avenue, Rosebank, Johannesburg 2196, South Africa • Penguin Books Ltd., Registered Offices: 80 Strand, London WC2R 0RL, England

IDIOT'S GUIDES and Design are trademarks of Penguin Group (USA) Inc.

International Standard Book Number: 978-1-61564-431-5
Library of Congress Catalog Card Number: 2013945262

16 15 14   8 7 6 5 4 3 2 1

Interpretation of the printing code: The rightmost number of the first series of numbers is the year of the book's printing; the rightmost number of the second series of numbers is the number of the book's printing. For example, a printing code of 14-1 shows that the first printing occurred in 2014.

Printed in the United States of America

Note: This publication contains the opinions and ideas of its authors. It is intended to provide helpful and informative material on the subject matter covered. It is sold with the understanding that the authors and publisher are not engaged in rendering professional services in the book. If the reader requires personal assistance or advice, a competent professional should be consulted. The authors and publisher specifically disclaim any responsibility for any liability, loss, or risk, personal or otherwise, which is incurred as a consequence, directly or indirectly, of the use and application of any of the contents of this book.

Most Alpha books are available at special quantity discounts for bulk purchases for sales promotions, premiums, fundraising, or educational use. Special books, or book excerpts, can also be created to fit specific needs. For details, write: Special Markets, Alpha Books, 375 Hudson Street, New York, NY 10014.

Publisher: *Mike Sanders*
Executive Managing Editor: *Billy Fields*
Senior Acquisitions Editor: *Brook Farling*
Development Editorial Supervisor: *Christy Wagner*
Production Editor: *Jana M. Stefanciosa*

Cover Designer: *Laura Merriman*
Book Designer: *William Thomas*
Indexer: *Johnna VanHoose Dinse*
Layout: *Brian Massey*
Proofreader: *Krista Hansing Editorial Services, Inc.*

Contents

Appendixes

Introduction

Welcome to the world of real estate investing! How you use your rental real estate, how you manage it, how you finance it, and when you choose to sell it all play a role in how profitable your investment is.

Like everything related to money, whether in business or the general economy, the profitability of real estate goes in cycles, some logical and some illogical, such as the boom and bust we've seen over the last 10 years. The fact is, the earth's population is increasing, but the supply of land upon which to build stays the same. The principle of supply and demand says that, over time, increase in demand with a limited supply of product results in the product's increase in value.

The same is true of your rental property—over time, its value will go up. In the meantime, it's important to understand how to cash flow your property, or make your monthly income exceed your monthly expenses. That's where property management comes into play.

Rental properties can and will make you money. Personal real estate investing is even more solid today than it was a few years ago. To be successful, you, the landlord, must understand the fundamentals of property investing, recognize the basics of good and bad investment properties, and have the right guide to steer you through the property and renter cycles. You must also recognize some of the pitfalls of the many rules, regulations, and laws that could stand between you and financial success.

Idiot's Guides: Making Money with Rental Properties walks new and seasoned rental property investors alike through the twists and turns of rental ownership. In these pages, we shed light on common rental theories and concepts that affect all property owners. We explore new and emerging trends, study successful marketing tactics, and highlight current fads like the new "share economy" (where people share or rent parts of their primary residence to vacation travelers). We also define the most common terms, forms, and formulas landlords and property managers use day in and day out. Use this book as a handbook and reference guide as you get started, and refer to it again as you progress through the property and renter cycles.

Kimberly's favorite investment story is about her first rental property. It was 1995, and Kimberly and her husband, Eric, had purchased a condominium in San Francisco for $89,000. They had just graduated from college, and they'd scraped and saved until, within a few months, they had enough for the down payment on a 400-square-foot condo.

The property included a washer/dryer, kitchen, closet, and an area just big enough for a Murphy bed; the window looked out from under the onramp to the Bay Bridge; and they called the top-floor unit a "penthouse." The condo really wasn't much to talk about, but it had all the necessary features, and for an extra $60,000, they added a parking space. It turned into a fantastic rental property, and within a few years, they were renting it for $3,900 a month.

Kimberly likes to think of all her real estate investments as tools in a toolbox. Some she uses to develop cash, some she uses to fund the next property, and some she sells to accomplish larger goals.

In 2001, for example, as the events of September 11 unfolded and the world stood still, Kimberly and Eric were completing a home they had been building for the previous 15 months. Just as air traffic was frozen after the attacks, so was the real estate market. Kimberly and Eric couldn't sell their primary residence, which would have enabled them to raise the needed down payment to purchase a new home.

However, even in bad times, the least-expensive real estate in the best neighborhood always sells. Only 2 months after the tragic attacks in September, Kimberly and Eric sold their San Francisco condo for more than $400,000—a return of more than $300,000 on their initial investment of $89,000—which gave them the cash they needed to finish building their new home.

Regardless of your real estate experience, certain important fundamentals are essential for you to remember and understand. Throughout this book, we share these fundamentals, along with new and emerging rules and trends that are the cornerstones of daily real estate and rental activities.

To get you started, here are three principles to keep in mind: always treat your rental property as a business and make decisions accordingly; respect and appreciate your tenants—they're the clients and customers to your business, and without them, you won't survive; and, finally, it's your responsibility as a property owner to maintain the safety and integrity of your investment.

Throughout this book, we reinforce these concepts while also giving you the confidence you need to operate your property successfully and make money on your investment.

Note: This book represents the opinions of the authors, and even though we've carefully researched the information we share, we do not give legal advice. When in doubt, always seek professional advice, legal or otherwise, about your specific rental property.

Also, it's beyond the scope of this book to list every state and local law that might apply to real estate investing in your city or state, so take the time to check your current local regulations and laws before making important decisions.

How This Book Is Organized

We've organized the book into four parts:

Part 1, Real Estate Basics, gives you a brief overview of real estate and helps you establish your expectations, as well as understand and define what investment success means to you.

Part 2, You and Your Property, covers the other element in property management—the property. Here you learn how to find the right property, understand the best rental option for you and your property, and get the property ready to make money.

Part 3, You and Your Tenants, stresses that being a landlord is all about the process of establishing value, collecting rent, and protecting your financial investment. This part also covers the ever-expanding and complex world of finding the right tenant at the right rate to rent your investment, an often overlooked area in the property management world.

In **Part 4, The Business Side of Rentals,** we discuss the importance of treating your rental property as a business. We also look at the bigger picture of property management—the laws, rules, and rights established by the federal government and state and local governments. We also review your rights and the rights of your tenants under these guidelines.

Don't forget to check out the appendixes at the back of the book. We've included a glossary, important contact information and further resources, and rental management forms you'll find handy.

Extras

Throughout the book, we've shared tips, notes, and cautions to make the reading experience more enjoyable and informative. Here's what to look for:

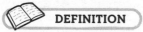 **DEFINITION**

These sidebars explain words and phrases used in property management.

$ REAL ESTATE ESSENTIAL

These sidebars share both interesting bits of info you need to know and stories from other real estate professionals so you can learn from their experience (and mistakes!).

RENTAL REMINDER

Learn what to do—and what not to do—in these sidebars.

WATCH OUT

These sidebars advise you on what to avoid and why. The more hazards you remove from your path, the more successful you will be.

Acknowledgments

Thank you to the Alpha team for believing there's still a need to understand the ins and outs of real estate investing, and for giving me the opportunity to share some of what I've learned over the years. Thanks to Lisa Iannucci for her professionalism, expertise, and attention to details that made this a great project. Thank you to Zoya for giving me my first job in real estate and showing me what you'd learned that gave me the foundation for everything since. I'd also like to thank my office team, Janine and Shawna, for holding down the fort while I typed away at my computer. A big hug to my family, Eric, Travis, and Hayden, for their support and laughs. And a special thank you to all the property owners and tenants who have been our customers over the past 20 years and who allowed me the opportunities to cultivate all the knowledge included in this book. —Kimberly

I'd like to thank Kimberly Smith, who is a tremendously intelligent expert in her field, for taking on this book and dedicating herself to completing it and making it a great resource for the readers. I'd also like to thank my agent, Marilyn Allen, for always having such faith in me. I'd also like to thank Alpha's Brook Farling and Christy Wagner for their tremendous input that makes this book even better. And finally, I'd like to thank my family for their ongoing support and love. —Lisa

Trademarks

All terms mentioned in this book that are known to be or are suspected of being trademarks or service marks have been appropriately capitalized. Alpha Books and Penguin Group (USA) Inc. cannot attest to the accuracy of this information. Use of a term in this book should not be regarded as affecting the validity of any trademark or service mark.

Real Estate Basics

Have you always wanted to own a property and have it make money for you? Do you daydream about real estate properties and being a landlord? Do you want an investment that will help you make more money? If so, you've come to the right place.

You're probably filled with lots of questions and concerns about how and where to get started—we know we had many when we first got started. You're probably also wondering about the type of property to buy, the type of landlord you should be, what income you can expect to earn, and the opportunities for future financial returns. In Part 1, we address all these issues and more. In the following chapters, we give you the knowledge to move forward and invest in real estate that's right for you.

Being a landlord can be a lot of fun. You get to meet interesting people, solve problems, develop pride of ownership, and create wealth. Let's get started by learning more about the world of real estate.

In Part 3, we take you through the steps of finding that perfect tenant by marketing, communicating with potential renters, and then closing the deal. We also cover what you need to know to keep your tenants happy and how to work with them should something go wrong.

Getting into Real Estate

People the world over dream of owning real estate. Even better, people the world over have been successfully navigating the real estate business for hundreds of years, so you don't have to reinvent the wheel if you want to invest in rental property.

Owning real estate can be a lot of fun and a great way to make money. However, like anything related to business, real estate also comes with some risks. In this chapter, you get a better idea about what's involved with owning rental property. Do you have the time to manage it? Can it really make you money? Can it contribute to your investment goals? What type of property is right for you? Armed with the answers to these questions, you can better shape your rental property goals.

In This Chapter

- A look at types of rental properties

- Choosing the right real estate for you

- Finding your property niche

Understanding Real Estate

If you're thinking of getting involved with real estate, before acquiring any piece of property, you first need to ask yourself what kind of real estate you want to buy. Maybe you've always wanted an apartment building or a timeshare. Maybe a condo or cooperative intrigues you. Maybe you want a single-family home you can fix up and rent out.

Why does this matter? Because your local laws might prohibit you from handling your rental property a certain way. If you want to buy a condo and rent it weekly, for instance, you might discover later that this arrangement is against your local regulations. As another example, it's against the law to rent out a residential property in New York City for less than 30 days, so buying a condo in this area for investment purposes might not be the best idea if you're looking to rent it on a short-term basis.

Keep in mind, too, that real estate jargon is different in different parts of the country and even different parts of the world. For example, a unit in a building on the U.S. East Coast is called an apartment, but in Europe, the same piece of property might be called a flat. So know your market, and understand the terms you're dealing with.

Types of Real Estate

Let's review the types of real estate available for you to invest in. For the purposes of this book, we focus most of our attention on investing in a single-family home versus a condo, but it's important to know what other types of real estate are available for you.

 REAL ESTATE ESSENTIAL

Real estate agents are licensed on a state-by-state basis and are called Realtors only if they're a member of the National Association of Realtors. Agents are divided into two categories: a *broker* is an agent who has at least 2 years' experience and has the overall responsibility of the office; a *sales agent* is licensed with the state but must hang his or her license with an official broker. It's becoming popular for states to regulate mortgage brokers. In California, for example, mortgage brokers are required to be licensed real estate agents.

Apartment   An apartment is a residential unit located in a larger building. A tenant leases an apartment from a landlord for a specific period, often a year at a time. Individual apartments cannot be bought and sold, but the larger building where the apartments are housed can be bought and sold.

Apartment/multiunit building   An apartment building is a larger structure made of several apartments. The building is owned as an entire complex. Individual units are not independently owned, as in a condominium building.

Owning an apartment building offers the potential for higher cash flow and means you're spreading your income over multiple tenants. However, it also means you're responsible for maintaining the entire building's interior and exterior, including the common areas and each individual unit.

Buying an apartment building is a little more complicated than buying an individual unit, so you need to know a bit more than the basics. For example, buying a building with up to three units is similar to buying and financing an individual condominium or single-family home. However, buying a multiunit apartment building with four or more units is more like getting a business loan and requires much larger upfront fees than typical residential mortgages. The good news is, once an apartment building has been properly financed, any new owners can take over the mortgage.

Condominium   A condominium, or condo for short, is a residential building with multiple units in which each unit is individually owned. Each owner has exclusive right to his or her own unit and has a "common" interest in the common areas. Condo can also refer to a single unit within a condominium building.

Flat   A flat is a condominium that's generally an older, single residential property that's been subdivided into condominium units with one unit per floor. This term is more often used in European countries.

Tenants in common (TIC)   A building with multiple units and multiple owners. Each owner has an undivided interest in the whole property.

WATCH OUT

Don't invest in any TIC without first learning more about the unusual rules connected to TICs. For example, you can sell your interest in the TIC, but you can't will or bequeath the property to your heirs. Ask your real estate agent to obtain the building's specific rules, and have a real estate attorney review them before you purchase.

Cooperative ownership (co-op)   In this situation, you buy shares in the corporation (partnership or trust), but you do not specifically own your own apartment unit. Basically, you're a stockholder in the building. Co-ops generally limit how you can rent your property and may not produce the highest financial returns.

Duplex/triplex A residential property under one ownership that may contain two or three units. Each unit has its own outside entrance. Also known as an attached single-family dwelling.

Townhouse Also referred to as a row house, a townhouse is a hybrid of a single-family home and a condominium. These individually owned residential properties are connected by a common wall, and the owner owns both the structure and the land beneath the structure and generally part of the common areas, like sidewalks, open spaces, and recreational facilities.

House/single-family residence A self-standing residential property under single ownership, designed to be inhabited by one family.

Timeshare/partial ownership In this newer form of communal ownership, you buy the right to use a property for a fixed amount of time, with expenses prorated based on ownership percentage. This type of ownership is often seen in resort areas and is designed more as a hotel alternative rather than investment real estate.

Unfurnished Rentals

When you think about rental properties, you might automatically think of 12-month unfurnished rentals. For a long time, this was your only option when it came to investing in real estate.

Unfurnished rentals are houses, apartments, and other types of residential property that come without any furniture and utilize a legal lease, typically for 12 months. Rent is typically paid at the first of the month, with one month's rent collected as a security deposit. Sometimes the last month's rent is also collected in advance. Some utilities, such as water and garbage collection, may be included in the rent, but other expenses such as electricity and cable are generally not included.

Continuity and consistency are two benefits of investing in unfurnished rentals. You know what your monthly expenses are, you get paid on a specific day of the month, and you know exactly how much income you'll receive, assuming there are no unexpected maintenance issues or bad tenants. We think of these types of rentals as "blue chip" stocks, or a good standard investment that will have consistent returns in both a good and bad economy over time.

Corporate Monthly Rentals

Another kind of rental you can own is a corporate monthly rental. You lease this residential property to a tenant for a minimum of 30 days on a month-to-month lease. The rental is completely furnished with housewares, a fully equipped kitchen, and electronics. Most utilities, including cable and internet, are included in the monthly rate.

Corporate housing was originally used by corporate travelers, hence the name. But today, corporate monthly rentals also have become lodging options for all travelers and even displaced homeowners.

Traditionally serviced corporate housing properties are a multibillion-dollar industry in the United States, according to statistics released by the Corporate Housing Providers Association, and they're growing as an investment opportunity for owners of private residences. We refer to corporate housing rentals as "technology" stocks; they have some ups and downs on consistent revenue returns, but they give you, the investor, an opportunity for higher returns.

Vacation Rentals

Vacation rentals are residential properties in resort areas leased for less than 30 days to vacationing individuals and families. According to statistics released by HomeAway (homeaway.com), the world's largest marketplace for vacation rentals, the vacation rental industry is made of more than 3.3 million individual rental properties and generates more than $85 billion in annual rental income.

Vacation rentals are rented on either a nightly or weekly basis, with some repeat clients. Many properties are also seasonal. For example, Lake George, New York, enjoys its most popular season during the summer, when rental requests are high. The rest of the year, however, rentals are much slower but not nonexistent. Other vacation rentals, such as in Hawaii, enjoy a consistent rental season year-round.

Vacations rentals can be very lucrative for you, but know that they require a lot of your personal time investment to find regular, weekly tenants. When one renter leaves, you must find the time to prepare and *flip* the property. Be sure you research the seasonality of your vacation rental market before you buy an investment property. Determine the length of the vacation season in that market as well. Renters might want a vacation spot for only a few months out of the year.

 DEFINITION

There are two kinds of **flip** in real estate. When purchasing a property, *flip* means to buy, fix up, and sell a property for a profit within a short period of time. In reference to rentals, *flip* means to clean, inspect, and prepare the property for the next tenant's arrival.

A vacation rental may sound perfect, and the rental rates are high, but if the actual high-demand season is only 2 months long, you might not be getting the annual return you were looking for from your investment.

Remember, too, that private residences rented less than 30 days are subject to lodging tax and may be prohibited or restricted by the city or your community's homeowner's association.

Student Housing

One of the best ways to achieve rental property success is to find a niche rental market with consistent demand and provide and manage rentals in those markets that produce higher returns than just a traditional unfurnished rental condo.

Student housing is one of those niche rental markets. It's not for everyone, but it can be an interesting investment opportunity. If you have the patience to deal with students, you may find a great income opportunity in this area.

Generally, you'll work with two groups of students, graduate students who have a normal rental budget, and undergraduates on tighter budgets who typically house-hunt in groups, looking to split the costs among three to eight people. Although each individual might have a smaller budget than, say, a professional couple or family, house-sharers have a buying power that should not be ignored. A property that might be out of the range of a single renter could be in high demand if marketed to a group of renters instead.

If you're considering investing in student housing, take time to visit the housing offices on local college or university campuses and ask what's currently available, what the students are looking for, and if there's an easy way to connect with students looking for housing.

Decisions, Decisions

Now that you know the different types of real estate properties available to you as an investor, what's best for you and what makes a better rental? Is it best to purchase a single-family home or a condo? Should you opt for an apartment building or a cooperative?

There are many factors to take into consideration when deciding on the right type of investment property for you. In the following sections, we discuss some things you should keep in mind while determining what property is best for you.

How Much Time Do You Have for Upkeep?

How much time do you have to take care of your rental property? Some types of property take more time and upkeep than others. For example, single-family homes, especially if they're older properties, take more time to manage and require a more active, hands-on landlord than a condo might. Single-family homes typically require regular yard maintenance, exterior painting, roof repairs, and more.

On the other hand, if you own an individual condominium, you're required to maintain only the unit's interior. Generally, the *homeowner's association (HOA)* maintains the upkeep of the exterior and the common areas. As the unit owner, you pay monthly fees to the HOA, the association creates a financial reserve from these fees, and then it uses that money to manage major exterior updates or repairs, such as a new roof, when necessary. For investors with little time, a single condo can be a great, worry-free way to go.

> **DEFINITION**
>
> A **homeowner's association (HOA)** is a regulatory body established to govern a building or community. HOAs are generally run by a professional management company and governed by an elected group of homeowners.

What Are You Willing to Pay Out Each Month?

Another factor to consider is what costs you're willing to pay each month.

Single-family homes come with monthly costs like trash removal, heating and water bills, and lawn mowing fees. Some of these costs, such as heat and water, may fluctuate depending on the season and the occupancy of your property. Depending on whether your home is vacant, has one tenant, or has multiple tenants, your monthly costs will vary.

If you own a condo, you pay a monthly assessment, regardless of whether someone is living in the unit. However, most condos include the costs of heat, exterior maintenance, trash, building insurance, and water in the fixed monthly fees.

What Are Your Investment Goals?

Is your goal to build equity in your rental property? Create a positive monthly cash flow? Create a large tax deduction? Have a property you can use from time to time when you want to get out of town? Or rent it until the real estate market gets better when you can sell it at a profit?

Be sure you're clear on your real estate goals, particularly what you expect to get out of the property and why. For example, if reselling your property for a profit is your goal, you need to remember that resale value depends on the property's location, among other things. Typically, single-family homes are easier to resell and hold their value over the long term. However, a condo building with 500 units may have 10 or more units for sale at any given time, making it difficult to sell your particular unit at a competitive price. Co-ops generally limit who you can sell your property to and may not produce the financial returns you're looking for.

You might be getting the picture that you have a lot of choices when it comes to investing in real estate and how to pay for it. Understand these options and decide what's best for your financial goals, what's best for the amount of time you're willing and able to invest in the project, and what's best for your property.

Think of it like this: what's the best and highest use for your property? What will give you the best annual return and preserve your equity in the property? Sometimes the best choice is a combination of both.

Sure, you can always rent your residential property for 12 months or longer—unless, of course, your property is in a community that mandates renters. In high-vacation-demand areas like Naples, Florida, or Paris, France, for example, homeowner's associations have become stricter and sometimes limit rentals to one tenant per year with a minimum 3-month rental. What's more, some cities and states regulate the taxation of rentals more than 30 days but less than 12 months, so you need to understand whether you need to collect and submit tax on your property. This is something very easy to research prior to buying.

 REAL ESTATE ESSENTIAL

Before you buy a property, research the builder. Sometimes Kimberly's best investments have been the ones she turned down. Early in her career, she purchased some great condos. One day, she walked into a sales office selling under-construction high-end condos. Excited about the property, she assumed building permits and city checks were enough to build a great building. A few weeks before closing, however, she finally got to walk around the condo and was not impressed. The building had numerous structural issues. Had she researched the developer beforehand, she would have learned his previous developments were in court for faulty construction. Kimberly is still glad she decided not to buy the property.

Success Story

Adriane—an Arlington, Virginia, resident—took her first foray into corporate housing when she and her children accompanied her husband, a military officer, on his tour of duty. It was during this overseas assignment that she gained the valuable knowledge about temporary housing that would serve her well in the coming years as a real estate investor.

Upon returning to the United States, Adriane and her husband purchased their first income property. Soon afterward, they rented the property, and the income they collected as rent immediately began off-setting their expenses. Hoping to continue the trend, the couple expanded their real estate investment portfolio by acquiring a second investment property.

However, with changing market conditions, the couple wasn't recouping their expenses. One property had a viable tenant, but the second sat idle for several months with no solid rental prospects.

"What started out as a real estate investment had gradually become a financial drag resulting from a lack of qualified leads in a tenuous housing market," said Adriane.

Recalling her overseas housing experience, Adriane began researching the need for similar housing in her area. After consulting with numerous real estate experts, she decided to convert her investment into a corporate housing rental in hopes of attracting and increasing the pool of quality renters. Further research led Adriane to Eric Smith, founder of CorporateHousingbyOwner.com (and co-author Kimberly's husband).

"I really came to rely on Eric's professional judgment. He not only walked me through every step of making the transition, but also he helped me do so effectively and efficiently," recalled Adriane.

This decision proved to be the turning point in a cycle of negative cash flow. After applying a fresh coat of paint and installing new carpet in their rental home, Adriane was able to create an environment worthy of their targeted audience by installing contemporary fixtures, high-end furnishings, modern housewares, and luxury linens. As a result, the couple secured their first tenant within 3 days of listing their fully furnished property with CorporateHousingbyOwner.com.

"Furnishing our unit enabled us to share our vision of what this home would look and feel like, making it easy for potential clients to see themselves moving in and living here," Adriane said.

Her first tenant not only referred her to the next qualified renter, but is now a repeat customer. Adriane said, "CorporateHousingbyOwner.com has made a believer out of us, and we plan to list other properties with the company to realize our goal of earning passive residual income on real estate."

That said, the couple realizes corporate housing remains a constant learning process. "We are learning as we go," Adriane said. "We continually reassess our expenses and adjust our rates accordingly so we remain competitive in order to attract quality renters. Yes, it's a learning process, but one we're excited to be a part of!"

The Least You Need to Know

- Before you delve into investment real estate, determine what your financial goals are.
- Think about and research what option is best for you before you decide what type of property to invest in.
- Purchase a property based on the amount of money you have to invest and the time you have to care for the property.
- Ask lots of questions. You can never have too much information when it comes to real estate.

CHAPTER 7

Ownership Structures and Financing

Throughout this book, we emphasize that successful real estate investment is about buying the right property and knowing what's right for you, as the property owner. In Chapter 1, we talked about property choices. In this chapter, we show you what you, the investor, need to know to be connected to your real estate investment. This is one of the most important chapters because it focuses on protecting you, your identity, and your cash flow.

Types of Ownership

Once you know what type of property you want to invest in, it's important to be sure you protect yourself legally. You can help protect yourself and your investment by considering how you plan on owning your rental property.

Unfortunately, lawsuits are a way of life these days. Sometimes bad things happen to good people, and sometimes renters think they can get rich quick at your expense. It's impossible to guarantee nothing bad will ever happen in or on your rental property. A lightbulb could burn out over the basement stairs, and your tenant could trip and fall in the dark. As the owner of the property, you could be held responsible for this.

Owning an investment property is the same as owning a business, and you should treat it with the same respect. You're taking a financial risk when you purchase rental property, so you want to ensure that you're protected from any kind of liability, your privacy is protected from identity theft, and you're doing what you need to do to avoid unnecessary taxes in the future.

Your risks vary depending on the structure, the state, and even the country in which you own. As a new investor, it's important to take the time to learn about both your ownership options and your risks. By setting up an ownership structure around your investment property, you can significantly reduce your liability and, most important, protect your wealth. Purchasing a property is a very important decision, so consult with a licensed attorney or financial planner who specializes in investment properties before making a final decision.

> **REAL ESTATE ESSENTIAL**
>
> When you buy real estate, you purchase the physical structure, the land or space, and everything permanently affixed to that space. You also purchase the "elements of ownership," or the nature, extent, amount, and quality of rights you can possess in connection to the property. The elements of ownership equates to what you can do with the property. When you own something, you have the right to control, possess, enjoy, and dispose of the property as you like, in accordance with the laws governing the property.

In the following sections, we outline some general types of ownership structures you might be interested in.

Sole Proprietorship

A sole proprietorship means just you. If you want to purchase investment real estate under the protective umbrella of a business entity, a sole proprietorship is simple and straightforward and the easiest type of business to start. No forms are required to set up a sole proprietorship, but you might need to register or get a business license to lawfully operate in your state.

For individual investment owners like you, business or real estate licenses are not yet required to own or manage your own rental properties, but getting these licenses anyway can provide a level of protection against potential liabilities.

As an individual owner, or person in charge, you are fully responsible and personally liable for the property. As a result, all your personal assets could be attacked if a renter filed a lawsuit. The good news, however, is that you need to complete only one tax return, and sole proprietorship is easier and involves less paperwork than other types of ownership.

Unlike with a limited liability company (LLC) or a corporation (more on these in a bit), you generally don't have to file any special forms or pay any fees to establish yourself as a sole proprietor. All you have to do is indicate that your business is a sole proprietorship when you complete the general registration requirements that apply to all new businesses.

Most cities and many counties do require businesses—even tiny home-based sole proprietorships—to register and pay at least a minimum tax once they're created. In return, your business receives a business license or tax registration certificate. You may also have to obtain an employer identification number (EIN) from the U.S. Internal Revenue Service (IRS) if you have employees, a seller's license from your state, and a zoning permit from your local planning board.

Start by choosing a name for your business. If you don't choose a name, the company name will default to the name of the person who owns the company. If you're using any name other than yours, you need to register that name with the state. This name, or the name under which you will be doing business, is referred to as "doing business as" (DBA).

Once you have a name, visit the websites for the Internal Revenue Service (irs.gov) and the Small Business Association (sba.gov). These sites have the information and forms you need, all available for free.

Technically, setting up a sole proprietorship requires no paperwork, but once you start doing business, you'll need an employer identification number (EIN) or federal tax identification number for your business—think of it as your business's Social Security number. You can find all the information you need about setting up an EIN at the IRS website.

The IRS has an entire section devoted to sole proprietorships and provides you with any and all other forms you might need during the operation of your business. The SBA is more instructional on your business entity and links you to the necessary state and federal sites, if needed.

Partnership

Pretty straightforward, a partnership results when you buy property with someone else or a group of other investors. The Uniform Partnership Act defines a partnership as "an association of two or more persons to carry on as co-owners of a business for profit."

You and your partner(s) determine in advance what percentage each of you owns. Generally, this percentage is a reflection of how much upfront money you brought to the deal.

With a partnership, you share the good times as well as the bad times. You also share responsibility if a lawsuit is brought against the partnership, usually the same percentage as what you own.

WATCH OUT

Partnerships can go bad, so don't just buy into a property with the guy who sits next to you at work if you don't him know well. You should have a full understanding of the credit history and legal history of potential partners. You don't want to be left holding the bag if your partnership turns bad.

Corporation ("C" Corp)

This type of ownership gives you the best protection from liability but takes a lot more work to set up and manage. In the eyes of the IRS, you and your corporation are totally different entities. That means you need to complete two tax returns at tax time. Also, you'll have your Social Security number, and the corporation will have its own tax identification number (TIN).

By setting up a corporation, or incorporating, you may be able to obtain more long-term financing options, so it's important to evaluate this option closely. Generally, beginning investors prefer the more simple forms of business ownership.

Limited Liability Company

The limited liability company (LLC) is a combination of a partnership and a corporation and is a very popular way to own real estate.

The LLC offers both liability and tax advantages. You can file one tax return between both you and the LLC, just like in the basic partnership.

And if you set up separate bank accounts for your personal accounts and the LLC, you reduce your financial responsibility if things go wrong. For example, if a tenant sues the property, only the property's assets can be tapped in a judgment.

Keep in mind, however, that LLC rules require the use of an attorney in all legal matters, including tenant evictions.

Individual Retirement Account

A new and emerging investment trend is to buy real estate under the tax umbrella of an individual retirement account (IRA). Traditionally, real estate investors have been able to defer certain taxes under the tax shelter of a "1031 exchange." With this, you can sell one investment property and roll the proceeds, under certain legal guidelines, into one, two, or three new similar properties. This allows you to avoid paying capital gain taxes.

Today another tax-deferred option is available for real estate investors. In an IRA ownership, you can sell your stocks and bonds and move the cash into a managed account without causing a tax event to occur. You can use funds from that account to buy an investment property and place it in a management program. You can't manage your own property under this tax shelter. You also may be required to put a 50 percent down payment on the property.

Rental income from this property is deposited directly into the IRA-managed account and grows tax deferred. To learn more about this type of investment ownership, find a self-directed IRA manager and start asking questions.

Trusts

The two main reasons to own real estate in a trust is to protect your identity from identity theft and to facilitate ease of transfer in the case of your death. Setting up a trust is relatively easy, but it should be done as part of your financial and estate planning process and not as a side transaction.

In many states, public ownership records are available online. Anyone can search a specific address and learn who you are and what your primary address is. If you own the real estate in a trust, only the trust information is displayed, and your identity is protected.

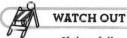

WATCH OUT

If they fall into the wrong hands, your Social Security number, bank account number, credit card number, and other valuable identifying data can be used to run up vast debts. Some unscrupulous identity thieves even commit crimes while using their victims' names. It's essential to protect yourself and your personal information.

Making Sense of Mortgages

A mortgage is a loan that helps you pay for your real estate. What type of mortgage you choose depends on several factors.

What are your investment goals from Chapter 1? For example, when Kimberly started investing in real estate, her first goal was ownership. She thought to herself, *How can I acquire the most number of properties utilizing the bank's money?* So she did her best to keep her capital investment, or the money out of her pocket, as low as possible.

As she matured as an investor, she looked at her investments differently and took new approaches to financing. For example, in one case, she took a shorter-term mortgage to reduce her profit and taxes now. This enabled her to own the property debt free in 15 years, which meant she could utilize the income to pay for her children's college education.

Also think about how long you plan on owning the property. Standard loans on residential properties are 15, 20, or 30 years.

If you plan on owing the property for more than 10 years, you should get a fixed-rate mortgage to reduce financial liabilities in unforeseeable future economic environments. With fixed-rate loans, the interest rate remains the same across the duration of the loan. It doesn't increase, but it doesn't decrease, either. Most people choose this straightforward option on their primary residence.

Also be sure you won't incur any penalties if you pay off your loan earlier or get your loan refinanced.

RENTAL REMINDER

Even if you get a 30-year fixed-rate mortgage, you can voluntarily increase your principal payments to significantly reduce the interest you pay over the life of the loan. You don't have to do this all the time. You can pay just the basic rates when you have other expenses to cover, like a new roof.

If your goal is to sell the property sometime in the near future and use the cash to send your kids to college or take that much-dreamed-about trip around the world, you need to plan ahead to ensure that your investment helps make that goal a reality.

In addition to helping you achieve your financial goals, choosing the right mortgage can help you build equity in your real estate property. The value of the property will increase over time, and as you pay down your mortgage, or the money you owe on the property, you'll receive more money when you ultimately sell the property.

If, because of the location of the property or the current real estate market, you don't expect to see a large increase in the property value, you need to set up a mortgage that you can pay down so you can gain equity somehow. In this scenario, you wouldn't get an interest-only loan.

An interest-only loan is a mortgage loan upon which you pay only the interest on the loan with no principal payments for a fixed period, typically 5 to 7 years. After that period, you have some options. You can refinance the mortgage, pay the remaining balance in a lump sum, or start paying off the principal, in which case the payments will rise. Interest-only loans are a popular option if you want your monthly payments to be as low as possible. But watch out if your goal is to grow equity in your investment. Fifteen years from now, you may discover you owe just as much as you did on day one.

Another mortgage option is an adjustable-rate mortgage (ARM). In this case, the rate starts low and goes high. Most ARMs have an initial fixed-rate period during which your rate doesn't change, followed by a much longer period during which the rate changes at preset intervals.

ARMs differ from fixed-rate mortgages in that, after the initial period, the interest rate and monthly payment move up and down as market interest rates fluctuate. This can be helpful if you need more cash flow in the beginning to make improvements on the property. But watch out. You never know what the future interest rates can end up being. Think interest rates are low and worried they might go up, but you're not really paying attention? That happened in the 1980s, when 30-year-fixed mortgage rates flirted with an 18 percent interest rate.

> **RENTAL REMINDER**
>
> Do you know your credit score? Run a free credit report on yourself today. As a result of federal regulation, the big three credit bureaus—Equifax, Experian, and TransUnion—give you a free credit report once a year. If you find something on your credit report that shouldn't be there, stop, investigate it immediately, and clean up your report. The better your credit report, the better the terms you can get on a mortgage. This could save you thousands of dollars in interest over the life of your mortgage.

More Mortgage Matters

Here are a few other things you need to know about mortgages:

If the conditions are right, the Federal Housing Authority (FHA), part of the U.S. Department of Housing and Urban Development (HUD), can insure your loan so you can get a better deal. This means you typically have a lower interest rate, lower closing costs, and a lower down payment. Plus, you should have an easier time qualifying for the loan. Both you and the property need to meet criteria established by the FHA, however. Learn more at hud.gov.

Annual percentage rates (APRs) enable you to better compare one mortgage to another. The APR is a percentage that compares the fees you pay to the total amount of money you financed. How to calculate an APR is regulated by the federal Truth in Lending Act. Numerous apps and online calculators are available that calculate APR, including one at the U.S. Department of the Treasury's Office of the Comptroller of the Currency's site, occ.gov.

As you investigate and compare mortgages, you might come across points. Points are percentage points that enable you to adjust your mortgage interest rate lower. You pay your points at closing, and the amount is based on your loan amount; 1 point = 1 percent of the loan amount.

When comparing two loan options, be sure you review both their APRs and the points needed to reach that APR. If you plan to have the same loan for a long time, reducing the APR in the beginning can make financial sense. If you don't plan to keep the property or the mortgage for several years, you have less reason to invest the cash up front to reduce the APR.

The down payment, or earnest money, is the amount of cash you need to bring to closing. Think of it as the amount you're investing in the property. On an investment property, most banks generally require at least a 20 percent down payment. So if the condo costs $100,000, you'll be expected to invest $20,000 out of your pocket into the purchase of the property.

Questions to Ask Before You Borrow

Before you sign on the dotted line for any mortgage, be sure you have all your numbers up front. Here are some questions you should ask to be sure you have everything you need to know:

- How much will the monthly payments be?

- How much cash will I need at closing?

- What is my interest rate?

- What happens if my interest rate changes?

- Over the term of the loan, how much interest will I pay?

- Are there any fees at the end of the loan?

- Are there any fees or penalties for paying off the loan early?

- Is the loan transferable to another owner?

You can approach a mortgage in hundreds of different ways, and we can't cover all the mortgage possibilities available to you in these pages. Our goal here is to get you thinking about your mortgage choices and encourage you to research different banks and brokers. All have different philosophies on the best solution for any property.

The Least You Need to Know

- Before you purchase any real estate, research your options to determine what type of ownership is best for you.

- Visit IRS and SBA to easily access the registration and tax forms you need to complete.

- Just like finding the right property, you need to find the right mortgage. A variety of mortgages are available to choose from, so find one that fits your needs and helps you to meet your financial goals.

CHAPTER 3

What to Look for in a Rental Property

Buying a home to live in is one thing, but buying investment real estate you plan to own, manage, rent, and hope to reap income from is a different process. For example, when you buy a home for yourself, you're probably not thinking about the property's price per square foot because you're not renting it out and setting a rental rate based on that number. But you do need to think about this before buying an investment property.

In this chapter, we explain how to calculate the price per square foot, understand a good deal and a not-so-good deal, and consider several other important points when evaluating potential rental real estate.

In This Chapter

- It really is all about location
- Calculating costs, taxes, and more
- Looking around the neighborhood

Location, Location, Location

You've probably heard the adage that real estate is all about "location, location, location," and it's true. When debating whether to invest in a rental property, you can't just look *inside* the walls of a property. You have to look outside, too, into the community and neighborhood. The right location can single-handedly ensure that your property is or is not rented.

To gain a potential edge over other rental properties, look for homes in urban areas, near train stations and airports, and close to universities and hospitals. Typically, these locations rent well and have the best resale value.

Before purchasing, be sure to take some time to gauge the changing look of the neighborhood you're interested in. Is it an older neighborhood that has held up over the years, or does it need a revitalization to become popular again?

RENTAL REMINDER

> When you're looking at neighborhoods, keep an eye out for new construction. If many properties are under construction in the area, it means the area is growing. It might also mean the market may become saturated and rental and resale rates will drop.

Also be sure your property is close to great schools. Parents want the best for their children, and quality education in a safe school is always a priority. Learn about the local school district. What alternative, charter, or private schools are available? What's the reputation of each school? That's a big factor with new residents, regardless of whether they're renting or buying.

If you're not sure how to evaluate a location, start by creating a spreadsheet to track properties and trends. Before Kimberly invests in a new property, she creates a list of furnished and unfurnished rental rates and for-sale prices per neighborhood and per building. Then she notes how long it takes to rent or sell specific properties.

Say you discover that two similar properties are for rent in the same building. One is listed at $2,000 per month, and the other is $1,500 per month. Watch both properties closely. If the $1,500 property disappears from the ads, but the $2,000-per-month property is still for rent some time later, that's a clue that $2,000 per month might be too much to ask in that neighborhood and $1,500 per month is probably too low. Based on this, if you were to purchase a similar property in that neighborhood, you should start out listing it for rent at $1,750 per month.

Also, this might sound odd, but you should take note of daily rates at local extended-stay hotels and standard hotels. (These are frequently published and easy to find.) Are the rates going up or down? By tracking these rates, you can better understand local trends.

You also can create a formula to compare nightly rates to monthly rates and to convert a nightly rate to a monthly rate. Say the only extended stay in the area successfully rents for $69 a night, including cable and a free breakfast, or $2,070 per month. Your plan is to buy a new high-end loft and rent it for $3,000 a month. No matter how cool your loft is, you'll probably find there's no demand for a loft in that neighborhood at that price. Your goal shouldn't be to buy in only trendy neighborhoods; you also need to understand which neighborhoods can really turn a profit for you.

To track for-sale and rental statistics, start by asking a real estate agent or check such websites as Zillow (zillow.com) and Trulia (trulia.com) for aggregated sales data. Keep in mind that sites like these are rarely 100 percent on point for accurate data. However, they do offer a great starting point for information and allow you to see a spectrum of information in one spot.

Finding for-rent statistics and vacancy rates might be a little harder, but you can try local real estate agents and the local *Multiple Listing Service.* If any local universities offer degrees in real estate, check with them for local statistical reports. Also check with your local Board of Realtors, Office of Economic Development, or state office. Ask for any information available tracking local real estate trends.

> **DEFINITION**
>
> **Multiple Listing Service (MLS)** is a real estate database. Traditionally, such a system was available only to real estate agents, but today they're open to the public via the internet. The systems, however, vary from one area to another. In some, rental properties are included, while others might list only for-sale properties.

What's the Price per Square Foot?

When you find a property you think will make a great investment and yield a great payoff, you need to evaluate the property's price per square foot. Here's the formula for calculating this number:

> Price per square foot = Asking price ÷ Total square footage

Actually, the better way to think of it is the price per *bedroom*. Keep this in mind especially if you're interested in purchasing a single-family home or condominium. Great investments are usually the ones with the most bedrooms and the least amount of common space to take care of. More space, such as bonus or family rooms, are great perks for a home you're going to live in, but it's just added liability for a home you plan to rent. Your goal should be to purchase the property with the smallest square footage and the most number of bedrooms.

Everything being equal, a 1,000-square-foot two-bedroom condo should rent for approximately the same price as a 1,700-square-foot two-bedroom condo if they're in the same building and have the same features. However, if the larger property needs a new carpet because of wear and tear, for example, that's an expense you must pay for and figure into your calculations. In this case, carpet for the larger condo will cost you almost twice as much as carpet for the smaller property.

What's the Price per Unit?

If you're interested in investing in a multiunit building, evaluate the price per unit. Here's the formula:

Price per unit = Asking price ÷ Number of units

Let's say you're interested in two buildings. One has ten one-bedroom units, and the other has five two-bedroom units. Which has the highest income potential?

If both properties were selling for the same price of $1,000,000, the price per unit on the 10-unit building would be $100,000, and the price per unit on the five-unit building would be $200,000.

Now let's look at rent potential. For the buildings to have the same rent potential, the same ratio would need to be applied. For example, the one-bedroom units would rent for $1,000 per month, and the two-bedroom units would rent for $2,000 per month. In this scenario, both rentals have the same rental potential.

But let's look at vacancy liability. If in the one-bedroom building you had a total vacancy of 1 month, your loss of income would be $1,000; in the two-bedroom building, your loss would be $2,000.

When evaluating properties, numbers are important, but don't let them be the only determining factors in your investment choice. Remember that supply and demand, as well as other market factors, play a major role in your ability to achieve the highest return from your investment.

Let's look at another example. Say you're looking at one property with six one-bedroom units that rent for $1,000 a month, and another property with three two-bedroom units that rent for $2,000 a month. Both properties produce $6,000 a month in gross rent. Which is the better option? Everything being equal, we'd buy the property with six one-bedroom units. If you have one vacancy in the one-bedroom-unit building, you're looking at missing out on only $\frac{1}{6}$ of your total rent, not $\frac{1}{3}$, until you can get it occupied.

 WATCH OUT

If you're purchasing a condo as a rental property, avoid a first-floor unit. Renters might not feel as safe in a first-floor unit, which can negatively affect your rental success. Also, some first-floor tenants use their rental to advertise a business they're conducting in the unit, which is against the rules of the homeowner's association.

Also don't forget to look at the entire market for your area so you can understand the supply and demand situation. If your area has a total of 100 one-bedroom units available among all the buildings but has only 20 two-bedroom units, the demand for the two-bedroom units might be higher. Think about investing in a two-bedroom.

However, if you still want to buy a one-bedroom unit, consider this: 99 other one-bedroom units in the area are competing with your rental, so you need to determine how you're going to persuade someone to rent your property. You may need to invest in more upgrades or special features, or offer perks such as a free second parking space or extra storage.

By knowing your price per unit, you'll be able to determine which building is the best one to invest in and where to go from there.

How Much Are the Property Taxes?

Understanding the local property taxes of the building you're interested in is a must! Do not be fooled by a low sales price only to discover later that the actual cost of owning that property is significantly higher than you expected because of the property taxes.

WATCH OUT

Property taxes vary significantly by state. In fact, some states, like Texas, have no income tax and collect a lot of their revenue from property taxes.

High property taxes might make it difficult for you to earn a profit and still have cash on hand to keep up with maintenance expenses. On the other hand, lower taxes could mean less support for local schools and parks (local property taxes vary from state to state and county to county and affect local neighborhoods in various ways) and make the area less desirable to renters.

How's Area Employment?

The lack of employment opportunities can affect a real estate market. Look at Detroit, Michigan. In this city built on automotive jobs, the real estate market collapsed when the auto factories shut down. In its darkest days, the city tore down vacant homes and left empty lots instead, which it saw as an improvement over empty houses.

Before you purchase a property, research the job and industry opportunities in the area. Jobs mean employment, which means wages, which means renters. The better economic future for the area, the greater the demand for your property, the higher the return on your investment.

What About Crime?

For better or worse, crime statistics are available for most neighborhoods. Ask your local real estate agent where to find this information, or visit the local police department and ask for any reports or records on your neighborhood. Some areas even provide crime-mapping statistics.

The Douglas County Sheriff's Office in Omaha, Nebraska, has a website dedicated to the crime mapping in the area (omahasheriff.org/crimes-and-prevention/crime-map). If you look at the statistics, you'll see the breakdown of crimes occurring in that area. Each color represents a different type of crime.

Look at the types of crimes occurring in the area where you're considering buying a rental property. Is there a problem with teens and crime? Vandalism? Drug dealers? Has crime activity increased or decreased over the last 10 years? Look at the historical data, and evaluate the trends.

Consider Future Development

Don't just look at where the neighborhood has been; look at where it's going, too. What does the future of the neighborhood look like? Is redevelopment or revitalization happening?

 REAL ESTATE ESSENTIAL

> Investing in a neighborhood at the beginning of a redevelopment project or revitalization effort can have huge payouts. But keep in mind, as mentioned earlier, it also could backfire if too much new construction takes place in the area.

Housing starts are a sign of increased demand and investment into the area. Rehab of older buildings is also a good sign. Revitalization efforts are more political and strategic, which generally results in improved living conditions and higher rents. These specifically designated zones of both residential and business areas have been identified for community development and may have tax or other financial incentives available.

After years of suburban sprawl, the need for access to public transportation is making a comeback and having a positive impact on rental rates. Take a tip from developers who are flocking to new transportation-oriented developments and determine whether your investment property can connect easily to these arteries or see if there's potential for new routes or rail lines in the area. Tenants and investors want more options these days, and they'll pay for them in certain cases.

Any Amenities?

Last, let's not forget about parks and other fun stuff. When people are looking to move to a particular area, they're often attracted to more than the number of bedrooms and bathrooms a property offers. Potential renters also want to know what there is to do nearby a property they're considering renting. They want plenty of parks and recreational activities to keep the children busy and great restaurants and shopping to keep the adults busy.

Note any neighborhood features as you're scouting locations. The more local attractions and amenities your rental property is close to, the more perks you can add to your for-rent or for-sale features list.

 REAL ESTATE ESSENTIAL

A recent trend is giving a property a "walking score." This means your property is rated on how easy is it to walk from it to such places as the park, restaurants, and shopping. To find out the score in your neighborhood, visit walkscore.com and type in the address of the property you're interested in.

We've given you a lot to research and think about, but remember this: the keys to finding a good property for your investment are to stay within your budget, find a good neighborhood, and find as many positive features as you can to attract potential renters and future buyers. In the end, your ability to achieve the financial return you're looking for is determined by a combination of buying the right property at the right price, renting it at the right rate, and selling it for the right price. A little extra time spent on research now, before you buy, means more money in your pocket later.

The Least You Need to Know

- Run the numbers on every property you're interested in before buying so you know what you can expect in terms of price per square foot or unit, as well as property taxes.
- Go beyond the four walls when evaluating potential rental property. Also check out the neighborhood, schools, community, and amenities.
- Never underestimate the extra income potential connected to the "fun stuff" in and around the property.
- Learn about the neighborhood's past, but also understand where it's going to better understand potential revenue growth.

CHAPTER 4

The Keys to Real Estate Success

You wouldn't start a new job and expect to know everything the moment you stepped through the door the first day, and have every day after that go perfectly, without any sort of training. You need to understand what you're supposed to be doing and learn the ins and outs of your new role. But when it comes to buying rental property, many people think they can be successful right from the start just by buying a piece of property and renting it out. It doesn't exactly work that way.

Kimberly once met a young couple who had just bought their first investment property, a one-bedroom condo in downtown San Francisco, with the goal of renting it out for a while to cover all their expenses and then eventually selling the property for more than they paid for it. They were so excited and ready to become the next big real estate moguls.

Their plan sounded great … except for the fact that they'd purchased the property for $1 million. With a loan amount that high, there was no way they were going to earn enough from renting their property to cover their monthly expenses. The couple didn't have the real estate knowledge they needed to recognize this problem before they purchased the condo.

In This Chapter

- Know before you buy
- The facts on finances
- A look at what makes a property profitable
- Important calculations to consider
- Achieving profitability

Success in real estate has very little to do with luck. It's more about knowledge. Like any investment market, real estate has up-and-down patterns and cycles. By taking the time to learn about real estate, you become a more knowledgeable investor who understands these cycles and can make money in good markets as well as in bad ones.

In this chapter, we clue you in on what you need to know about investing so you don't make the same mistake this young couple did. This chapter is about achieving success. It's why you picked up this book in the first place.

Thinking Financially

In Chapter 3, you determined what type of property you want to invest in. You learned how to assess a property, the neighborhood, and nearby amenities so you could tell if the property had money-making potential before purchasing it.

When evaluating any real estate investment, you need to think about and calculate such things as *property cash flow*. To determine whether a property is right from a *financial perspective*, you need to figure out how you're going to *leverage your investment capital* (the money you have) against the money from the bank and understand what your *equity* is (the total value you have). You also need to determine your *potential appreciation* (money growth) and, most importantly, do some *risk assessment* (money you could lose).

Does all this sound like a foreign language to you? If it does, don't worry. We walk you through it all, and before you know it, this will become second nature to you, too.

> **RENTAL REMINDER**
>
> Landlording can be financially rewarding. Buying the right real estate is a secure investment, and if you manage it correctly, it can provide a solid income and pave the way to more property investments. But you do need to invest time, money, and energy into your rental property in order to yield the financial results you're looking for.

Cash Flow

Probably the first thing you want to know is if the property you're interested in will provide cash flow. Simply put, is the property going to be a good return on your investment and worth the risks you may encounter by purchasing it?

Rental property risks come in all shapes and sizes. It could be as simple as a tenant who stops paying his rent. But the bank still wants its mortgage payment each month, regardless of your ability to collect rent on the property. Can you handle that risk? If you don't have extra cash just sitting in your bank account to pull from when this happens, you may need to reconsider how you invest in a property.

Your income on your property is determined by the amount of rent you can charge. What's the current rental market look like right now? Talk to people who live in the area, read the real estate and business sections of the local paper, contact the regional offices for economic development or city planning, and think about the current rental market in your area. You might be surprised at the amount of information you can find even talking with the local mailman!

Here are some questions you could ask—the mailman or others:

- What kind of neighborhood is this?

- Are rents in the neighborhood going up?

- Are more people moving into rentals or purchasing homes?

- Are new apartment buildings being constructed?

- Are new single-family homes being built?

- What may be available in the near future?

- Is there growth in the schools?

- Are new businesses coming into the area?

Even though this information may be available through local business offices, it's nice to know what people think about the way the neighborhood is progressing. You might find out that the neighborhood is growing or that underlying issues exist that can't be shown in a statistical report. If the neighborhood is growing, your property has a better chance for a greater increase in cash flow. If the neighborhood isn't growing, you may need to reconsider your purchase if you want to make money.

REAL ESTATE ESSENTIAL

Investing in rental properties comes with financial positives as well as negatives. On the plus side, you have cash flow, tax deductions, an increase in equity, and consistent residual income. On the negative side, you could have a large capital investment, ongoing expenses, the potential for unexpected expenses, and little or no equity increase.

Remember, the market goes through ups and downs. Your market might not be doing well right now, but in 6 months or a year, the tide may turn and the possibility of cash flow may increase. So don't always cross a neighborhood off your list permanently.

Remember that the real estate market runs in cycles. Just because now might not be the right time to invest doesn't mean it won't be right in the future.

Profit and Loss

Whether you're trying to make money today or down the road, investing is about making cash. When you buy a stock, it's easier to calculate how much cash you made on your investment because you know exactly what you bought it for (the purchase price) and then what you sold it for (the sale price); the difference is your profit. There really aren't any variables or expenses that make a difference.

That's not the case when you invest in real estate. You can count cash, profit, and expenses in many ways, and how you calculate it is different from how Uncle Sam wants to count it at the end of the year for taxes or capital gains.

When it gets complicated, it's always best to go back to the basics, so let's take a minute to talk about the profit and loss (P&L) statement. This form records income as well as expenses you incur over a period of time, like monthly or annually. Appraisers and other real estate professionals who are interested in determining value of property used for income purposes often make use of a P&L statement. If you use accounting software, you can also use it to develop a budget for your rental property and create a sample projected P&L statement for what the future could look like.

When setting up and reviewing a profit and loss statement—and you should do this both monthly and annually—you need to know the following:

- Gross income = the total amount of rent collected

- Gross expense = the total amount of property expenses

- Gross debt service = the amount you pay on your mortgage

- Gain or loss = how much cash you can expect from the property

RENTAL REMINDER

Gross income is the total income you earn. Net income is your gross income *minus* any expenses you incur.

To figure out how much profit you could make with a rental property, you use a simple formula based on cash flow:

Gross (total income) – Total property expenses = Profit (or loss)

The following table helps you calculate your monthly property expenses and create a budget plan. This budget gives you the information you need to evaluate your real estate investment and ensures that you buy a property that meets your financial expectations.

It's understandable that determining income and expenses can be a challenge if you don't actually own the property yet and haven't been paying the bills. However, if you start with a general P&L statement form, you can fill in the blanks using the numbers for existing properties that either you, a friend, or your real estate agent already own and compare those numbers to what you might see on the prospective property.

By examining these costs and understanding the value of each expense, you can estimate the total expenses you might incur with the new one. Then, once you understand the income and expenses connected with a property, you can better determine if it's right for you to purchase.

Tools are available online to help you calculate all these numbers. You input numbers specific to your property, and the site analyzes your investment property and creates 30-year performance projections with key financial metrics, such as cash flow, cap rates, and return on investment. You can also get reports to send to the bank to help secure a loan or to financial partners if you don't want to do this by yourself. There's no exact science to calculating financial returns on your investment, so run your numbers through two or three different sources to compare results.

RENTAL REMINDER

Expenses aren't just the physical costs of the property. Don't forget to calculate for lost rent/vacancy or other items, like building a reserve account for unexpected maintenance items.

Property Expenses

Expense per Month	Cost
Mortgage	
Taxes	
Insurance	
Homeowner's association dues	
Electric	
Heat	
Water	
Sewer	
Gas	
Oil	
Propane	
Wood	
Trash removal	
Cable	
Internet	
Telephone	
Maintenance	
Landscaping	
Snow removal	
Supplies	
Vacancy	
Nonpayment of rent	
Management fee (if outsourced)	
Advertising	
Legal	
Accounting	
Reserves (cash for future maintenance)	

Leverage

Leverage is how you get the most out of the money you have. You do this by tapping into the money the bank will give you to purchase a property. Leverage is important in investing in real estate because the less cash you put down on each property, the more properties you can actually buy. If the properties go up in value, your rate of return (the money or equity you get when you sell) goes up exponentially. However, if the properties go down in value and you have a lot of debt on the property, the result can be negative equity (you could be underwater, or owe more to the bank than the property is worth).

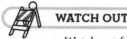 **WATCH OUT**

Watch out for zero-down investing! This can seem attractive for the high-leverage investor but should be approached with caution. If you're a long-term player, leverage will generally work in your favor if the markets you invest in appreciate in the long run and your income from the properties can pay for the monthly debt service. Otherwise, find another option.

Think of leverage as using the bank's money to make your own money. However, you need to understand that the bank's money actually costs you, so be sure you don't end up just making the bank money and getting none for yourself. When starting to look at financing your rental investment, ask yourself how much of a first mortgage you can and should take should you take to ensure your investment produces the cash you expect. Should you take a second mortgage? How much money should you put down? You might want to keep your first mortgage under a certain value to get a lower interest rate. Or you might want a second mortgage to minimize the amount of cash you need to put down.

Based on the type of property you're looking to buy, the bank may require a 20 percent equity investment. So if the property costs $100,000, for example, you'll need to give the bank $20,000 to buy the property.

There are many different ways people choose to finance investments, and you need to think about what works best for you. Often investors choose to finance multiple investments in different ways based on a number of factors, including how long they plan on keeping the property and what they believe the economic outlook is for the next few years. Ask your accountant, real estate agent, mortgage broker, and even your friends to find out what they suggest.

Equity

Equity is the amount of capital (money) you invest in the property plus the increase in property value. For example, if you sell the property for more than you bought it for, this increase is added to your original investment to calculate your total equity.

Over time, if the value of the property increases, so does your equity. This might allow you to refinance the property and take out cash for property improvements, to buy your next property, or to send your kids to college.

Investment Life

Investment life is the period of time—months, years, or decades—you plan to hold on to a property. This period of time may also change as the market changes. You might have planned on holding the property until you retire, for example, but if the economy becomes a bit shaky, you may decide to sell before you lose any more money.

However, know that the longer you plan to own your property, the fewer risks you might need to take because you can weather some of the bumpier real estate cycles and wait for it to come around again.

Appreciation

Appreciation occurs when the value of your property or investment goes up. Real estate investors expect appreciation on their properties based on the principle of supply and demand. The population is always increasing, and the size of the planet is limited, so there will always be an increasing number of people who want to buy a fixed amount of property. And when there's an increase of people who want something, and there's only a limited supply of that item, the price or value of that item goes up. Some high-demand cities, like San Francisco, generally have higher appreciation than other cities such as Colorado Springs, Colorado, but over time, the values will still go up.

> **REAL ESTATE ESSENTIAL**
>
> Property rates increase if there's more demand for housing than there is supply.

One city in North Dakota, for example, became a hotbed for housing because of new oil development. An oil company expanded its operation and moved 300 employees to the city. As a direct result of the new increase in demand for housing, the property prices rose significantly. However, if the city hadn't experienced new oil development and 100 of the 1,000 residents moved away and only 90 moved in, the prices would start to go down.

Large urban cities with geographic boundaries that are highly developed, meaning the city cannot sprawl or grow larger in area, generally have larger increases in property values. Both San Francisco and New York City, for example, are surrounded by water that limits the city to grow.

Remember, the best formula for appreciation and profit is buying in the right neighborhood at the right stage of a real estate cycle. Timing a real estate cycle can be difficult and very speculative, unless you plan to hold the property over a longer period of time than just one cycle. If you buy properties without equity or cash flow solely because you want short-term appreciation, you're engaging in a risky investment because you don't have time to develop property equity. If the real estate market dips, you could owe more on the property than it's worth. Instead, buying for moderate long-term (10 to 20 years) appreciation is safer and easier.

To learn whether your property has the potential for high appreciation, look at long-term neighborhood and city-wide trends you can find online or request from your real estate agent. Pick an area that will hold its value and grow at an average 5 to 7 percent pace. Combine this with a reasonable cash flow from your property and buying a property that will increase in equity, you have a formula for success.

Other Considerations

If you were baking chocolate-chip cookies and you forget to add the chocolate chips, your cookies wouldn't taste like chocolate-chip cookies.

Likewise, sometimes people think of real estate investing too simply and then get frustrated and disappointed when surprises pop up or things don't go the way they'd planned.

Real estate investing is not just about real estate. Yes, it's partially about the real estate property, but it's also about you, about the money, about the time involved, and about what you can do that might or might not make you more money and take more or less time or risk.

> **REAL ESTATE ESSENTIAL**
>
> It's not enough just to *try* to make money with rental property. You have to make a commitment, have a goal, and create a plan. That means asking yourself some questions and answering honestly: Why do you want to be a landlord? What type of landlord do you want to be? Do you want a monthly income or a large future payout? How does this investment complement your overall portfolio? How long do you want to be a landlord? Could you live in the same property as your rental? What if you move away? How much of your savings and other investments can you invest? What type of return do you want? Can you afford to lose money in the short or long term? Is your spouse/partner on board? Have you considered investing with a partner? What's your exit plan?

Do You Have the Time?

Time is an important factor when you become an investor. Will you have the time to collect the rent, fix the leaky faucet, or show the property to the next potential renter? Remember, single-family homes and multiunit apartment buildings require more of your time, energy, and financial resources than a condominium, where you're responsible for only the inside maintenance. If you travel for work and barely have time to take care of your own home, you'll need to appreciate this factor as you calculate your expenses and your success formula. However, the trade-off may be lower price appreciation with the condo, compared to the single family home.

A family Kimberly knows put four kids through private colleges with the money earned from investing in apartment buildings. The father loved his job with the church, but it didn't pay much, and the family didn't have a lot of monthly cash flow. They did have some cash saved, which enabled them to get approved for a loan. The family purchased two side-by-side four-unit apartment complexes, furnished them, and rented them weekly for just a few hundred dollars each. The neighborhood where the apartments were located had limited low-end housing options. The units were great for construction workers and lower-income families and were always rented.

To protect their investment, the family weekly cleaned each unit as part of the rent. The rentals were always in demand and consistently rented, and as a result, the parents were able to send all four kids to college. After the kids graduated, the parents sold the properties to finance their retirement. By capitalizing on their time, the family was able to produce higher financial returns on their investment property. Maybe you can do the same or something similar.

What About the Risks?

Risk is a consideration people sometimes forget to review because who wants to think about what might go wrong? However, the best-laid plans include a plan to reduce or eliminate risk, so you always need to ask yourself, "What if my assumptions are wrong?" In other words, do you have a Plan B?

For example, if you bought a property solely with the goal of achieving appreciation and it didn't appreciate in value as you planned, it becomes a financial risk. If that happens, can you rent it for positive cash flow? If so, that's your Plan B.

If you bought the property with an adjustable rate loan and the rate suddenly went up, what would you do? Would this put you at a negative cash flow, or do you have a Plan B? Did you put additional cash aside to compensate for the potential of an increased interest rate? If you're renting out the property, did you include gradual rent increases to cover the increase in the interest rate? If so, that's your Plan B.

What if your property has a few vacancies, leaving you with a negative cash flow? Will it break your bank? What if you bought a property to use as a vacation rental and the city where it's located suddenly passes a law against vacation rentals? What would you do? Can you now rent the property monthly as corporate housing? If so, that's your Plan B. You always need a Plan B when faced with these and other potential risks.

Investing in real estate will test your personal definition of *risk tolerance*. What do you value most, making a profit or not losing your initial investment? Which do you want more, increased growth or stability? Can you financially and emotionally handle financial setbacks? Can you afford a financial loss today? Can you afford a financial loss 10 years from now? Or can you afford *not* to take the risk?

Think about every possible scenario that can go wrong, and plan for it. Expect the best, but prepare for the worst.

Buying investment real estate for the first time can be a little risky, and we guarantee you'll look at your priorities and understand new aspects of your personal risk tolerance as a result of this adventure.

Before purchasing a property, Kimberly asks herself, "What do I get, or what do I earn, as a result of this investment?" She follows that question with another—one most people don't ask: "What if I *don't* make this investment?" By identifying what opportunity you might miss out on, you may discover that your risk tolerance is higher or lower than you thought.

REAL ESTATE ESSENTIAL

Say you have two small children and are worried about paying for their college education. You love your job, but it doesn't pay as much as you hoped. So your question might be, "If I *don't* invest in a rental property, how will I be able to afford to send my kids to college?" Having a clear goal—such as affording to pay for your child's college education or affording to pay for your retirement—is a great motivator for investing in real estate.

A friend of Kimberly's in the real estate business believes real estate investment property will be the alternative to Social Security for the next generation. Think about it. Social Security is a program you invest in while you're young so you can receive fixed monthly payments when you retire. Sounds just like the return you earn on an investment property—except you have a lot more control over the future.

The Bigger Picture

To make a profit, you need to find the right property at the right time and price; properly prepare and maintain that property; set the right rental price; keep the property occupied and, therefore, the rent coming in; and keep your costs, or expenses, low. Admittedly, it's a lot to think about.

It's not surprising we often see property owners focus on just one element, such as the rental rate, and forget about the bigger picture. You could have the perfect property in the best neighborhood and set the rental rate that covers your monthly expenses and still yields a hefty profit, but if the property is vacant, no one is paying rent, and your investment return is $0.

You need to consider all the various pieces of the puzzle—the occupancy rate, the monthly rent you'll charge, your expenses, and even your relationship with your tenants.

Occupancy rate refers to the ratio of days a property is rented versus the number of days it's available. Basically, it's all about keeping your property full 365 days a year. How do you fill as many days as possible? When do you start marketing for the next tenant? How do you keep your property rented during seasonal downturns? We address these questions and more in Chapter 9, but you should be thinking of items even before you buy.

If your rental rate is too high or too low, that's a bad thing. Set your rate too low, and you're leaving money on the table. Educated renters might not look at the property because they assume something's wrong with it because it's below market rate. Set your rate too high, and your property may sit vacant and produce zero return on your investment.

When it comes to expenses, remember the adage, "It's not what you make, but rather what you don't spend." Keep detailed reports on your income and expenses to be sure you really understand the property's true expenses and, therefore, understand the true profitability. We discuss expenses in detail in Chapter 7, but again, it's something you should think about from the start.

Once you have chosen the perfect property, your ability to attract and retain tenants depends on each customer's experience with you and your property—particularly in competitive markets. If you don't make your renters happy, another investor will.

The Keys to Profitability

After you've purchased a rental property, you can't just sit back and wait for the rental money to roll in. You still have work to do.

There are three crucial elements to running a successful and profitable rental:

- Properly prepare and maintain your property.

- Strategically market your property.

- Maintain great tenant relations.

WATCH OUT

We put these elements in a specific order because a good investor takes the time to properly prepare the property before trying to find the right tenant. Don't jump the gun by marketing a property that still needs a lot of work. You'll lose both time and money.

How you maintain your property—paint, carpet, landscaping, appliances, and such—is vital. A clean unit is the first step to creating a first impression and creating a positive reputation.

If you want to charge competitive market rates for your property, your unit must reflect that rate from the first day. Even if you list your rental below market rates, don't expect that any tenant will put up with mold in the bathroom, worn carpet, or a dirty kitchen.

To get the annual occupancy you want from your rental, it's critical to strategically market your property. Take the time to create a marketing plan, and treat your rental like a business. In addition to online marketing, see if you can advertise in any good local publications. Can you make any real estate agent connections that will get you the hard-to-find tenant?

Finally, it's essential that you maintain great relationships with your tenants. They're your customers, and your source of income, so you want to keep them happy.

How quickly are you able to connect with a tenant? Do you have all your leasing and property documents ready ahead of time? How well do you serve your tenants' needs during their stay? How well do you close your relationship with the tenant through the departure process? If you do all these things well, you'll soon earn a good reputation—and repeat business.

The Least You Need to Know

- It's essential that you consider all the elements to determine whether a property will make you a profit.

- Know what your Plan B is. Always plan for the unexpected and have a solution to every problem you can think of.

- Property appreciation can be a guarantee over the long term, but don't get trapped in the short term.

- Keep the bigger picture in mind. It's all about profitability.

You and Your Property

Few experiences are more empowering than when you receive the keys for your new real estate property and you get to walk through the front door knowing the property belongs to you and only you.

Now you have expenses, and you probably also have things to fix. Services need to be turned on, and you need to find some tenants. But where do you start?

In Part 2, we review some of the basics you need to know as you begin your landlording adventure and get your property ready for renting.

Landlording Basics

You've purchased the right property, with the right mortgage, under the right ownership structure. Now you get to roll up your sleeves and really get to work.

Your property is a reflection of you, and you should approach the management of your property with this mentality. When Kimberly opened her first property management office, she always made sure to sweep the sidewalk, wash the windows, and keep the office organized and clean. She believed that if potential customers saw that she couldn't even manage her office, how could they expect her to manage their property?

Start thinking about your rental property as your personal brand. Be proud of the product you deliver, and you'll find continued success.

In This Chapter

- Tips for getting started
- Setting up the right systems for success
- Detailing everything in writing
- Leases, agreements, rules, and clauses
- What about pets?

Tips for Success As a Landlord

This book is filled with tips for landlording success, but we wanted to give you some of the most basic ones now as you get started. Keep these pointers in mind as you move forward. They will make your life as a landlord simpler while growing your business and your profit.

Possess Key Qualities

All good and successful landlords have developed similar qualities and talents. You should, too. Here they are:

Confidence: When you're confident, you believe in yourself and the decisions you make. By learning more about being a landlord, you also develop the confidence to make the right decisions.

Leadership: A good leader motivates others to achieve the tasks at hand. Leadership when managing vendors and dealing with tenant issues is essential.

Professionalism and fairness: You will be presented with problems that need to be solved on a daily basis. Your ability to be professional and fair in your decision making goes a long way toward developing good vendor and tenant relationships and having continued rental success.

Awareness: You'll save time and money if you're aware of potential problems as they're brewing, whether with the property itself or with your tenants. Address problems early, before they get out of control.

Organization: Get organized. Start by setting up three boxes or filing drawers labeled "Property," "Maintenance," and "Tenants," and use them to keep track of items that can cost you money.

Communication: You'll be talking with a lot of people—vendors, real estate agents, tenants, community members, and more. It's okay to have fun, but remember to communicate clearly and stay professional.

Time management: This isn't the same as being organized. It's about controlling what can be controlled during each 24-hour day. Most importantly, it's about planning ahead, which enables you to be as efficient as possible. Manage your time wisely.

 REAL ESTATE ESSENTIAL

Make time every day to plan and prioritize. Start your to-do list with tasks that will make, and save, you money. Don't start your day until you complete this plan for your time.

Keep It Simple

Whether it's tenant communications or property renovations, the simpler you keep things, the better.

Say you purchased a six-unit apartment building and think it would look nice if each unit has a different color of carpet. That's not keeping it simple.

First off, you'll spend more money upfront because you'll miss out on any discounts you could get from buying in bulk, or in a higher volume, and decorate all units at once. Later, chances are you'll need to patch the carpet in one or more units. You can't keep just one extra piece of carpet on hand for repairs. You have to keep six—one of each color.

It's nice to offer options, but you need to keep your bottom line in mind at all times.

Know the Law

We go over some of the laws you should be aware of throughout this book, but it's impossible to go over every single one, especially those that might pertain specifically to your state or town.

It's your responsibility to look up and know the federal, state, and local investing, real estate, and management laws that apply to you. It's easy to look them up on reliable sites online, so don't get in trouble because you returned a deposit late and didn't know the law specified how much time you had to do so. Or don't end up in litigation because you refused to rent to an individual who owns a service dog.

When you know the law and you're not just guessing at it, you have more authority in all your tenant interactions.

Trust Your Gut

Not everything in property management is about specific rules, laws, and policies. Sometimes you just need to slow down for a minute, think through a situation, and trust your gut.

If something doesn't feel right about a potential vendor, for example, don't hire him. If a salesperson is trying to sell you a new roof and you're not quite sure she's on the up and up, get a second opinion before you shell out any cash. If a potential tenant tells you about his or her job and something seems off, get a reference before you rent.

Micromanage Your Property

This isn't something you typically hear, right? In many cases, micromanaging is frowned upon. When you're doing a job, do you want your boss looking over your shoulder, scrutinizing every detail of the work he gave you, pointing out where you've done something wrong or different from the way he'd do it? No, you want to get the work done and get it back to him. That's what's important.

It's a bit different when it comes to real estate investing. When you've invested in a property and you want to turn a profit, you need to micromanage every little detail. Don't take a laid-back approach to renting out your property. Successful landlords know they need to be hands-on.

You need to provide tenants with a property manual, map, and guide on how the property works that contains key information they need to know, such as what to do with the trash or who to contact for maintenance emergencies. You should inform tenants on how to disconnect hoses at the end of the season or who to call if the pilot light goes out on the furnace.

The more information you provide your tenants, the more likely they are to take care of the property.

> **RENTAL REMINDER**
>
> Stay in your property for a night before you rent it out. Many issues won't come to light until you live like your tenant. Then you'll know exactly what you need to do to prevent a negative experience (and likely negative review) related to your property.

Focus on Your Tenants

It sounds simple enough, but give your tenants your utmost attention. Maintain good communications with them at all times. Doing so pays off time and time again with repeat business and referrals.

Don't think of tenants as "bothering" you when they reach out to you. Successful landlords know that being "bothered" comes with the territory. Always make yourself available to your tenants by giving them your cell phone number and email address. And be sure you respond in a timely manner!

Treating your tenants well and responding to them quickly is the best way to ensure you maintain a great reputation.

Establish Systems in Place

Your number-one goal of owning rental real estate is to make money. To help make that happen, you can't spend all your time running around trying to get something fixed on the property. Instead, you should have systems in place that help you get and stay organized so you can accomplish your landlording tasks efficiently and cost effectively.

Start by creating as many organizational systems as you can. For example, Kimberly makes liberal use of binders and folders with pockets and dividers. She has a binder or folder for each of her properties in which she keeps documents, records, and maintenance logs connected to that property.

> **REAL ESTATE ESSENTIAL**
>
> Numerous cloud-based property management programs are available to help you keep track of details on your property. We share a few in Appendix B.

Store appliance warranties and operating guides in a labeled binder or folder, too. If the property came with a stove, you were probably given an operating manual when you signed the contract. Put it in the binder. As you purchase new items, get in the habit of storing the operating manuals in the same binder or in another logical, easy-to-access location.

If you don't have operating manuals for your systems, look online for them. You can often search for the brand, make, and serial number of a product and download the operating manual. Save a copy to your hard drive, or print it out and store it for future reference.

Maintenance Logs

Maintenance logs are a must for you to keep track of what gets fixed, when it gets fixed, and by what vendor. Save copies of all your maintenance logs in a folder or file. Also save any quotes you obtained on work to be done, any invoices you received on work that was already done, and receipts of items you purchased.

Track the date of purchase and the make, model, and serial number of all appliances and mechanical items on the property, such as the furnace and water heater. You need these for insurance and maintenance, and they'll come in handy when you need to order replacement parts.

It might seem easy enough to remember these items in your head, but the benefits of recording all the details and storing them in one location are worth it. For example, if a tenant damages the carpet in his unit, you'll want to hold him accountable. You need to prove when the carpet was purchased in order to establish what you can charge the tenant for its replacement.

Or say a toilet is leaking and you have called a plumber to fix it. The plumber says it was fixed, but it keeps leaking. You'll want to keep track of how many times you had to call the plumber back to fix an ongoing problem and hold him accountable for the work he said he did.

In your maintenance log, keep a list of possible maintenance items both inside and outside the property, and put together a seasonal projects list so you know up front what needs to be handled when—and so you're not surprised by something later.

On your winter maintenance list, include handling snow removal and checking the pipes so they don't freeze. The spring list should include watching for stagnate water and possible mold. In the summer, your list should include air-conditioner maintenance, and in the fall, preventing pests is a big concern.

Also note on your calendar those recurring items that aren't tied to a specific season, such as changing filters.

Keys and Property Access

Great landlords go out of their way to ensure that their tenants feel comfortable and secure in their rental. To provide a secure property for your tenant, you should have a system in place for managing security issues.

Maintain information on any keys, security cards, garage door openers, and the like you give your tenants. In fact, stop reading this book right now and make a copy of the key to your rental property, label it, and put it away for safe storage.

WATCH OUT

When making duplicate keys, use the oldest key as your master. Each duplicate has slight variations and won't work as well, making it difficult to unlock the door.

For security purposes, do not write the full property address on the keychain. If you lose the key, it can be traced back to your property, which might force you to re-key all the locks on your property. That can be quite an expense! Kwikset manufactures locks homeowners can re-key themselves without calling a locksmith. These could be a worthwhile investment, especially if security in your area is of concern.

You'll need keys for you, your tenant, and any vendors who need access to the property. You should store the master and these spare keys in a key box (these are available from property management supply stores), or you could just put them in an envelope in a filing cabinet if your office is outside of the building. Wherever you decide to locate it, be sure it's safe. There's nothing more embarrassing than calling a locksmith to get into your own property because you lost your key.

You'll also want to write down the make, model, and code of the garage opener, if your rental has one, so you can replace it if it's lost. Record the serial numbers of any and all access cards, too, so you can have them deactivated if they're lost or misplaced.

Finally, ask yourself these questions and put systems in place for handling the issues they raise:

- Who has access to the property besides me?

- Are the security codes for the garage changed between renters?

- What should I do if I suspect a security issue?

- How should I handle keys and locks when a renter moves out?

Emergency Plans

Nobody wants to think about it, but it's vital to create a plan of action for natural and man-made disasters. Is your area prone to floods, hurricanes, earthquakes, tornadoes, extreme weather, or wildfires? If so, make a plan to better protect your property and ensure your tenant is as safe as possible.

Start by talking with your insurance agent, neighborhood police department, or local fire department. These sources will have great information that can get you started.

Changing Information

Throughout the book, we give you key information on landlording, but there's so much more out there for you to learn. Laws change all the time, trends come and go, and tips and shortcuts are always being found that can help you to do your job better. So stay informed.

You can join a property manager organization such as the National Association of Residential Property Managers, attend trade shows and conferences, take real estate classes, or follow informative blogs. Or set up a Google Alert for terms like *landlord* or *rental law* to be sure you're up-to-date when anything new comes about.

Get It in Writing

You just purchased a very expensive investment—your rental property. Your goal for that property is to make residual income from it for the life of your investment. It's essential that you protect your rental property by getting all arrangements in writing.

Always give a receipt when your tenant gives you a security deposit, for example, and note the amount specifically listed in the written agreement. Otherwise, at the end of the lease when your tenant wants his or her security deposit back, you'll be in trouble if you didn't provide a receipt originally or you don't have it in the written agreement. You can purchase state-specific leases online or at local office supply stores that help you better maintain this information.

 **WATCH OUT**

> Oral agreements are legal for month-to-month tenancies and, in most states, for leases up to a year. However, they often lead to disputes when the parties remember the agreement differently. (That's another good reason to get everything in writing.) If you do accept an oral agreement, keep in mind that oral leases that exceed 1 year automatically become a month-to-month agreement at the end of the first year. Also, the amount of notice needed for rental increases or termination typically is calculated based on the time between rent payments. If you collect rent monthly, for example, you'd need to give 30 days' notice. Check your state and local statues. Oral agreement statutes may vary.

Be sure you have every detail in writing—the terms of the lease, pet rules, smoking rules, departure notice requirements, and even authorization you have to enter the property for maintenance issues. Your tenant must agree to and sign the agreement.

Rental Rates

One thing you need to get in writing is the rental rate for your property. As a new landlord, how you price your property is vital to your financial success. If your rent is too high, the property will sit vacant and you'll lose money month after month. If the rent is too low, you'll be leaving money on the table you'll never be able to get back.

Smart pricing hits the appropriate target market and optimizes your income. But how do you determine the optimal rental rate? Rental rates are generally determined by the area where the property is located, the style and quality of the property, and the number of bedrooms. Remember those notes you made earlier on the local market rates to determine how they were trending? Review those notes now to help you determine the right rental rate for your property.

Keep in mind, however, that there are a few items tenants may be willing to pay a higher rent for, such as parking—especially secure parking, a washer/dryer in the unit or in the building, security systems, air conditioners, pet acceptance, or extra storage.

When you decide on your rental rate, be sure it's included in writing in the lease.

> **$ REAL ESTATE ESSENTIAL**
>
> Should you offer a discount if a tenant pays multiple months in advance? It depends. What's the value to you? You don't have the hassle of collecting rent every month, but is there any value to you for getting this money in advance? Perhaps you have a large credit card bill with a high interest rate you could pay off with this money. Or could you use the cash as a down payment on your next property? Will you have cash flow issues in later months when you're not collecting rent because you used the money now? Be sure there's a monetary value to you for receiving rent in advance before you offer a discount.

Rental Agreement Versus Lease

Do you know the difference between a rental agreement and a lease? Few do. Before you rent your property, you need to understand how these two contracts differ and decide what's best for you and your rental.

At first glance, rental agreements and leases can look very similar. Both list the terms of the rental contract, such as the rent and deposits required, number of occupants, and basic rules for tenants to follow.

The main difference between the two contracts is the length of the tenancy, or how long the tenant will rent the property. A lease is generally for a longer, fixed amount of time, typically for 1 year, while a rental agreement is generally month-to-month. A rental agreement is just as legally binding as a lease, but it allows for either party to get out of the contract with a written 30 days' notice.

A lease agreement is the document you have your tenants sign once the application process is approved but before they move in. It's the most important document in property management. It outlines definite beginning and ending dates and protects the tenant against rent increases or changes until the end of the term. You cannot break a lease or force tenants to move without cause unless they fail to pay rent or violate other terms of the lease or applicable laws. (You could, however, evict a tenant for selling drugs or damaging the rental unit.)

Like any contract, for a lease to be valid, it must meet certain legal requirements:

Mutual agreement: All parties must reach a mutual agreement regarding all the terms of the contract.

Consideration: The contract must be supported by some form of legal payment, typically rent.

Capacity to contract: The parties involved must have the legal capacity to contract.

RENTAL REMINDER

Anyone can sign a lease, but not everyone will be legally responsible for the signing. For two parties to be in a rental contract, each party must be a competent adult at least 18 years of age. As a landlord, you can legally contract with someone under age 18 if that person has been declared a legal adult through a court-issued emancipation, military service, marriage, or court order.

Legal objectives: The objectives of the contract must be legal.

Signatures: The lease must be signed by the landlord because the courts consider the lease as a conveyance of real estate. A lease need not be signed by the tenant because through possession and payment of rent, the tenant is accepting the terms of the lease.

Description of property: A description of the property must be included in the lease. Generally this is the address of the property.

Create a boilerplate, or template, lease agreement you can use for every tenant. Lease terms are state-specific, and you can find these online or request them from your attorney for your state. In fact, your attorney is likely to have templates he or she can customize for you. Have a lawyer review any template you're planning to use. It should take your attorney no more than an hour to read your agreement and provide feedback. It's a small price to pay to protect yourself for years to come!

Rules and Clauses

Certain items must be included in a lease to make it valid, as noted in the preceding section, but above and beyond that, you have the right to include more.

A lease is designed to provide a level of legal protection for the tenant as well as for the landlord. However, landlords frequently add clauses to leases to account for future tenant issues based on what they've experienced with current or past tenants. That's fine for you to do, but be sure to have a real estate attorney review any additional clauses you include in your lease.

More often than not, if Kimberly adds a clause to a lease, it's because she wants the tenant to take a policy seriously, not that she expects to be fighting them in court. For example, if she includes a "no smoking" clause in the lease, she's found that tenants are less likely to smoke in the property than if she just asks them nicely.

Disclosures

In addition to the clauses, there may be items you need to disclose to cover yourself on future liabilities. Some disclosures are required by law on specific properties. The most common disclosure is the lead-based paint disclosure required on properties built before 1978.

Congress passed the Residential Lead-Based Paint Hazard Reduction Act of 1992, also known as Title X, to protect families from exposure to lead from paint, dust, and soil. Section 1018 of this law directed the U.S. Department of Housing and Urban Development (HUD) and the Environmental Protection Agency (EPA) to require the disclosure of known lead-based paint and lead-based paint hazards before the sale or lease of most housing built before 1978. (You can learn more at hud.gov.)

A lead disclosure form must meet the specific requirements set by the EPA. In addition, tenants must receive a copy of the EPA booklet, "Protect Your Family from Lead in Your Home." (To learn more, log on to epa.gov.)

Landlords are required to disclose any information regarding the safety of conditions of the rental property prior to having the tenant sign a lease or rental agreement.

Penalties for not complying with EPA disclosures can range from a reprimand up to criminal fines of $11,000 per violation. You also could be ordered to pay up to three times an injured party's actual damages.

 WATCH OUT

Don't lose money because you didn't give the tenant a lead-based paint disclosure and then get fined. Keep a copy on file so you can send it to potential tenants when you send them their tenant application information.

Other Policies

Here are a few more common policies you might want to add to a residential lease:

Guests: With this policy, you can limit the number of guests and the length of time they can stay in your rental property. Typically, a guest shouldn't be allowed to stay for more than 2 weeks within a 12-month period. Guests who stay longer could be considered additional occupants and then can be asked to leave or added with an addendum to the original lease and subject to a rental increase.

You could word the guest policy like this:

> *Lessee* shall not permit any persons, other than those listed on the lease and minor children born or adopted into the household during this tenancy, to reside on the premises for more than 14 days every 12-month period without the prior written approval of the *lessor.*

DEFINITION

The **lessor** is the person who rents or leases property to another. In residential leasing, he or she is often referred to as the *landlord*. The **lessee** is the person to whom property is rented or leased. In residential leasing, he or she is often referred to as the *tenant*.

State laws specify how many occupants can legally reside in a specific size of rental, so adding additional permanent occupants may be a violation of the law and be terms for eviction.

Roommates: Roommates are different from guests. There are official roommates who are listed on the lease, and there are those who come and go without your knowledge and without your having the opportunity to properly screen or interview them.

You can put a policy into your lease or rental agreement stating that you are to be notified if there's a change to or addition of a roommate and that you make the final decision regarding the admission of a new roommate.

The biggest problem with roommates is the lack of individual responsibility. Roommates frequently try to pass off responsibility for rent, damages, or other problems to the other party.

Specify in the lease who will take responsibility when one roommate moves out. Also in the event of a security deposit transfer, note that the transfer will take place between the occupants and will not affect the existing deposit on file with the lessor. For example, you can write this in the agreement:

Lessee understands that if an occupant or occupants occupying the unit decide to vacate the unit and want to be removed from the lease or rental agreement, these actions must be approved by the lessor. If lessee wants to substitute for another person for the remainder of the term, the lessor must also approve all changes. The lessor has the right to interview and accept or deny any applicant per the lessor's policy.

Subletting: There's a difference between roommates and subletting. A sublease is a lease given by a lessee for a portion of the leasehold interest, while the lessee retains some reversionary interest. Think of it like this: you've rented the property to someone; they then rent part of the property to someone else and collect rent from them. You don't collect rent from the subletter.

It's best to just say no to sublets. Often you rent the property to someone, they decide to sublet, and they charge a higher rent than what you are charging them and pocket the difference. In most cases, you won't have any idea you have a new tenant.

Subletting gets even more complicated when you stop getting paid rent and have to proceed with an eviction. Check with your local state laws for the best course of action here. In most states, you need to evict both the original and the subletting tenants separately.

Lease assignment: To throw one more situation at you, a lease assignment is different from subletting. A lease assignment occurs when the tenant finds a new tenant to take over the lease and the tenancy is transferred from one person to another.

Be sure you stay involved in the process and qualify the new person the same way you did the original tenant.

Smoking: You have the legal right to choose whether you want your property to be smoking or nonsmoking. You cannot discriminate against a tenant just because he or she smokes, but you can require they not smoke inside the property. Smoke is a very difficult smell to remove from inside a property, and often a property previously occupied by a smoker is less appealing to future tenants.

You can word the policy like this:

> Lessee agrees that no persons shall smoke cigarettes, cigars, pipes, or other items inside the premises.

Talk to your insurance agent about the pros and cons of smoking versus nonsmoking rentals. There may also be some financial benefits on your insurance premium to being a nonsmoking property.

Bed bugs and pests: Bed bugs have become a common occurrence in rental properties and can cost thousands of dollars to eradicate. The National Apartment Association has created strict guidelines that can require tenants to be financially responsible for bed bug eradication should they be found in the tenant's rental unit. Check with your local state agencies to better understand the laws that apply to your property.

Lease agreements often contain a clause about pest control issues, including the responsibilities of the tenant to comply with procedural treatments, move or treat furniture, or even vacate, if necessary.

You can word the policy like this:

> If bed bugs are found in your rental property as a result of your activity, you may be required to pay all reasonable costs of cleaning and pest control treatments incurred by us to treat your dwelling unit for bed bugs. If we confirm the presence or infestation of bed bugs after you vacate your dwelling, you may be responsible for the cost of cleaning and pest control treatments.

As a landlord, you have a responsibility to treat any pest problems immediately or risk it spreading, which could result in legal action from your tenants.

Illegal activities: Obviously, you don't want illegal activities taking place in your rental property, but it's beneficial to state the obvious and include a clause in the lease. Word the policy like this:

> Lessee agrees no resident or guest shall engage in any type of illegal activity on or near the premise. Lessee agrees that any violation of this policy shall be cause for termination of tenancy.

WATCH OUT

Should you suspect any illegal activity, do not try to investigate on your own. Call your local police department to report the situation.

Noise complaints: This is a common complaint, so give yourself some leverage to deal with noise by including a policy in your lease. Word the policy like this:

> Lessee agrees to refrain from making loud noises and disturbances so as to not disturb others around them.

However, keep in mind that "loud noise" is subject to interpretation. Depending on how well insulated your property is, this may or may not be an issue.

Parking: If you offer parking as part of the rental agreement, be sure you are specific as to where the spot is, the size of vehicle that can be accommodated, and ramifications if the parking policy is violated. Word the policy like this:

> Lessee understands parking spaces are unit specific. Parking details for this unit are as follows:
>
> _____
>
> _____
>
> Lessee understands that vehicles may be towed if not parked in designated parking space. Any parking cards, garage openers, and the like not returned will result in an additional charge of $_____.

Property alterations and decorating: You may be okay with the tenant painting a wall a different color, but be sure he or she doesn't break through drywall to, say, add a door without getting approval from you. Word the policy like this:

> Lessee will not, without the prior written consent of lessor, make any alterations, improvements, or additions.

Military representation: The purpose of this clause is so you can know if any resident in your property is currently a member of the armed forces. This information is important because military personnel are subject to additional laws and may be able to break a lease if they are deployed or for other circumstances.

Word the policy like this:

> Lessee …
>
> ❑ is
>
> ❑ is not
>
> … an active member of the armed forces.
>
> Lessees' individual identification number is: _____.

Liquidated damages: This clause is a good idea. This is an amount predetermined by both parties as the total amount of compensation an injured party should receive if the other party breaches a specified part of the contract. To be enforceable, the liquidated damages clause must set forth an amount that's reasonable to the breach. Check with your specific state; some have statutory guidelines on what's a reasonable amount.

Facts About Fido

Every landlord has a good and bad pet story to tell you. But pets are a way of life, and you need to accommodate them, so start thinking about your pet policy now.

If you have a property that's not in a high-demand area, allowing pets might be an attraction to potential tenants. Yes, pets can cause damage to rental properties, but they also can increase the rental rate on your property to cover any potential damage. You can demand a larger security deposit, too.

You might even be able to charge a higher departure fee if a pet is involved. (Be sure you use the fee to have the carpets and upholstery cleaned to make the property ready for the next tenant who may be allergic to pets.) Most tenants with pets expect this, and they're happy to oblige.

If you decide to allow pets, be specific with the clause. What type of pets? How many? What size? Be sure you outline the rules on what you can expect your property (inside and out) to look like while the tenant lives there and upon departure. Spell out in your contract if the pet chews through the wood floor, for example, who's responsible for damages.

Be sure your lease also has a clause for undisclosed pets. Word the policy like this:

> Pets shall not be allowed without the prior written consent of the lessor. Lessee agrees to pay $_____ for any undisclosed pets, plus cover the costs of any damage incurred as the result of any pet.

If you do allow pets, ask potential tenants the following questions so you get a better idea of what animals they might bring with them:

What type of pet do you have? Some animals are more rental-friendly than others.

How many do you have? It's wise to limit the number of pets to one large animal or two small animals.

How old are they? Are they trained? You don't want a puppy marking up your carpet or chewing your door. Be sure the animal is at least 1 year old and house-trained.

Are they noisy? Dogs like to bark, especially at strangers, which can be annoying and disruptive to neighbors. Set a policy that the dog will be outside only when supervised by the owner. You may even set hours (for example, the dog can't be outside after 10 P.M.) to ensure the dog isn't barking late at night.

What breed dog are they? Most breeds are fine, but you might want to prevent breeds that could be considered dangerous to the families living around you.

> **WATCH OUT**
>
> A dangerous animal might require you to change your homeowner's insurance. Some dog breeds are even prohibited by local laws.

Are they up-to-date on vaccinations? You don't want animals who are carrying or exposed to disease living in your property. Ask for proof of up-to-date vaccinations.

Finally, ask for letters of recommendation. These can be helpful, especially if they're from a previous landlord. Many pet owners already have these available.

The Least You Need to Know

- Creating systems in place prevents problems and obstacles later.
- Get everything in writing to protect yourself from potential problems and litigation.
- Write clauses that outline what you will and won't allow in the property.
- Consider allowing pets but then increasing the rental rate for tenants with animals to repair any damage the animals cause.

CHAPTER 6

Preparing Your Property for Tenants

Sometimes it helps to think of your rental property as a product. What makes your product better than the one down the street? If you were buying a used car, for example, you'd shop around and compare one car to another. You wouldn't buy the car that's rundown with high mileage and ripped seats, would you? Or would you opt for the one that has a new engine, a good security system, and other upgrades? Typically, you'd buy the car that's clean and upgraded.

You have to think of your rental property the same way. You can't just toss your property into the rental market and hope someone wants to live there, whatever condition it may be in. You must put in the necessary work and properly prepare your rental so it has the best chance of getting rented. This means sprucing up the property, cleaning it, and adding some finishing touches that will help seal the deal.

In This Chapter

* Sprucing up your property
* Ensuring your property is safe
* Going green to make more green
* Making use of inspection reports
* Renting a furnished property

Making Your Property Look Good

Appearances are everything, and first impressions are vital. That applies to your rental property, too. It needs to make a good first impression on prospective renters. A little sprucing up can keep it looking good and running smoothly, and do wonders for improving your occupancy rate.

RENTAL REMINDER

Spend an evening in your property to ensure everything works properly and get a better idea of what your tenant will see and experience.

Start at the curb. What impression does it make? It is welcoming? Will a prospective tenant feel good about inviting his or her friends to dinner? What image does the yard and the outside of the structure convey? Is this image in line with the rent you intend to charge?

Once you make it to the front door, what does it convey? Welcoming? If not, think about replacing the door, painting it, or upgrading the doorknob.

Inside, replace old, outdated linoleum flooring with new tile or laminate. If your rental has carpeting throughout, get it cleaned or consider replacing it.

Do any rooms look dark and dingy? Upgrade the lighting with a new light fixture. Is the unit hot and stuffy? Consider adding ceiling fans.

Dirty light switches and even outlet covers can leave a bad impression. This is a simple upgrade. Replacement covers don't cost much, and they're easy to replace, so swap out with clean ones before showing your property to possible renters. (Be careful when working around electricity.)

Want to make a room pop? An inexpensive can of paint has the capability to make a property look fresh and new. Don't use anything too drastic, too bold, or too bright, or a color that could go out of style in a year or two. Still, one or two walls painted with a tasteful accent color can freshen up a property and turn a plain-Jane unit into a highly wanted property. Check out pictures online or in decorating magazines for ideas.

In the kitchen, replace old counters, if possible. Do the cabinets look dingy and outdated? If so, you could paint them or put new fronts on them. At the very least, scrub the outsides so they look better. Clean the insides very well, too. Check out the refrigerator and stove, and clean as necessary. Be sure the dishwasher is in good working order, too. If you can, upgrade the appliances with eco-friendly versions.

Bedrooms should have a clean, fresh, relaxing feel. Install new, neutral-colored blinds in the windows (so you can avoid numerous screw holes in your walls from tenants trying to install blinds themselves), and be sure they're in good working condition. An overhead ceiling fan with light package is also a nice touch.

A dirty, old bathroom can make or break a rental, so eliminate grime and mold before even thinking about finding a renter. Make sure all caulking is free of mold, dirt, and discoloration. If the showerhead has 10 years of grime and mineral buildup on it, clean it well or consider switching it out with a new low-flow showerhead that looks nice and saves water. Snake the shower drain now to avoid a tenant complaint for a poorly draining shower later. Upgrade older cabinets by lining drawers with contact paper. Look at all the details, like the inside of the medicine cabinet and the top of the shower curtain rod, and be sure everything looks new.

Sometimes upgrading and sprucing up a property can be overwhelming. But take it one room at a time, and you'll get through it. Remember, your property must be a reflection of your rent, especially if you want to maximize your income. Charging less than market rate doesn't mean you can expect tenants who will live with mold in the bathroom, worn-out carpeting, or a dirty kitchen. If you're charging higher than market rate, your renters will expect their unit to be upgraded and clean. Meet your tenants' expectations, and develop a positive reputation for future rentals.

Cleaning It Up

Cleaning your property is essential between renters. There are three types of cleans you can do: annual (or seasonal) cleans, make-ready cleans, and maid-service cleans.

Annual or Seasonal Cleans

During a seasonal clean, your goals are to keep things working longer, prevent damage, and check on a few items. Make a point to check the following during an annual clean:

❑ Furnace/air-conditioner   ❑ Bathroom drains and vents

❑ Stove   ❑ Toilets

❑ Refrigerator   ❑ Washer/dryer, including vents

❑ Kitchen sink   ❑ Water heater

❑ Disposal and drain   ❑ Water softener

❑ Dishwasher   ❑ Garage

❑ Microwave and vent

WATCH OUT

Not cleaning a dryer vent annually—if not more frequently—could start a fire.

Give a copy of this checklist to the tenant, and explain that you'll do these cleaning checks annually or seasonally and need access to the property. You can take a good look at the condition of the property when you do the cleaning.

Not completely sold on the idea of seasonal cleans? Get down on your hands and knees and look under your refrigerator. If you haven't vacuumed out the dust balls annually that collect here, you'll find a refrigerator motor that's insulated in dust and dirt and working harder than usual. As a result, it's costing more to run, is pulling more electricity, and could burn out faster.

Take a good look at all your rental property appliances annually to be sure they're working at their peak efficiency and safety.

Make-Ready Cleans

When you're in between renters, your cleaning list should start with the same items on your annual cleaning list. After that, you should complete a more detailed cleaning of the property.

Remember, at this point, you have a vacant property so you need to get it back up to like-new condition, the expectations a new tenant will have.

Wipe down the baseboards, doors, doorframes, windows, and window sills. Pull out the refrigerator, and clean behind it. Pull out any furniture, and clean under it. Clean the front of the cabinets and inside the drawers.

Does any exterior cleanup need to be done? Check gutters for clogs, window wells, and other hard-to-reach areas. If there's a yard, consider zeroscaping it—take out the grass and replace it with rocks and plants that need less water and maintenance. Have the exterior of the windows cleaned as well.

> **RENTAL REMINDER**
>
> Make a to-clean list to refer to so you can ensure you don't miss anything from year to year.

Maid-Service Cleans

There's absolutely nothing wrong with hiring a professional cleaner to clean your rental property. You can spend more time on things that are more important for your time and leave the cleaning to someone who knows what they're doing.

Before you hire a cleaning company, do a little research to ensure that the company is trustworthy and reliable and comes with spotless recommendations.

You also can encourage your tenant to have a professional company come in and clean the inside of the property during tenancy. You could also build a maid-service cleaning into your rental rate. If you have more than one property, you should be able to negotiate a lower per-unit cleaning rate, too.

Making It Safe

Liabilities are a part of owning a rental property, but successful landlords take the time to limit their liabilities as much as possible. You don't want to get stuck in court because a tenant fell down your stairs due to improper lighting or a wobbly staircase rail you could have quickly and easily fixed. You also don't want to end up in litigation because you didn't follow a state or federal law. Some states require carbon monoxide detectors in all rental units, for example. And unfortunately, some tenants will go out of their way to find things that are wrong with a property, or something wrong you did or didn't do, just so they can make a fast buck.

It's essential that you make your rental a safe environment. Here are some ideas:

Security: The front door should be solid and weather tight, with sufficient locks. Change locks and access codes on the property between tenants. You also can ask your insurance company or local police station for advice on how to secure the property. Conduct periodic security inspections that can be as simple as driving by the property and checking the outdoor security lights.

Electrical safety: Electrical outlets located near sinks should be ground-faulted for safety. Bathrooms also should be properly vented per state and local building codes. Light fixtures should have working bulbs and switches.

Fire safety: State fire codes often require entry doors that share a common hallway to be fire rated, which means the door must be able to sustain fire for a specified period of time. If you're required to have fire-rated doors in your common entrances and you don't have them, you could face severe penalties.

Your property should contain smoke detectors and carbon monoxide detectors, and you should test them to be sure they're in good working order. You can generally call your local fire department to come and inspect smoke detectors in hard-to-reach areas.

RENTAL REMINDER

Kimberly always leaves a small fire extinguisher under the kitchen sink for her tenants. This $10 investment could save big bucks in the long run.

The number-one fire-prevention advice for any building is to ensure it's up to code and all fire-prevention equipment works. Check with your local fire department because fire codes and laws differ from state to state.

To stay up-to-date on the latest research, technology, and safety practices, consider investing in a copy of the National Fire Protection Association's (NFPA) *Fire Protection Handbook*. This handbook includes security information and tips and explains how to make a comprehensive and effective security plan for your property. Visit nfpa.org for more information.

Accessible and usable: Be sure the bedroom, bathroom, and closet doors have working handles and open and close properly. Windows should open and close and have functioning locks.

Safe flooring: The property's floors should be solid and sealed properly to keep water leaks from seeping through and causing damage below.

 REAL ESTATE ESSENTIAL

> Once when Kimberly was taking a prospective tenant on a tour of a few condominium properties, they walked into a condo to find a steady stream of water pouring into the property from the unit above. Unable to reach the off-site building management, they had no idea who the upstairs property owner was. Instead, they called the fire department, who broke into the upstairs unit and turned off the water.

To protect yourself in case of litigation, also have an inspection log sheet that lists when you went to the property and any action you took.

Take all tenant complaints seriously. Document each complaint, and respond promptly. Make necessary repairs or improvements in a timely fashion, and do not hesitate to call the police or ask the tenant to call the police if you suspect suspicious activity.

Green Is the New Black

By green, we mean eco-friendly, and by black, we mean profit. You can take care of the planet and pocket more cash at the same time.

Renters are more energy and environmentally conscious today than they've ever been before. They're looking for homes that have energy-efficient features and appliances. They want Energy Star refrigerators, stoves, washing machines, and freezers. In fact, studies show that 60 percent of tenants *demand* eco-friendly features in their rental property.

Having these items in your rental shows that you not only care about your property—after all, these appliances will save you money in the long run—but you also care about the environment.

Real estate investors are under a common misperception that green practices are more costly than nongreen practices. But the truth is, there are many ways you can incorporate environmentally responsible practices into your rental property without breaking the bank.

Easy Ways to Go Green

If you're looking to go green, take these basic ideas into consideration:

Recycling: Make it easy for the tenant to recycle. Leave recycle bins in accessible places within the property with instructions on what can be recycled and when recycling will be picked up. If you rent a condo, leave instructions with the tenant on where to unload the recycle bins when they're full.

Lightbulbs: Replacing bulbs with compact florescent light (CFL) bulbs that are more energy efficient will most likely lower your electric bill. Energy-efficient bulbs also last longer and require fewer changes.

Toilets: Upgrade older toilets with newer, low-flow toilets. It can shave dollars off your water bill while saving water. Most modern toilets are low-flow anyway.

Cleaning products: When you prepare your property for the next tenant, have it cleaned with eco-friendly cleaning supplies. These nontoxic products are on par, cleaning-wise, with chemically laden cleaning supplies.

Appliances: Upgrade old refrigerators, dishwashers, and washing machines with energy-efficient models. These appliances can drastically reduce your water and energy bill while helping to save the planet. The U.S. government and some states also offer tax rebates for upgrading some appliances with Energy Star ratings. Check out the Environmental Protection Agency's Energy Star site (energystar.gov) for more information.

Thermostats: Programmable thermostats can help regulate the temperature in your rental without causing spikes in electricity when the air-conditioner or furnace has to work overtime to keep up.

Wireless thermostats take it a step further, enabling you to connect your thermostat to your computer or smartphone via Wi-Fi and easily monitor and control the thermostat from there.

Some thermostats are even motion sensitive and can be set to an automatic-away mode if movement isn't detected within the property for a certain period of time.

WATCH OUT

Be careful if you purchased a property in a new green building because some use thermostats that prevent a property from getting cooler than 72°F (22°C). This can be a bit uncomfortable during hot summer months. If this is the case for you, protect yourself by adding a disclaimer to the lease pointing out this fact. That way, no tenant has an excuse for getting out of the lease early.

If you've already purchased a property that isn't already eco-friendly, you can make some green upgrades to it. Installing energy-efficient windows and doors is one of the most important steps you can take to seal your home against the elements and, in return, save money that isn't wasted on heating and cooling. Your potential tenants will appreciate the features and are often willing to pay more for them. As a bonus, upgraded windows will increase the resale value of the property.

You also can upgrade flooring to more environmentally conscious material. Bamboo, for example, is a fast-growing grass that's strong and stable. When it's recycled, it's pressed together, making it stronger than both traditional hardwood flooring and regular bamboo flooring.

Making a property greener and more energy-efficient is not only an environmentally conscious decision in real estate, it's also a great marketing tool. Take the time to understand some of the green terminologies and set yourself and your property apart from your competition. You'll make more money, more "green," as a result.

LEED Certification

If you want to go a step further on the green scale, you can make your rental a LEED property. LEED (Leadership in Energy and Environmental Design) is a U.S. standard for rating properties developed by the United States Green Building Council (USGBC).

According to USGBC, making a property LEED-certified can:

- Reduce use of electricity, water, and other resources

- Reduce operating costs

- Boost the value of your property

- Provide a safer and healthier environment for tenants

- Make you eligible for tax rebates and other incentives

Building owners can have their building LEED rated and then achieve certification ranging from "certified" to "platinum," depending on how many green features are incorporated and the building's energy-efficiency rating. Each specific feature you install is worth a certain number of points on the LEED chart, which corresponds to a certification level.

In existing buildings, a LEED rating means green features added to improve the building's energy efficiency have helped minimize the negative impact the building has on the environment. Following LEED standards can result in a 50 percent reduction in water usage and optimized energy performance, as well as help the development of alternative green power sources like solar power.

To learn more about LEED rating and certification, go to usgbc.org/leed.

Getting an Energy Audit

A great way to get started on making your property green and implementing the changes that would have the biggest impact is to have your property energy audited. An energy audit assesses your property's water and energy use and provides a rating. A professional auditor inspects your property's energy systems and identifies how much energy it uses and how it's used. Using the results, the auditor identifies efficiency and cost-reduction opportunities.

RENTAL REMINDER

Save money on your electric bill by asking your utility company about time-of-use rates. Some utility companies offer different rates for off peak hours. For example, you could save 50 percent on your electrical bill just by doing your laundry after 7 P.M.

Once you've upgraded the unit with eco-friendly features, be sure to add this to your rental description when you market it. Use keywords such as *green, energy-efficient,* and *eco-friendly.*

The Importance of Inspection Reports

You should have had a professional inspection done prior to purchasing your rental property. You can use that report as a reference tool. Now that you've cleaned it up, spruced it up, and made it safe, be sure you document the condition of your rental property in your inspection report.

In addition, you should have completed your own inspection report prior to finding your first tenant. Again, use this report to check the physical and mechanical aspects of the property and ensure everything is in working order. What should you include?

General:

- Lights—are they all working?

- Window, window tracks, blinds, screens—are they all clean and working?

- Smoke detector—are they present in every room and working?

- Entrance door—does it have a deadbolt? Is the lock working?

- Walls—are they all clean and free of large marks and scratches?

- Air-conditioner and/or furnace—are they working?

- Carpet—is it clean and in good condition throughout?

Kitchen:

- Floor, countertops, faucet, drains, and disposal—are they all clean and working?

- Cupboards and drawers—are they all clean and working?

- Appliances—are they clean and working?

Bathrooms:

- Tub, toilet, sink—are they all clean?

- Floors and countertops—are they clean?

- Faucet and drains—are they clean and working?

- Shower—is it clean? Is the shower curtain or door clean?

- Medicine cabinet—is it clean and empty?

Other:

- Washer and dryer—are they clean and working?

- Water heater—is it free from any leaks or deterioration, and is it properly vented?

- Patio/balcony—is it clean and free of trash?

- Doors—do all the locks work?

- Garage/garage door (if applicable)—is it functioning smoothly, and are security elements in place to prevent injury?

- Keys—do all keys work in their corresponding doors?

Also include in your inspection report a date- and time-stamped video of all rooms, from top to bottom. This is your opportunity to evaluate if everything is working and note any damage before a tenant moves in.

Furnishing Your Rental

To optimize your rental income, you can furnish your property and rent it as a nightly vacation rental or monthly corporate rental. If done correctly, furnished rentals can easily bring in about $10,000 in additional annual income. Keep in mind that furnishing a rental requires a significant number of items, and the average upfront costs of furnishing an 800-square-foot property is about $10,000. (It can be more if the property has an office and additional bedrooms.) You'll soon make that money back, though, and the initial furnishings are tax deductible.

Before you get started shopping for and filling your rental, remember this: keep it simple and cost-effective. Don't spend too much time running around and stressing yourself out trying to get everything just right.

And don't spend a month shopping while your property sits vacant. Get it done quickly. Remember, time is money when it comes to your rental property, so furnish your property quickly and cost-effectively so you can get a tenant in there. Sure, you can shop for bargains, but don't spend too much time or gas going from store to store or waiting for multiple deliveries. We recommend shopping in just three stores for your items.

When decorating your rental, think about how the property is going to be used. If your end goal is to rent it to a corporate executive, decorate it so it's up-to-date, stylish, and comfortable. A corporate rental shouldn't look like a dorm room or your grandmother's cottage.

> **$ REAL ESTATE ESSENTIAL**
>
> Antiques generally aren't the best choice to furnish your rental property because a small, fragile chair, for example, could break if improperly used.

Think about the style and quality of furniture you're going to choose, and be consistent with the style and décor throughout the property. For example, a kitchen with pink floral wallpaper and a living room with contemporary black leather sofas isn't cohesive. Keep everything gender neutral and practical. Chairs should be comfortable and sturdy. Also be sure your property has a good workspace for the renter who wants to work from home.

Remember, style, comfort, and attention to detail will maximize your occupancy rate and boost your annual rental income.

Accessories

You can buy just about everything you need for a furnished rental—linens, kitchen supplies, decorations, and such—from big-box discount stores. You can also shop hotel supply stores or warehouses. Just like furniture rental companies, accessory rental companies enable you to buy items directly and take advantage of their bulk buying power.

You might be able to find housewares rental companies in your area. Or check out appliance rental companies.

Kitchen Items

You can purchase kitchen items one at a time, or you can buy everything in one order from the Lodging Kit Company (lodgingkit.com). Call and ask for the corporate housing kitchen package in the quantity you need. Then if one plate gets broken, you can order just one replacement plate and they'll all still match.

Have one clean, fresh set of dishes in the cabinet. Get a set of cooking utensil sets, too. Do not buy white utensils; they stain easily and will need to be replaced often. A knife set in a butcher block stand is also cost-effective and keeps the kitchen well organized. Drawer organizers are a must. We also recommend purchasing a higher-quality set of pots and pans. Nonstick pans won't last and will need to be replaced frequently. When purchasing a coffee maker, try to find one that's as basic as possible so you can easily replace the glass carafe if gets broken.

Buy simple and easy-to-use appliances like toasters, blenders, and microwaves. Fancy versions can be frustrating if a tenant can't figure out how to use them.

Keep everything as fresh as you can. Some items are used regularly and get icky with wear. You don't want to furnish a rental home with burned oven gloves or stained kitchen rags. Replace those items between tenants or as needed.

Electronics

If you expect to get top dollar for your high-end rental, your entertainment electronics need to complement one another and appeal to a high-end tenant. Technology such as an Apple TV or an iPod docking station can go a long way. Give your tenant an enjoyable audio and video experience, but you don't have to overdo it.

Tenants expect flat-screen TVs these days. Include at least a 42-inch flat screen TV in the main living room. It's a good idea to have a TV in the master bedroom, too.

Tenants want access to news channels and sports networks, so you could provide extended basic cable service. You can charge the tenant for pay-per-view movies or additional services.

Consider providing high-speed Internet service with a modem/router located in the property, too. A wireless modem is a plus. Be sure to leave detailed instructions on how to access the Wi-Fi.

A radio and CD player are also must-have items.

Furniture

Be sure your rental property furniture is comfortable and usable. Try to get all your furniture from one location with one delivery fee, if you can. You can do this by employing a consistent decorating style throughout the property. Also keep in mind that a patterned upholstery fabric generally hides wear and tear, while wood can be water stained, so if that's a concern, steer clear. Furniture rental companies or staging companies generally have a liquidation area for slightly used furniture that may allow you to buy complete sets at a great discount. Costco and Sam's Club are also excellent sources for furniture items.

When it comes to your budget for furnishing your rental property, don't get carried away. A $5,000 couch won't translate into more rent money, so buy the nicest couch you can find with the smallest price tag. However, don't go too cheap-looking and then expect to charge high rents.

WATCH OUT

It's tempting to use old items from your house or from a garage sale in your rental, but it's best to buy everything new. Don't risk turning off a tenant, and potentially getting a bad review, because you cut corners and put your old blender in the kitchen.

Dining room furniture: Furnished rental properties should have some way of accommodating in-house dining. Whether it's a formal dining room or a kitchen counter with stools, you must have a comfortable place for your tenant to enjoy a meal alone or with others. Consider arranging a place setting complete with a move-in gift of food to create a welcoming presentation.

Family room furniture: The feeling of home to prospective tenants is central to a successful rental. Furnish the family room with a sofa, coffee table, end tables, television and related electronics (as mentioned earlier), and proper lighting. Your renter needs to be able to imagine enjoying his or her evening relaxing in front of the TV, reading a book, or just hanging out.

Bathroom

Unsightly bathrooms have cost landlords more leasing deals than any other single feature, so pay close attention to this room.

Decorative items should complement one another in style and color. Provide a complete set of matching towels twice the potential number of occupants.

Provide a wastebasket, soap dish, plunger, and toilet brush in appropriate places. Cleaning supplies in the room are optional but recommended. Provide replacement lightbulbs for light fixtures, too.

Bedroom

You'll need a bed for the bedroom. Avoid a bed frame with a footboard, however, because it can add limitations for taller tenants. You also should have at least one bedside table and dresser, as well as a clock radio and TV in the master bedroom. The closet needs to be fresh and clean—a quick coat of paint can do wonders—and stocked with hangers and a laundry basket.

For linens, you need a mattress pad, sheets, pillows, blanket, and comforter set with accent pillows. Don't go overboard on expensive linens or pillows. Think of these as disposable items you'll need to upgrade as soon as they get soiled. Also avoid real feathers; some potential tenants could be allergic. Keep all bedroom linens fresh and free of stains.

Phone

Having a phone in the property is optional, but it's highly recommended so your tenant can call for help in case of an emergency. Discuss with your tenants whether you'll invoice them for long-distance calls, turn off the long-distance feature with your phone company, or include unlimited local and long-distance rates in your rental price.

Tenants should not be disturbed with your personal phone calls, so avoid using this phone line for personal reasons. If you plan on returning to the property at a later date, transfer your existing line to a voicemail box and establish a new phone number for the tenant. Phone companies will charge a set-up fee for a new line.

> **RENTAL REMINDER**
>
> Voice over Internet Protocol (VoIP) phones are a good way to cut down on costs and provide complimentary long distance to the tenant.

You can download a complete itemized list of what you'll need to furnish your rental from corporatehousingbyowner.com.

Property Manual

We recommend preparing a detailed property manual and leaving it inside your property for your tenant. Have fun talking to merchants in your area to get helpful information and discount coupons to welcome your tenant and ensure they enjoy living in your property.

This booklet, at a minimum, should include information on the following:

Unit instructions:

- Arrival
- Departure
- Building map
- Key
- Building access
- Parking
- Thermostat
- Trash
- Major appliances
- Electronics
- HOA rules and regulations

Emergency numbers:

- Fire
- Police
- Hospital
- Maintenance
- Property manager

Neighborhood information:

- Amenities
- Transportation
- Shopping
- Restaurants
- Schools
- Urgent care
- Hospitals

Things to do:

- Sports
- Parks
- Entertainment
- Inside tips

The Least You Need to Know

- When thinking upgrades, consider energy-efficient or environmentally safer options.

- Be sure your rental home is clean and safe before your new tenant moves in.

- Create inspection reports to be used before the tenant moves in and when the tenant moves out.

- Renting a furnished property can cost you more up front, but you'll more than make up that expense quickly.

Property Management and Maintenance

You've purchased your rental property, and you've ensured it's clean, safe, and ready for occupancy. Welcome to the property management phase of landlording!

When you purchased your property, you acquired the right and responsibility to repair and maintain it. By law, landlords are required to provide properties that meet basic structural, safety, and health standards. Your specific state might have some different or stricter laws and requirements, so be sure to check. If you don't fulfill these duties as a landlord, your tenants have the legal right to withhold rent, sue you, or move out without notice.

In This Chapter

- Assembling your property team
- DIY maintenance or hire out?
- Handling complaints
- Preparing for emergencies

The Property Team

Being a landlord is a 24-hour, 7-day-a-week, 365-day-a-year job. A friend once told Kimberly, "It may take a village to raise a child, but in the world of property management, it takes a team to run a building." At any given moment, something can break or need to be replaced or upgraded. You may be the best handyman in the world and able to fix everything, but there's no way you can be available all the time. As a result, you need a team to call on for repairs and other aspects of property management.

WATCH OUT

If you repair something and it harms someone, you might be liable and suffer considerable financial losses—maybe even prison time. Check with local building officials to see what repairs you are allowed to make and what repairs should be left to licensed professionals. Also, to avoid paying unnecessary fines, know the local requirements for your properties. Is a carbon monoxide detector required? Are you legally required to change the locks and carpeting between each tenant? Research this information before you get started.

Who's Answering Phones?

Who's going to answer the maintenance emergency call 24 hours a day, 7 days a week? In the beginning, this might be you. If it is, you can set up a free phone number for emergencies through a service like Google Voice (voice.google.com). You can easily forward this number to a specific phone so that one week calls come to you and the next week calls go to your handyman.

You can also hire a phone answering service that will always answer the tenants' calls and can determine whether the issue is really an emergency that should get you up in the middle of the night or whether it can wait until normal business hours.

Whatever you decide on, remember your goals—focus on your financial success, set up the right team, and don't get bogged down with troublesome phone calls.

Assembling Your Team

So who is on your team? It depends. Maybe you need someone to answer the phone in case of an emergency if you're not available. Or someone who is going to repair the heater when the weather is below zero.

Start by creating a list of service providers who can take care of specific issues. Your list can include, but isn't limited to, the following:

- Handyman

- Heating and cooling (HVAC) specialist

- Plumber

- Electrician

- Locksmith

- Cleaner

- Carpet installer

- Exterminator

- Landscaper

- Snow removal company

If you're planning extensive renovations, you might need a team of architects, engineers, and general contractors as well.

To find any one of these vendors, check with your local trade or business organizations for references and referrals. If you're looking for a builder or contractor, for example, check with your local builders' association. Need a landscaper? Check the local landscaping trade association.

Vetting Potential Team Members

Once you have a few potential professionals to choose from, you can start checking them out. Ask the following questions when vetting prospective team members:

- How long have you been in business?

- What's your project or company philosophy?

- How do you manage your projects?

Also ask for references. When you call those contacts, ask for their honest thoughts on working with the professional. What did they like and not like?

Schedule times to visit workers on other job sites. As you're there, observe whether they're doing a job that would be similar to yours. If your job is larger and the contractor has worked on only smaller jobs, is he capable of handling your job?

Be sure the vendors you choose have any required licenses, insurances, and warranties. You don't want to be liable for any accidents.

Find out if the professional guarantees the work he's doing. Most contractors provide a long-term warranty that says the work they do will last for a minimum period of time. If anything were to happen with the work before then, they'll cover the cost of the replacement repair.

When working with the vendor for the first time, meet him at the property to give him access and monitor his work. If you're comfortable with his level of service and he's properly bonded and insured, you can give him the keys and allow him to work on his own.

Why is it important for the vendor to be bonded and insured? Let's say you give the plumber the keys to your rental property that's currently occupied. You previously got written permission from the tenant to enter the property, and the plumber goes into the property and fixes the leak. The tenant later returns home and claims an expensive watch is missing. If the plumber is bonded and insured, you're off the hook. If he's not, you're responsible for the missing watch.

Should You DIY?

It costs money to have repairs done by a handyman or contractor, so if you have the skills and experience, you might be able to tackle some repairs yourself.

You can do plenty of repairs without needing a license, such as painting, patching drywall holes, and changing washers in faucets. You could also change locks, install carpet and tile, replace windowpanes, and cut the grass. Just be sure you have the experience and the time to do these repairs correctly.

> **RENTAL REMINDER**
>
> Don't worry about *not* having a task to do. When you are a landlord, there is never a dull moment.

Some repairs you shouldn't—and legally *can't*—do without a state-specific license. Plumbing, electrical, and structural construction work fall in this category. To ensure the safety of your tenants, only qualified service personnel should do these and other repairs that could result in a condition that could harm the occupant. In many states, single-family, owner-occupied properties are the only ones you could fix without these state laws requiring a license.

Just as the electrical company always wants you to check for buried electrical lines before you dig, you should also check with your local building officials to find out what you can and cannot do.

The Importance of Maintenance

Normal wear and tear will occur on your rental property. Maintaining the property is a two-part job; you have responsibility for maintaining it, but so does your tenant.

Establish the maintenance rules in writing and have the tenants sign them to acknowledge they have read them and agree to comply. Rules should be reasonable and directed at keeping your property in excellent condition. They should emphasize the tenants' responsibility to report any issues as soon as they occur. Failure to report a leaking water heater or faulty wiring could ultimately be dangerous to the property, the tenant, and you.

Outline how you want the tenant to report a maintenance issue, too. For example, do you have an online maintenance form accessible on your website, or do you want tenants to call or email you? Maintenance requests are always best to get in writing so you can keep track of the dates and details. (Check out the sample documents available in Appendix C.)

If your rental unit is unoccupied, it might be a good idea to engage in some preventive maintenance before the next tenant's occupancy. Use this time to test the functionality of a microwave, snake a drain pipe, or clean a gutter.

RENTAL REMINDER

Before purchasing expensive maintenance equipment, check with the hardware store and find out what tools and equipment you might be able to rent by the hour instead.

Sometimes when we focus all our energies on more pressing items, we overlook the smaller things—in this case, daily wear and tear. For example, fireplaces and wood and gas stoves need annual inspections to prevent gas buildup or other possible hazards. Be sure to schedule an annual furnace inspection and schedule seasonal maintenance on heating and air-conditioning units.

Also set up a filter replacement schedule and keep replacement filters next to the furnace. Clogged filters can cause a system to underperform or even break.

A common issue with air-conditioning units is that a tenant runs them at full blast and they freeze up. If a tenant calls to say the system stopped working, talk them through what happened and suggest they turn the system off for an hour to unfreeze it and then turn it back on.

The Complaint Department

You have a legal responsibility—and a good business responsibility—to properly process tenant complaints in a timely manner.

It helps to be a good listener. Sometimes the problem isn't with the property as much as it is with the current circumstances in the tenant's life. Taking 15 minutes to listen to the tenant process her complaint can go a long way in resolving the issue.

> **REAL ESTATE ESSENTIAL**
>
> It's worth listening to and checking out tenant complaints, no matter how crazy they sound. Kimberly once managed a three-floor apartment in San Francisco. One warm spring day, a tenant had her windows open. When she called to say she had rats jumping through her windows, no one took her complaint seriously. After her third call, maintenance went to her apartment and indeed found rats jumping through her windows! The property next door (built about a foot away) was being renovated, and the workers had stirred up a rat colony. The rats were now escaping the building by jumping to the next building—through the tenant's window!

Next, ask the tenant to follow up with a complaint in writing. This gives the tenant time to process his or her issue and gives you a good basis to start your remediation of the issue. It also gives you written documentation should there ever be legal action related to this complaint.

Establishing the Rules

Make clear to your tenants, in writing, what's considered an emergency and what isn't. You want to avoid 2 A.M. phone calls asking you to come remove a moth, but overflowing toilets, leaking pipes, and electrical sparks are something you need to address before serious damage occurs.

When you became a landlord, you became the boss. Every landlord has a different approach to dealing with tenants. You should be friendly and professional, but beyond that, choose a level of interaction that works best for your personality and comes naturally.

Remember, there may come a day when you have to tell a tenant no or track someone down for unpaid rent. It's hard to get them to take you seriously if they think of you only as a drinking buddy.

Handling Tenant Complaints

How you handle a complaint depends on a variety of factors. For example, handling a dispute between residents of a co-op or condo depends on what's written in the building's bylaws or *covenants, conditions, and restrictions (CC&Rs)*, while a dispute between single-family home neighbors in a homeowner's association may be handled differently.

> **DEFINITION**
>
> **Covenants, conditions, and restrictions (CC&R)** are restrictions on the use of a property. Generally, CC&Rs are established and maintained through a homeowner's association.

Regardless of how it's handled, your goal is to solve the problem before it gets to litigation. Once lawyers become involved, it costs you money, so litigation should be the last thing on everyone's mind.

Sending Complaint Letters

You, as the landlord, might send complaint letters, too. Say you've already approached a tenant who continually throws large, noisy parties. Sending a complaint letter to the tenant is usually the next step to keep documentation of how a complaint is handled, especially if the tenant is in violation of the building's bylaws, proprietary laws, or house rules.

Noise complaints are probably the number-one reason tenants have problems with one another. If you're getting more than your normal share of noise complaints, it might be time to educate your tenants about local noise laws or any noise-reduction requirements that are in their lease or bylaws.

If the tenant still won't respond to a complaint letter, it may be time to contact the authorities. In most areas, noise complaints can be filed anonymously. A visit from the authorities is usually enough to stop the person in violation from continuing.

Emergency Preparedness

We touched on emergency preparedness briefly in Chapter 5, but let's take a more detailed look now. A successful landlord thinks ahead, contemplates worst-case scenarios, and ensures steps are taken to reduce the risks when something does happen.

Create a Plan

One of those steps is creating a plan of action that you provide to your tenants. This plan tells them what to do in case of various emergency situations and should include emergency numbers and evacuation plans. Although every person is truly responsible for his or her own evacuation, you can be sure the evacuation goes smoothly.

 **REAL ESTATE ESSENTIAL**

Be sure you have in-case-of-emergency contacts for each of your tenants.

Create a list of local emergency numbers, as well as evacuation and escape plans, and share these with all your tenants. You may want to permanently attach the numbers and evacuation plans to the inside of the front door.

In the preparedness plan, include a property escape plan that includes a map of the building with the exits clearly marked. Also list the most structurally secure rooms in the building, in case your tenants would need to seek shelter.

Plan for Everything

Start by being prepared for anything Mother Nature could throw your way based on your specific location—hurricanes, tornadoes, earthquakes, fires, floods, and such. Believe it or not, planning for a natural disaster is actually a little easier because, for some, you get some advance warning.

Hurricanes: If your property is located in a potential hurricane area, have a clause in your lease that tells the tenant what to do in case of a hurricane warning. You'll need to secure your rental property, too, to minimize damage the storm might cause. This could mean boarding up windows and doors, bringing in outside items that could fly away or create more damage, and so on. Check out the list of things to do at ready.gov/hurricanes.

REAL ESTATE ESSENTIAL

A watch means conditions are possible for a hurricane, tornado, or other severe event to develop. A warning means a hurricane, tornado, or weather occurrence has been seen in your area.

Tornadoes: If your area is prone to tornadoes, instruct your tenant on what rooms in the property provide the most shelter. Typically, the basement is the best choice. If that's not available, a windowless interior room, such as a bathroom with a bathtub, is a good idea.

Like other acts of nature, you'll need specific insurance to cover tornado damage. Damage as the result of a microburst, or strong downward gust of wind, is generally covered by your traditional homeowner's policy.

Earthquakes: You don't get advance warnings with earthquakes like you might get with other natural disasters. If your property is in an earthquake zone, your best bet is to plan for the unexpected.

To reduce the impact of earthquakes, the Federal Emergency Management Agency (FEMA) suggests repairing deep plaster cracks in ceilings and foundations, anchoring overhead lighting fixtures to the ceiling, and following seismic building standards.

When an earthquake strikes, instruct your tenants to stay away from the elevators and shield themselves under a sturdy table or other piece of furniture until the shaking stops.

Fires: Fire may or may not be an act of nature. But regardless of the cause, fires can spread quickly. Be sure the property includes fire extinguishers, smoke detectors, and carbon monoxide detectors, and instruct your tenants on what to do in case of a fire.

REAL ESTATE ESSENTIAL

To keep up-to-date with the latest research, technology, and safety practices when it comes to fire, check with the National Fire Protection Association at nfpa.org.

Floods: Flooding can result from hurricanes or other strong storms or be the result of a water leak or backed-up water or sewage lines. Not all property insurance covers flooding, so check with your insurance agent if you're not sure what your coverage is. And as with the other potential disasters, be sure you provide clear instructions to your tenants on what to do if flood waters start to rise.

We've covered only a few of the emergencies you could face here. Think about what others might occur in your area, whether natural disasters or man-made, and make a plan for each of them. You can never be too prepared when it comes to protecting your property and your tenants.

The Least You Need to Know

- As a property manager, it helps to have a team you can turn to when you need help with something, be it landscaping, snow removal, plumbing, or a host of other tasks.

- It's essential that you (and your team) maintain the property to keep your tenants happy and safe.

- Handle all complaints, whether you receive them or dole them out, quickly and professionally.

- Prepare an emergency manual that instructs the tenant on what to do in case of any kind of emergency.

Landlord Rights and Responsibilities

We've given you a lot of information so far. You know you need to treat your rental property as a business and make decisions accordingly, never letting your actions get personal. You know you must respect your tenants as your customers and clients. After all, you can't survive in this business without them. You know it's essential that safety come first with all maintenance aspects at your property, and if you don't know how to fix something, you should hire someone who does. And maybe you're picking up on the fact that just when you think you have figured it all out, the rules will change. It's important to keep an open mind. Your long-term success depends on it.

Also keep an open mind as you read through this chapter. This is the legal chapter, the one with all the jargon, the lingo, the legalese. Call it what you will, but it's part of being a successful landlord, and you need to know it.

Whatever you do, don't bypass this chapter and skip to the next one. It's important that you take your time with this chapter.

In This Chapter

- Your responsibilities as a landlord
- What you can—and can't—do
- A look at tenants' rights
- What about rent control?

The Implied Warranty of Habitability

As the landlord, it's your responsibility to provide the "implied warranty of habitability." This legal doctrine, established in the 1970 case of *Jarvins* v. *First National Realty Corp.*, makes it the landlord's responsibility to maintain and repair the rental property. This isn't a state-specific rule. It's applicable all across the United States.

So what does this mean? At the very minimum, you need to do the following:

- Keep the basic structural elements of the building—the floors, stairs, walls, and roof—safe and intact

- Keep all common areas, such as hallways and stairways, safe and clean

- Keep the electrical, plumbing, sanitary, heating, ventilating, and air-conditioning systems running safely

- Keep any elevators on your property operating safely

- Supply cold and hot water and heat in reasonable amounts at reasonable times

- Provide trash receptacles and arrange for trash pick-up

- Manage known environmental toxins, such as lead paint, dust, and asbestos so they don't pose significant dangers

Also, in most states, you need to provide rental property that's reasonably safe from the threat of foreseeable criminal intrusions, and exterminate infestations of rodents and other vermin.

Some states have ruled that the implied warranty of habitability requires the property owner to maintain the property only according to what's required in his or her state and local housing codes. You can look up your local codes to find out exactly what you're required to do. Normally, substantial compliance with the code is sufficient.

Other states view the implied warranty of habitability as unaffected by housing codes. In these states, the issue is more whether the unit is fit for human occupancy. A housing-code violation doesn't necessarily mean a unit is unfit for human habitation; conversely, just because there's compliance with the housing codes doesn't mean it *is* fit for habitation.

In situations in which the court makes the determination, requirements may be imposed on a property owner that are more substantial than the local or state codes require.

Housing laws, such as state or local building codes, and housing and health codes normally list specific standards by which property should be constructed and maintained. These conditions and requirements vary by state and municipality, but they generally apply to the rental units and the common areas of the property. You need to find out what those are and be sure your rental property measures up.

> **REAL ESTATE ESSENTIAL**
>
> If you own a condominium or other property that has a common area managed and maintained by a homeowner's association (HOA), don't assume the HOA is on top of it or watching out for specific things that could affect your rental. If you see something wrong or notice something that needs to be fixed, submit a written maintenance request to the HOA.

Your Rights as a Landlord

It might seem like all the laws favor your tenant, but believe it or not, you do have some rights as a landlord.

First of all, you have the right to maintain your rental property. This means you can make most types of repairs yourself, without official licensing or certification. This right, however, may be restricted only to you and not a maintenance contractor. For example, based on most state laws, you could remove lead-based paint from the property. However, if you hire someone to do the job, they need to be licensed. This could also apply to asbestos removal.

When dealing with potential tenants, you have the right to properly screen them. This includes requiring permission for the release of credit, criminal, and eviction history. You also have the right to verify the information provided on the rental application and to refuse to rent to anyone who lied on the application. In addition, you have the right to charge a tenant a security deposit and keep that deposit if the tenant damages the property.

You have the right to establish rules associated with your property, such as prohibiting your tenants from smoking in your rental. Additionally, you have the right to restrict or prohibit pets in your property unless the animal is a service animal like a seeing-eye dog.

You have the right to require your tenants to pay for their own utilities, as long as the utilities are separately metered and these items are specified in the lease or rental agreement. You also have the right to sell your property, even if it's currently leased.

Most importantly, you have the right to make a profit from your rental property.

You have other rights, too, but these are a few of the important ones.

> **RENTAL REMINDER**
>
> The rental business has a lot of moving parts. It's often in your best interests to consult an attorney if a situation arises that you're unfamiliar with. Also be aware that property law can be modified by a court decision at any time. Joining an organization like the National Association of Residential Property Managers (NARPM) or the Institute for Real Estate Management (IREM) helps you stay informed and ahead of the curve.

You Can't Do That!

Feeling overwhelmed yet? We hope not. Our goal isn't to overload you with legalese, but rather to ensure you're properly informed. The more you know, the better your chances of reducing your liability—and increasing your profitability.

On that note, we need to tell you some of the things you, the landlord, cannot do to avoid issues or lawsuits. The penalties for violation of these rules differ by state and municipality but generally include fines or possible jail time.

You cannot discriminate when renting your property. (We cover the specifics on discrimination later in this chapter.)

You cannot physically remove tenants from a unit without following the specific court procedures and obtaining the appropriate court approvals.

You cannot change the locks on a unit (often referred to as a "lockout") to force a tenant out of the property.

You cannot shut off utilities in an attempt to force the tenant out.

You cannot remove personal property, such as furniture, automobiles, or pets, without first obtaining the tenant's permission.

You cannot willfully destroy the property without proper permission from the local authorities.

You cannot modify the property without permission if it's protected by local or state historical authorities.

You cannot violate zoning ordinance that apply to your property.

WATCH OUT

Unless a dangerous emergency exists, you cannot enter a leased unit without the tenant's permission. For example, if a gas leak is reported and the source appears to be inside the tenant's unit, you are allowed to enter the unit.

In most states, you cannot make improvements to the property if it's leased that would otherwise require you to have a license, like an electrician. Check your state's laws, and watch for any changes that could affect how you do business.

The Covenant of Quiet Enjoyment

All 50 states have accepted the common-law concept of quiet enjoyment. Courts normally define this concept as an implied promise that a landlord will not act, or fail to act, in a way that interferes with or destroys the capability of the tenant to use and enjoy the rented premises.

The generally accepted definition of quiet enjoyment is, "The right of an owner or lessee legally in possession of property to uninterrupted use of the property without interference from the former owner, lessor, or any third party claiming superior title."

Written Permission

As a new landlord, it might be hard to understand that once you've rented out your property to a tenant, you don't have the right to just use your key and walk through the property anytime you want. By leasing the property to the tenant, you have given them the right to live quietly without your interference.

Always get written permission to enter from your tenants prior to doing any maintenance work inside your property, even if they've requested the maintenance. Tenants often request items to be fixed, but they don't always want you to show up anytime. By taking the time to get written permission to enter and specifying an acceptable time frame for entering the property, you're eliminating potential liability.

A simple solution would be to create a document or web version of a maintenance request form that also includes the following:

> By completing this maintenance request, you are indicating permission to enter has been granted to the landlord or the proper maintenance vendor needed to correct your request.

Grandfather Clauses

Some states and local codes provide for certain exemptions to code requirements for specific property types. Normally, single-family, owner-occupied properties are exempt from local and state housing codes. Other exemptions may be applied to older buildings built before certain dates.

Because some code requirements may result in major structural changes, lawmakers have provided grandfather clauses in the codes for all buildings built before a certain date. Sometimes the exemption date is the same as the date of the change in the code, but not always. Check before remodeling because your building might need to be brought up to code as a result of the remodel.

Other safety code requirements, such as door locks and smoke detectors, must be followed regardless of the age of the building.

Understanding Tenant Rights

Yes, this is a chapter on *landlord* rights, but we need to address some tenant rights here, too.

You have rights, and your tenant has rights. Understanding these rights reduces the chance that you will, even accidentally, cross the line between your rights and your tenant's. If you do, it could result in legal actions against you.

 **WATCH OUT**

If you think landlord-tenant laws generally favor the tenant, you're right. Traditionally, courts, legislators, and tenant-advocacy groups have supported tenants against landlords.

Following are some of the more general rights your tenants have that you should be aware of. Your tenants have the right to …

- View any property you have advertised for rent.

- Apply to rent any unit they want.

- Retain privacy and confidentiality of any personal information released to the landlord.

- Use and expect quiet enjoyment of the property once the property is rented.

- Live in a property that is safe and sanitary (right of habitability).

- Be protected from environmental conditions arising at the property such as radon gas, mold, or asbestos.

- Make reasonable modifications to the unit.

- Have a legal hearing of any disputes that arise or complaints made against them.

- Hire an attorney to represent them in a legal dispute.

- Demand payment of interest to them if interest has accrued on a security deposit.

- Withhold rent if you don't make repairs needed for the right of habitability.

- Deduct repair expenses incurred to maintain habitability.

- Receive proper notice regarding late rent, eviction, entry, and inspections.

- Participate in a rental-assistance program without your permission.

- Receive a timely security deposit refund if the property is left in good condition.

- Receive a complete itemized accounting of all deductions taken on a security deposit.

Now let's review some of things the tenant does *not* have the right to do:

- Damage the property

- Change the locks on the property

- Receive a full security deposit refund if property damage has occurred

- Break the lease or rental agreement without cause

- Stop paying rent without cause

- Break the laws applicable to the property

- Use the property for a purpose other than that stated in the rental documents

- Allow persons not listed in the rental documents to live in the property without authorization

- Abandon the property (if they expect an extended absence from the property, they must notify you.)

REAL ESTATE ESSENTIAL

In most cases, it's illegal for tenants to change the locks on the property because it bars you from entry in case of emergency. And typically, a state allows a landlord to enter a property if the tenant has been absent for 7 or more days. Some states require tenants to notify the landlord of any extended absence. Protect yourself by adding an absences clause to your rental documents. You can decide when you want the tenant to notify you.

Right to Entry Versus Right to Privacy

We've talked about your rights and your tenants' rights, but we also need to talk a bit more about ways you and the tenant interact and whose rights take priority.

You know you need to get written authorization or permission to enter a property prior to doing so, and you've studied the exceptions in cases when there may be a safety issue. So who wins when it comes to your right to entry and the tenant's right to privacy? Both issues have specific rules and regulations you must follow to preserve and protect both your rights and your tenant's.

Most states have specific laws regarding the landlord's right to enter an occupied rental unit. The good news is that most states also recognize the importance of allowing the landlord into the rental unit to make repairs or show the property to prospective tenants once a current tenant has indicated he or she will not be extending the lease. Check your current state laws and restrictions.

Most states also typically require a 24- to 48-hour written notice before you or a designated representative may enter a property. Of course, there are always exceptions. For example, if there's an immediate emergency that threatens the property or other occupants, you may enter without first seeking permission. Written notice can be in the form of an email or standard letter you mail, hand to the tenant, or post on the unit door.

Some states specify what hours are permitted for entry, but usually they allow for entry during times considered reasonable. If your state doesn't specify how you should gain access to a tenant's unit, we recommend you err on the side of caution and give the tenant a full 48 hours' notice.

In the case of an emergency, the landlord can always gain immediate access to the rental unit. If there's smoke pouring from the property or smoke alarms sounding from inside the unit, if you can smell gas coming from the unit, if water is leaking from the unit, or if you hear screaming for help from inside the specific unit, you may enter.

Permission Denied?

What do you do if your tenant says, "No, you cannot enter the property"? This becomes a bigger issue if the tenant has reported a maintenance item to fix and, if not fixed, the tenant has the right to stop paying rent.

First, start by carefully documenting all communication, attempted communication, and actions you've taken regarding the repair. This documentation is important if you're later sued for not providing a property that meets required standards. Many states allow you to enter an occupied rental unit even if the tenant is uncooperative, as long as you have a justifiable reason to enter and you've given proper notice.

However, never physically push your way into a tenant's unit. If the situation has deteriorated to this point, get an attorney involved. If there appears to be immediate danger, call the police.

> **RENTAL REMINDER**
>
> Don't enter an occupied rental unit alone. Bring a witness with you in case a tenant claims his or her personal items are missing. This doesn't have to be an attorney or the police. It can be someone on your property team or another employee.

Respect Your Tenant's Privacy

Just as you'd want a tenant to respect your privacy, you also need to respect your tenant's privacy. You may own and maintain the property he or she lives in, and you pay the taxes, but that doesn't give you the right to harass your tenants. A smart landlord doesn't get involved with the day-to-day activities of his or her tenants.

In fact, certain actions could be perceived as an invasion of your tenant's right to privacy and could result in a lawsuit against you.

Try to avoid contacting or visiting your tenant at work. Never call your tenant's place of work to criticize or comment on his or her actions as a tenant. This can be considered harassment. Spying on your tenant is also an invasion of privacy.

Do not interrogate visitors to the rental property. Keep your conversation with visitors to a casual hello and other small talk. Don't concern yourself with visitors who stay for only a day or two. If you notice visitors who have stayed past the allotted guest time documented in your rental documents, address this with your tenant directly.

Rent Control

We haven't talked about rent control yet, and it's not something you should take lightly. You should never purchase a property in a rent-controlled city without proper research and understanding.

Rent control is a state or local government regulation restricting the amount of rent and the amount of rental increases landlords can charge tenants, among other things. Rent increases, evictions, security deposits, unit improvements, and re-rental of units are the most common factors affected by rent control ordinances.

There are three major themes in rent control in the United States:

- The use of rent control to regulate the quality of rental dwellings, with controls used only to address violations of building codes, as in the case of New York City

- The use of rent control to regulate high rents, as in Massachusetts and California

- The use of rent control to regulate building quality and high rents, as in New Jersey

In most areas, an elected or appointed board of officials enforces rent control. The board is responsible for interpreting the rent-control ordinances set forth by the local government. Some rent-control boards have additional powers and are allowed to approve or disapprove a landlord's requests for rent increases, determine penalties, and request that the landlord ask for permission when making any changes to the unit.

REAL ESTATE ESSENTIAL

Local municipalities can establish fair rent commissions on a state-by-state basis. A fair rent commission is a group of appointed officials that has the authority to receive and investigate rent complaints, issue subpoenas, hold hearings, and order landlords to reduce rents for specific reasons.

Check your local state and municipalities for more information on how rent control could affect you. Take the time to protect your investment by understanding these restrictions *before* you buy, and stay alert about and involved with potential new laws and property regulations.

The Least You Need to Know

- Learning the law is vital to protecting your rental property investment.
- You have rights, and so does your tenant.
- You must provide a habitable property for your tenant.
- You cannot discriminate against your tenant.
- Rent control is not something to be ignored.

You and Your Tenants

Who's going to live in your new investment property? Who's going to call your rental "home"? In Part 3, we help you figure out the answer to those questions. We show you how to find the tenant who is going to write you a check or swipe a credit card every month and give you the profit you've been wanting.

Every landlord wants good tenants. Good tenants pay rent on time, don't break leases, keep the property clean and maintained, notify you about problems, and leave the property in good condition when they move out. Bad tenants can actually cost you money, not to mention the time you then need to spend marketing and trying to find the next right tenant. Finding good tenants is a key element in your formula for success in real estate investing.

In Part 3, we take you through the steps of finding that perfect tenant by marketing, communicating with potential renters, and then closing the deal. We also cover what you need to know to keep your tenants happy and how to work with them should something go wrong.

Finding the Right Renters

In the past, finding a good tenant meant running an advertisement in the local paper, answering the phone, and faxing out rental applications. By the end of the week, you may have shown the property a few times and, by Monday, you were reviewing rental applications to choose the most qualified renter.

Life isn't so simple anymore. Thanks to the internet, you have so many more places to market and advertise your property. Today the new tenant for your rental in Wisconsin might actually come from Japan after seeing your posting on Twitter, Facebook, or craigslist.

The key to managing it all and finding the right renter for your property is learning about what marketing and advertising opportunities are available, what's best for you, what to say, how to present your rental, and foolproof ways to turn "I'd like to know more about your rental" into a tenant signing on the dotted line.

Establishing Your Brand

We've said it before, but it's worth saying again: landlording is a business, and your rental property is your product. You need to establish your product in the marketplace.

What does that mean? Well, what do you think of when you hear or read the word *Pepsi* or *Subway* or *Microsoft?* You probably know what kind of products these words represent and what you can expect with each of them. Subway, for example, sells submarine sandwiches but makes it a point to cater to customers who want to eat out but eat healthier. You know what you're getting when you step into a Subway restaurant. Do potential renters know what they're getting with your rental property when they read about it?

Building your rental property's brand starts by establishing a relationship with your potential tenant. That begins with the look, feel, and style of your property. It builds when your tenant reads your advertisement and likes what he or she sees in your photos. Your goal is to get a potential tenant to read your ad, contact you for more information, see your property and like it better than another rental down the street, sign the rental documents, and move in.

If you expect to rent your upscale property to a business executive for top dollar, will she be impressed with dark photos and a bland, boring ad? If she comes to tour the property anyway—maybe it's in the right location for her—will she like the fact that your rental application is photocopied from a book? Probably not.

When she comes to look at your property, you're also looking at her to determine if she's a good rental candidate, right? She's watching you closely, too. Everything you do provides an impression of what kind of landlord you are. You want to show potential renters that you're the best at what you do and provide your tenants with quality service.

RENTAL REMINDER

Something as simple as providing a freshly printed set of application documents leaves a lasting impression. And that's your goal—leaving a lasting impression.

Even if this applicant doesn't rent from you, you still need to be aware of the impression you're making. Maybe she wouldn't rent this particular property because it's farther away from the train than she wanted or because she accepted a job in a different town. But that doesn't mean she won't give your property a second thought later if her needs change. When she does consider it again, how you presented yourself as a potential landlord will stick in her mind.

Also keep in mind that someone who looks at your unit today could easily refer a friend tomorrow or next year because you made that lasting impression and established a relationship.

Marketing for Success

Pulling out all the stops to ensure your property gets—and stays—rented takes some time and commitment, but it's well worth your effort. Devoting effort to marketing your investment property can pay off handsomely in the years to come.

When it comes to marketing and advertising your property, you have many ways to find potential tenants:

- Creating a website for your property
- Placing ads on rental websites
- Placing ads on free sites like craigslist
- Advertising and marketing with social media such as Facebook, Twitter, and Pinterest
- Pinning fliers to bulletin boards
- Taking out ads in newspapers
- Setting up online virtual tours
- Designing brochures
- Marketing to local real estate agents
- Taking out ads in rental magazines
- Making sales calls to local employers
- Placing yard signs on the property
- Placing ads in international magazines and newspapers

And that's just a few of your options.

Create a Website for Your Rental

If you're renting a single apartment, you probably don't need to create a website for it, but if you're renting a vacation home, building a website for your rental property is a good idea.

You don't need anything too elaborate when it comes to your rental website. There are free and low-cost ways to create a simple website. Blogger.com and Network Solutions (networksolutions.com) are two options.

Whatever route you choose, include a description of your property, several flattering photos, and your contact information.

Smart Ad Placement and Search Strategies

You can spend a lot of time and money writing and placing ads and designing brochures and fancy websites but still not get the results you're looking for. So it's essential that you understand how potential tenants actually search for and find your property. Then you can maximize where you spend your marketing dollars by placing ads where your potential renters actually look.

Potential tenants can search for properties in many ways, but in today's tech-savvy world, the most popular way is by searching online. Renters search a community's Multiple Listing Service, web listing sites, or craigslist. They search by property location, rental terms (nightly, weekly, monthly), or a specific mile radius from a desired location like an office. Other searches focus on rental rate, bedroom count, furnished or unfurnished, vacation rental, corporate housing, pet friendliness, move-in readiness, or property type (apartment, house, and such).

> **WATCH OUT**
>
> Be aware of websites on which you can place free listings, such as craigslist. These are popular places to list properties, but you might discover that an hour after you post your property, your listing is buried under 100 more. This might not be the most effective outlet.

If you want to attract someone from the medical profession because your property is located near a hospital, include the name of that hospital in your property description so it comes up in a search. If you want to attract a renter who is moving from out of state or even out of the country, you need to market your property on websites that have multistate and even international exposure, not just local appeal.

Local newspapers are a good advertising outlet, too. International tenants especially search online and on the websites of newspapers in the area where they're looking to move.

We talk more about where to list your rental later in the chapter, but start thinking about and researching how you can get tenants to find your rental now.

Craft Your Marketing Plan

Now that you know how renters search for properties, you can design a marketing campaign that fits your budget and your type of rental so you successfully reach your target tenants. A marketing plan lists your budget and what marketing tools you're going to use.

If, for example, you're marketing a vacation rental, your marketing plan might include the following:

- $1,000 budget

- Design a website

- Take out ads in travel magazines and newspapers

- Social media promotion on Facebook, Twitter, and Pinterest

- Hire a college student to help with marketing

Because most people find vacation rentals online, maybe you don't need a printed brochure. Instead you design a brochure that someone can download and print from your website. You don't want fliers, but you want to use social media to promote your product and decide you'll find a local college student who can work part-time to do this for you.

Your marketing plan should include how much each item costs so you know if you're sticking to your budget. How much are you going to pay your college student? Or will it be an internship? How much will it cost to place ads in the magazines and newspapers for several months? If you have a $1,000 budget and want to advertise in travel magazines, you're probably not going to have enough money. Instead, consider putting up banner advertising on travel websites, which are more affordable. If you haven't designed a website yet, who is going to design your website, and how much will it cost to keep it maintained? Elaborate websites can cost thousands of dollars. Social media is mostly free, but you can purchase ads on the sites, so what's your budget for that? All this should go into your marketing plan.

RENTAL REMINDER

As a general rule of thumb, you should dedicate anywhere from 1 to 3 percent of your total annual revenue to marketing your property. In a Corporate Housing by Owner "By Owner" survey, 43 percent of respondents invested more than $500 on their annual marketing plan. That's really not a lot of money to find the right tenant. It's important to remember that marketing your property is part of your investment. Stick to a long-term strategy that targets quality tenants.

Most importantly, your marketing plan should not rely on just one marketing tactic. For example, marketing your property by placing a For Rent sign on your Florida property might garner local interest from those driving by, but your perfect tenant might be someone in California looking to move to Florida. They won't know anything about it if your only marketing outlet is that sign. That person is looking online. You'll need a combination of various strategic marketing efforts for the best results.

Make Your Property Stand Out

As you're marketing it, one way to make your property stand out is to furnish it. Tons of unfurnished properties are available for rent, but very few homeowners are tapping the potential of offering a fully furnished short-term property for rent. Sometimes finding that information in a property search is the thing that brings a tenant to your rental.

A short-term rental can be used as corporate housing and earn nearly three times the rent. Short-term rentals also mean less wear and tear, with no furniture constantly being moved in and out. High-quality tenants—typically traveling executives—will seek out upscale furnished apartments, so be sure you market this feature if it applies to your rental.

You can use other incentives to attract quality tenants. Look for creative ways to attract tenants by including free perks in the rental price. Some ideas include a gym membership or gym equipment usage or a monthly cleaning service, which is bonus for you, too, because you know your place will be cleaned.

> **RENTAL REMINDER**
>
> Market your property even when it's rented. The old adage "The best time to find a job is when you have a job" also applies to rental property. Don't get too complacent. Always be looking for your next tenant.

Get Testimonials

A competitive renter's market means potential tenants are pickier about who they rent from. Today's tenants want to work with professional landlords and don't want to have to train a newbie landlord to do the job right. To show you have the experience tenants are looking for, get testimonials and add them to your packet of information you have available for potential tenants.

Ask current and former tenants to write you a short letter of reference testifying that they enjoyed your property and that you were amicable to work with. This little effort will make your rental property stand out to future tenants.

Track Your Success

If you have a website, you can use it to track where your visitors are coming from, including what search terms they're using to find your website. If you have a page on a third party's site you pay for, you should have access to similar statistics.

Understand the overall volume of the website and on your specific property listing. See how many views, clicks, and direct email leads you've received from your listing(s). You might notice trends that are useful to help you market your property in the future.

If you placed a banner ad on a travel website, for example, are visitors clicking on your ad? Was it worth spending the money? If you find out your ad isn't getting views and clicks, you can decide to spend your money somewhere else the next time.

On your own website, your tracking statistics might show that most of your visitors are coming from Europe. Next time, you might want to target your advertising in Europe to draw more tenants.

When you place in ad, consider using different phone numbers for different marketing efforts so you can track exactly where phone calls come from. Your newspaper ad can list one phone number, while another ad can list another phone number. That way, you can see which ad drew more phone calls. Or place codes in the ads and ask the caller to give you the code so you know where they saw your ad.

Write It Well

One of the main things that will win you tenants is what you put in your written ad. If you're not a writer, you might be dreading this part of marketing. You needn't be worried.

In your write-up, be honest in how you describe your property. To get started, brainstorm a list of words that describe your rental. *Modern, quaint, upscale,* or *upgraded?* Write as many adjectives as you can. Now make a list of words that describe the neighborhood. *Trendy? Quiet? Family-friendly?*

Keep it clear and simple. Use your descriptive words list when you're writing your advertisements and flyers. Use them on your property website, too.

Don't overpromote your property or say it's something it's not. Watch out for bait-and-switch wording, and don't try to lure tenants with false advertising. For example, don't say your property is sunny if it really only gets sun for an hour in the morning. *Bright* could more accurately describe your property and give a potential tenant the right image. Avoid slang words when describing your property, too, because some people might not understand them.

 **WATCH OUT**

Be careful with your wording in your advertisements, and be sure there's no possibility of discrimination by limiting who can rent your property.

There are generally four sections for a property description: the title, a short description, a longer description, and list of features or amenities. For a title, don't just write "Two-Bedroom Apartment." Instead, add adjectives specific to your property, such as "Upgraded and Bright Executive Two-bedroom."

For the short description, use two or three sentences to catch a renter's eye: "Comfortable, well-appointed studio situated in the heart of the Financial District with a 24-hour security concierge desk. This condo boasts a bright eastern exposure, with views of the Bay Bridge and the high-rises of downtown San Francisco. Condo features hardwood floors, stainless-steel appliances, in-unit washer and dryer, flat-screen TV, large queen bed, and large closet."

For the long description, write three or four paragraphs that describe the property, the building, the neighborhood, and any features you think you should highlight. Then for your amenities list, note 10 to 20 items that show additional value, like oversized parking, additional storage, air-conditioning, weight room, or mountain views.

Picture It

Photos and videos share a lot of information about your property. They're especially helpful for renters searching for properties quite a distance from where they live.

These visual aids can make the difference in whether a potential renter is interested in your property.

Photography Pointers

If you write that your rental is state-of-the-art and upper scale, the photos of your property had better reflect that, too. Otherwise, the renter is going to notice the difference and move on, which means lost money for you.

Your photos may be the only means a potential tenant has of evaluating your rental before actually making an appointment to see it, so it's important that your photographs be good quality, clear, and appealing. They have to make a potential tenant *want* to call and make that appointment. Remember, first impressions are everything.

Follow these tips to ensure your listing is picture perfect:

Lighting: Take pictures when lighting is at its best indoors and out. Take pictures on a bright and sunny day, and turn on all your lights. This sends a warm and inviting message to any potential tenants. Avoid backlighting. Tenants like to see details, so get the camera as close as possible to the item you want to feature.

Focus: Your photos should be in focus. No blurry images ever!

Quantity: Seeing is believing, so the more photos you can show of your property, the better. Potential tenants want to see as much as possible before they invest the time and energy in seeing the property. Take photos of the exterior and the interior, including the living room, kitchen, bathrooms, bedrooms, closets, and any other beneficial features.

Details: Potential tenants want photos with details. They want to see the brand-new stainless-steel refrigerator you mention in the ad, as well as the updated bathroom you brag about. Be sure those details are represented with close-up pictures.

Extras: What else can you take photos of? Get shots of the yard and pool, hot tub, parking space, neighborhood, views, and exercise facilities, if they're worth showing.

Staging: You might have heard of staging if you've watched any home renovation or decorating show. Staging a property means you set up furniture and a few decorative accessories to give potential renters a better idea of how the property would look when they move in.

You can rent furniture and set the table and light the room just for the right mood. Arrange pillows on the sofa, take wrinkles out of bedding, unplug and hide electrical cords, and make an effort to declutter rooms for clean photos. If you have a pool on the property, put out lounge chairs, towels, and glasses of lemonade, and take quality pictures of these and all areas. These types of photos can help potential tenants imagine what it would be like living in your property.

RENTAL REMINDER

For more information on home staging and finding a professional home stager, visit the Real Estate Staging Association at realestatestagingassociation.com. Here you can find consumer information and find a home stager to help you rent your property.

If you're not a good photographer, or if you don't have a digital camera, hire a professional who has the equipment and experience you need to get great digital shots of your property. It's worth the investment, and you actually might be surprised at how reasonable the cost is. Search websites like Obēo (obeo.com) for a local photographer who knows exactly how to get the best marketing photos for you.

Virtual Video Tours

In addition to photos, make use of videos, especially virtual video tours.

Think of all the money you spend promoting your rental property listings, and add to that the cost of your time and your gas to travel to appointments to show the property.

Now consider this: 81 percent of U.S. tenants make use of virtual tours when they're searching for a rental. Only 15 percent actually schedule and attend in-person tours. Virtual video tours are easy to make and even easier for your potential tenants to use, and they'll appreciate the effort you save them.

It takes only an hour or so to create a virtual tour, but then you essentially have an around-the-clock online open house renters can experience from the comfort and convenience of their home via their computer. If, after watching your tour, a tenant is interested in making an appointment, he or she can.

A virtual tour isn't a substitute for an actual walkthrough, but it is an important opportunity for you to display your property the way you'd like. Your goal is to entice the online shopper to take the next step and give you a call. With a virtual tour, you are in complete control of your listing and all the features that will make your listing stand out from other properties.

Remember, the goal of the virtual tour is to get your property rented. Film it as you walk through your rental, looking at things like a potential tenant would. Make it, at the very least, 30 seconds long to up to 2 minutes. Show every room, any special features, and any amenities of the property. Don't get carried away in length, or by adding music and other fancy extras. Keep it simple, and highlight your property's best aspects.

Listing Your Rental

Now that you have a fantastic write-up of your rental property, along with clear and flattering photos and an easy-to-use virtual tour of your property, you need somewhere to put it.

You could post your property listing on craigslist, or you could feature it on larger international sites, on topic-specific sites like student or corporate housing, or with your local real estate agent on his or her site.

Topic Sites

We don't know about you, but we think it's easy to get overwhelmed by the volume of choices one online search can return. Type in "one-bedroom apartment Denver" in Google, and you get 3.5 million results. So how can you get your property to the top of the list? That's where a well-optimized topic-specific website can make a huge difference in whether your property is seen and rented.

Examples of topics include student housing, corporate housing, nurse housing, by owner, university, medical, or sublet. Websites with specific topics like these work hard to develop long-term relationships with the renters who use their site and often have memberships in trade organizations that connect with these renters.

Take a minute to learn about a site before you pay to list your property. Find out how long the site has been around, what traffic it gets, where else the site feeds its listings, what membership or organizations it's connected with, and what reviews it has from other property owners.

craigslist

craigslist (craigslist.org) is a popular website and has many uses. craigslist is a great place to market your property for free, but it doesn't come without great risk of attracting the wrong type of tenant or wasting your time with the need to repost or speak with all the wrong tenants.

We've found that most property owners advertise on paid internet sites because they prefer to market their properties where quality renters will find them, not just on high-volume sites.

Wherever you choose to list your rental property, be sure to keep your listing updated. If you upgrade appliances, mention that in your ad. If you list the rental fee in your ad but then raise it, update it in the ad, too. Change your phone number or email address? Change it on all your marketing resources, too.

 REAL ESTATE ESSENTIAL

Tenants want to work with landlords who are organized and keep their information current. Tenants get frustrated when they contact a property owner because a rental fits their budget, only to find out the rent was raised months ago.

Smart Social Media Strategies

A successful landlord takes advantage of the latest techniques to help tenants and promote his or her property. In today's world of social media, that means using such tools as YouTube, Pinterest, Twitter, Facebook, and blogs to connect with the right tenant.

Unlike traditional marketing avenues, where you just put your message out into the universe, with social media, you send your message to people you've specifically connected with because they have something in common with you. For example, creating a Facebook page and having people like your property means they sought you out, so they're interested in what you have to say and promote.

You don't need to be a tech-geek to work these technologies. They're generally easy to understand, affordable, and, in most cases, free.

You can utilize social media with your personal account or set up accounts specifically for your property. One of the advantages of setting up a Facebook page or locked, members-only Twitter account for your property is that you can use this account as a way to communicate with tenants, send emergency alerts, or alert your tenants that the exterior windows will be cleaned next Thursday.

YouTube

YouTube (youtube.com) is about more than just watching the newest and funniest animal or baby videos. It's a video-sharing website where users can upload, view, and share video clips.

Whether you're publicizing your property, creating a virtual tour, or teaching a tenant how to change an air filter, all you need is a digital camera or camcorder and a video-editing program or smartphone app, and you can make and upload your video to YouTube. The exciting part is that someone in New York might see your video and like it. Then someone connected to that person can see your listing, too, simply because the New Yorker liked it.

Facebook

Facebook (facebook.com) fan pages are a must for most businesses—and that's true for your rental property business, too. Facebook is an easy way to stay connected to people interested in what you do and your properties, especially those in your local area. Facebook can also be used to spread the word about an available property you have, a special you're running, new amenities to your rental property's neighborhood, and such. A Facebook page doesn't cost anything to set up and maintain, so networking and marketing on Facebook can be beneficial to your business and your bottom line.

To start a Facebook page for your business, you must first have a personal Facebook account. If you don't already have one, just go to Facebook.com and follow the instructions on the main page. Do not create a *personal* Facebook account for your business. It's not only against Facebook's rules, but a Facebook personal account has a limit on the number of people you can friend, which could also limit the number of people who can connect to your business.

To create a Facebook page for your business, go to the Create a Page area at facebook.com/pages/create. You'll be given several categories in which you can place your business. Choose what's appropriate for you. We recommend Local Business or Place. Then you can narrow down your category—in this case, Real Estate—and fill in the rest of the information as needed. Read over and accept the Facebook Pages Terms, and you have a Facebook page for your rental property business.

> **RENTAL REMINDER**
>
> You'll have a temporary Facebook URL until you get 25 fans. Then you can choose a permanent URL (facebook.com/*your business*). Once you choose your permanent Facebook URL, you can't change it, so choose carefully!

Facebook gives you several opportunities to add images. One is your banner, or what Facebook calls a cover photo, which people see when they go to your page. There's also your profile picture, which people will see both on your page and when you come up in their main timeline feed after they like your page. You can also upload images into albums via your timeline.

The cover photo must be a size and format that won't distort when you upload it, so you might have to try a few photos until you find the one that works best. We recommend using something that will really symbolize your business. You can choose a logo for the name of your business or a beautiful photo of the building(s) you own. You can change it occasionally by hovering over the section for the cover page.

Your profile picture can be any size. We recommend making it something simple to remember. This is a great place for a logo, if you have one. If not, focus on something easily identifiable—*one* thing. If the image has a many pieces and parts to it, it will be hard to tell what it is due to the small size allowed. You can change it by hovering over the section for the profile picture.

Flesh out your page's "about" section. Potential customers will look here to find out more about you and your property, so make the most of it. You can write about the properties you own, awards you've won, organizations you're a part of, and so on. It's the first impression your customers will have of you, so be sure it's a good one.

Facebook isn't as interactive as Twitter, but it's still important to remember that social media is a two-way street. If you post multiple times a day, you could wear out your welcome. We recommend you don't post more than once a day.

Do respond to followers' posts and take an interest in what they're doing. Ask questions, check in with your followers, and respond respectfully to comments and concerns posted on your page. Obviously, the pages will vary from business to business and location to location, but the key to posting is to respect your fans and treat their concerns seriously.

People can find your Facebook page by simply looking you up, so it's important that the name of your Facebook page matches the name of your business. You also can share your Facebook page on your other social media sites, should you have them, as well as include the link on your business cards. If you don't have a website, you can also direct people to your Facebook account for more information on your business.

Twitter

Twitter (twitter.com) is the most active of all the social media sites and the one with the widest reach. So be sure to include it in your marketing campaign.

The idea behind Twitter is simple: you post up to 140 characters at a time on any subject or topic. For example, you might post "New property available in the downtown #Chicago area for #rent" (more on the # hashtags later). Anyone who searches for "Chicago" or "rent" will find your post, or "tweet." You also can post links to photos on Twitter (but not the actual photos).

> **RENTAL REMINDER**
>
> Social accounts are great for marketing your property, but don't post ads for your rental *all* the time or you'll be marked as spam. Instead, run contests (give away gift certificates to local restaurants, for example) to interact with your customers and encourage more people to like your Facebook page or follow you on Twitter. You also could talk about a great new restaurant in your rental's neighborhood or comment on national real estate topics.

To create a Twitter account, go to twitter.com. It's easy enough to sign up—just pick a username and type in your name and email address. If you're promoting Smith Property Management, for example, your username should be SmithProperty or something similar. If you use your name, your customers might not find you because many will look you up by your business name.

To edit your Twitter page, click on your username and then click the Edit Profile button. Add your business name—not your personal name—and a description of your rental property, as well as your location and website. If you don't have a website, you can always link to another social media site, such as your Facebook page.

Like Facebook, Twitter allows you to upload two images—a cover photo and your icon photo. The cover photo sits behind your icon photo, so instead of a logo, we recommend using a beautiful photo of your business location. Your icon photo should be your logo or something easily identifiable. It will be the image most commonly associated with your account, as well as the one in focus when people go to your page.

Before you start tweeting, it's important to understand hashtags. The hashtag is the # symbol, followed by a word, phrase, or sentence with no punctuation or spaces. For instance, #realestate is a hashtag that might be of interest to your customers. When you tweet using a hashtag—and know that the hashtag symbol counts as one of your 140 characters—those who search for that hashtag on Twitter will find your tweet and, therefore, your profile and business. Using many hashtags is considered bad Twitter protocol, as is spamming a hashtag with advertisements for your business.

Let's look at two examples of tweets using hashtags:

> *Good:* We're a brand new #realestate business in New York! We look forward to working with you!

> *Bad:* We're a #brandnew #realestate #business in #NewYork! We look forward to working with you.

You can tweet a lot of things—news about what your business is doing, questions to your followers, real estate trends you're noticing, and such. Twitter is the most open medium and the one that allows the most communication with your followers, as well as the biggest follower base. The same rules as Facebook apply: act respectfully. Nothing will turn off followers like being dismissed or receiving rude treatment.

Some of your tweets will be retweeted, or shared by others. For example, say you've tweeted about a great new restaurant in the area or an opening in your building. Someone who knows someone or liked your review may retweet it so all of his or her followers can see your post, too. You can track how many people have retweeted what you tweeted.

To reply to a question you get on your account, simply hit the Reply button, and answer. It's very simple to do, and Twitter supplies the username—*@soandso*—of the person in the reply.

RENTAL REMINDER

When responding to somebody, you will find that putting that person's username—*@soandso*—at the beginning of the Tweet means that only those who follow both of you will see it. If you're answering a question you think will apply to more than that user, move the username to the end of the Tweet.

It's important to remember that each tweet is limited to 140 characters. That's not much, so it's important to be concise in your tweets. Try to use proper grammar despite those limitations, as it's most professional.

Pinterest

Pinterest is a popular photo- and link-sharing website where users "pin" things they like to virtual bulletin boards. You can create a Pinterest account at pinterest.com by signing up with either your personal Facebook account (you can't use your business's Facebook page) or an email address (you *can* use your business's email address). Simply enter your name, email address, and other basic information. You also can upload a profile photo and link to a website in your profile.

Once you've created your account, you can upload photos of your real estate property or share links of people talking about your location. To do so, go to your profile, create a board, and name it. Then upload your photo and pin it to the board. Link it to your website, if you can.

When you upload something to Pinterest, you can add a description with certain keywords—similar to the hashtags you use in Twitter. When people look up words that are in your pin's description, they'll find what you uploaded and can then repin it to their own boards, where everybody who follows them or that particular board will see it.

Pinterest isn't the strongest social marketing tool, but it's very popular, so you might want to give it a try. The same goes with the other social marketing tools. Twitter may be great, but Facebook may be a dud, or vice versa. Pinterest works for some people, but not for others. Keep at it for at least 6 months, and see what happens. You'll discover which tools work best for you.

Social Media Management

If your head is spinning with the thought of managing all these social media outlets, you're not alone. There are tools that can help you. Social media management websites enable you to remotely access all or most of your social media accounts at once, sync posts up across the board, and schedule posts in advance.

Social media management websites act as an application, or app. The app logs into your account and posts with your permission. You have to approve a social media management website as an app in your account; it won't magically have the ability to post. You can remove the app at any time.

HootSuite (hootsuite.com) is the most popular way to wrangle multiple social media sites. You can manage Facebook, Twitter, and other profiles from its interactive deck, as well as schedule posts in advance. However, putting more than five social media accounts on a system means you have to pay a monthly fee, whereas five or under is free.

Another popular social media management site is TweetDeck (tweetdeck.com). This is solely for Twitter and can be installed on multiple platforms.

Seesmic, SocialOomph, CoTweet, Ping.fm, Twitterfeed, Spredfast, Buffer, and SocialFlow are a few other social media management tools you can use, and even more options are available online. If you're looking for a social media management site to handle all your new accounts, play around with a few and find one that best suits your needs. They're all organized differently and have different capabilities.

> **RENTAL REMINDER**
>
> Don't let your social media sites go cold just because you have a tenant in your rental property. Stay connected with the world—and your potential next renter—by posting fun things to do in the neighborhood or a review on a new restaurant around the corner. You never know who's watching.

Successful Property Tours

Many potential traditional tenants will want to tour your property in person prior to signing a lease. If your property is a corporate rental, many of your potential renters will be from out of state and will see your online photos and video tour only prior to renting the property. If your property is a vacation rental, the majority of tenants will be from out of the area and won't take a property tour.

How you conduct a property tour directly affects your chances of leasing your property. Start by staging the property for the tour. Get there a few minutes early and open the front door, turn on the lights, and make the property look inviting. It takes only an extra 5 minutes, and your goal is to get the property rented as quickly as possible. If the property is currently occupied, notify the existing tenant and get written permission to enter. Never leave a potential tenant alone in an occupied unit, and don't touch or move the existing tenant's belongings.

Think about how you'll conduct the tour. What room will you start with and end with? Tour the entire property, including its amenities and features that the tenant will use—even the parking space. Talk about these features as you tour the property. Be sure to bring all the keys you'll need to access any out-of-unit features. End the tour in a room that leaves a lasting impression on the tenant. For example, finish the tour on a balcony overlooking a view of the river or in the bedroom with a view of the fireplace. At the end of the tour, ask tenants what they thought about the property and if it meets their needs. Answer any questions they may have.

If you have more than one rental property to show the prospective tenant, think about which order to tour them in. A good rule of thumb is to end with the property you think the person will choose.

Too many choices can be overwhelming, so if you own multiple properties, try to limit your property tour to no more than five properties. Print out a map with your route and rental locations clearly marked, to make it easy for the tenant to follow you if he or she is beyond walking distance.

Making the Most of Inquiries

You're getting emails and phone calls inquiring about your rental, but are you effectively converting those inquiries into contract signings? Here are some tips to help convert a prospect into a renter:

Respect each lead: You never know how a lead will turn out, so don't let any stone go unturned. If you don't call back leads because you didn't like something they said or the fact that they had a pet, you may be missing out on the perfect tenant who's willing to make compromises in order to rent your property.

Mind the 24-hour rule: Potential tenants will contact you based on the information in your property description. As a general rule of thumb, either immediately respond to a tenant request or respond within a 24-hour time period. You can lose potential tenants or receive a bad review for your listing by being unresponsive to requests. Business travelers especially need to confirm housing as quickly as possible. Any delay from you could result in a missed opportunity.

Use the phone: Whenever possible, get a potential tenant on the phone. Email is nice and fast, but great tenant relationships are developed through personal connections. Take time to listen and understand your contact's needs over the phone, and you'll find that your tenants will do a better job of taking care of your property—and they'll likely stay longer, too! Chances are, the prospective tenant is sending out several queries, and you want to be the first to snag the lead by picking up the phone.

The Least You Need to Know

- Marketing your property is the key to investment success.
- Take time writing your property advertisement. The right words can mean the difference between a sale and a vacancy.
- Take great photos of your property and use them in the ad—along with a video virtual tour.
- Take advantage of free social media sites, such as Facebook, Twitter, and Pinterest, to spread the word about your rental.
- Once you hear from someone because of an ad, be sure you do everything you can to turn that inquiry into a rental.

More Renter Considerations

Ideally, you want the perfect tenant. Everyone gets along, they pay their rent on time, and no one causes any conflicts. But no matter what you do and how good you are to your renters, some of them will cause problems. These can range from simple noise complaints, or late-night parties, to far more serious issues. How do you qualify tenants, set up rental rates, and avoid getting stuck with a problem tenant?

You've purchased a property, upgraded it, and found a tenant interested in renting your property. What you do now establishes the framework of your relationship with your tenant that could last for years to come.

In This Chapter

- The importance of good communication
- Checking up on applicants
- Selecting and inheriting tenants
- Talking about rent
- Beware of scams

Start with Good Communication

Every relationship starts the same way—two people getting to know each other. Your relationship with your tenant is no different.

Start building the right relationship with your tenants on day one with good communication and an understanding of expectations. Your tenants should know what's required on their part when they fill out the application, sign the lease, and move into the property.

Don't just assume the tenants have read every word in the application or lease. Take the time to verbally review everything, from what references you'll check, to how the building works, to what you expect from them and what they should expect from you. Communication is the key to any successful relationship.

The Application Process

The rental process starts with a rental application and a tenant reference authorization form. You can use standard forms available online, or you can personalize these documents to better align with your expectations. We also provide some sample documents in Appendix C.

Remind potential renters that by completing a rental application, they're giving you access to their financial and other personal information. You'd be surprised how many tenants don't understand what they're authorizing by signing the application form. This is especially true with employment verification and references. Be sure they understand that you'll be calling their boss to verify their current employment.

To keep everything legal, do not start checking their information until you have a signed agreement giving you authorization to do so. Your rental agreement should include wording such as this:

> I authorize the verification of the information I have included on this form, as well as verification of my credit history, as they relate to my tenancy and to future rent collections.

Before you start the expense of running reports on potential tenants, ask for a photo ID and verify that they are who they say they are by matching them to the photo on their ID.

RENTAL REMINDER

It's okay to pass on the fees associated with running these checks to the applicant, as long as they're reasonable costs. You cannot charge for your time, however.

All application forms should include the following information for each adult who plans on living in your property:

Personal identification: Complete name of applicant, date of birth, Social Security number, current address, phone numbers (home, cell, and work), email address, and emergency contact information.

Employment information: Company name, job description/title, contact name, address, phone number, email address, and length of employment. If the applicant has been at the job less than 3 years, ask for previous employment information as well.

Rental questions: Current address and length of residence there. If less than 3 years, ask for previous residence information. Also ask for their current landlord name, if applicable, and his or her contact information.

General questions: How many people will be living in the rental property? How many and what type of pets will be living in the rental property? Have they ever been served an eviction notice? Have they ever refused to pay rent? How did they find this property? Have they ever filed for bankruptcy? Have they ever been found guilty in a court of law of criminal activity?

When you have a completed rental application from the tenants, give them a copy of your property lease or rental agreement for review while you do some checks.

Remember, once they give you a completed rental application, it's your responsibility to protect their personal information. Store the application in a secure location, or scan the form into your computer for future reference, password-protect the file, and shred the original document.

Reports and Checks

Now the process of qualifying the tenant begins.

Rental History Checks

There are two ways to verify rental history. First, start by running a rental history report utilizing their rental history and their Social Security number. Numerous websites offer specific reports, or your marketing websites should have a resource page from which you can connect with approved vendors.

Second, pick up the phone and call their current and previous landlords. During this process, also verify that the addresses listed on the application matches the addresses in your report.

Ask the previous landlords, "Would you rent to them again?" As you're having these conversations, remember that these landlords might not give you the entire story. Landlords can be sued for slander or making derogatory comments about the tenant, or the landlord may want to get rid of a bad tenant at your expense.

Finally, verify the potential tenant's eviction history. This can easily be done through a professional company like TransUnion.

Credit Checks

Another way to verify that your tenants will be able to afford your property and that they don't have anything of suspect in their background is to run a credit check. A credit check also tells you if other lenders have given your prospective tenant a loan and whether they've missed any payments, paid on time, or paid them off. In addition, a credit check shows how much debt a person currently has and whether he or she has been sued or filed for bankruptcy.

The best way to do a credit check is to run a credit report. You can do this online easily; you just need to find a good price and a report format you like to read. Almost all credit reports, no matter which agency runs them, go through one of the three national credit reporting agencies: Equifax, Experian, and TransUnion. You can also get more information on credit reports at usa.gov.

RENTAL REMINDER

If you reject an applicant due to bad credit, you're required by law to notify the tenant of the bad report. The Fair Credit Reporting Act requires you to provide notice to the person, including the name, address, and phone number of the credit reporting agency; a statement that the agency did not reject them; and a notice of their rights to dispute the report and the right to receive a free report.

Background Checks

Just as you called the previous landlords, you also need to call to verify employment information. Start by researching the company listed on the rental application. This is easy, thanks to a few quick internet searches.

Then pick up the phone and give them a call. Ask the employer to verify the information provided on the application. For example: "Do you currently employ this individual? Could you verify his or her hire date?" If there's anything that makes you suspicious about either the company or the contact the applicant gave, ask to speak with the human resources department.

This process can also include running criminal history reports. You can do these at the same time you're running a credit report.

If the applicant claims to be self-employed, you'll need to do some more research. You might even want to ask for a previous tax return or the company's financial statements and bank statements. Verify their income to confirm they'll be able to pay the rent due to you.

If the tenant lists other sources of income, such as alimony payments, child support, or Social Security, ask for the documents to back up this information.

Remember, running these checks now is what will make you residual income in the future.

Reference Checks

Personal references can be tricky. Yes, you want to have them, but who in their right mind would give you a bad personal reference? It can't hurt to call these reverences; just remember they probably will say only great things about the applicant.

Start by verifying that the people listed as personal references do exist and do know the applicant. Ask about the nature of their relationship and how long they've known the applicant. If you're not able to locate or verify these references, chances are, this is not a tenant you want to rent to.

Approvals and Denials

In a perfect world, everything about your potential tenants check out and you can let them know they can rent the property. All you need to do now is make arrangements for them to complete the lease and other rental documents.

But sometimes tenants don't check out. You can always say no to a potential renter if they have bad credit. No laws protect people under these circumstances.

However, if everything else checks out, you might still want to rent to them. As a result of the past economic downturn, many people now have bad credit. It's no longer a black-and-white issue when qualifying a tenant.

If you do decide not to rent to them, you'll need to let them know you've denied their application. If you deny a tenant, you have to give that person a good reason and an explanation of why you denied him or her. It's important for you to properly communicate the denial and avoid any possibility of discrimination. If you decide to deny tenants because of their credit history, you have a legal obligation to notify them of the reason for the denial. You can always deny a renter if you find a lie on the application.

To protect yourself from any possible litigation, properly complete a written denial letter. We give you a sample letter in Appendix C.

REAL ESTATE ESSENTIAL

A smart landlord has a specific predetermined approval criteria that applies to all tenants. This makes it easy for you to review the application and completed applicant checks.

Most credit agencies supply you with a form to use when you deny someone based on credit score. You must give this information to the denied applicant so he or she can investigate any discrepancies found on the report. If the tenants indicate they think something could be off on the credit report, you can encourage them to order a free copy of their report to review and correct, if needed, before you run their information. You should not give the tenant a copy of the report you receive. They need to get it directly from the credit agency.

Remember to protect their privacy and discuss their credit report only directly with them. Credit information is privileged, confidential information, and it's illegal to violate that confidentiality. If you have any questions, you can always talk with your credit report agency about the do's and don'ts of credit reports.

Choosing a Tenant

How do you decide who you want to or do not want to rent to? You get to decide based on the facts, your experience, and your gut instincts.

Let's start with "No, you cannot rent my property." Generally, this is because the applicants have refused to provide a required piece of information during the application process, you discover they lied on the application, or you found out they can't afford to pay your rental rate.

As you're reviewing the applicant's reports, look out for some potential warning signs. If the applicant has a credit history that shows late payments, this could mean he or she will also be late with their rent. Look at how frequently they happen and when they happened, and ask the applicant about them.

On the credit report, look at the total amount of debt and minimum amount of payments due, and calculate whether the applicant can afford to pay all those plus rent to you. If you get a bank statement, review the balance and check to see if any cash is available in case of a rainy day. Never assume that just because they want to rent your property, they can actually afford it.

In addition to the finances, check to see if the applicant has moved around a lot. If this bothers you, talk to the applicant about it.

If the criminal check shows past convictions, you'll want to understand all the factors, including what crime was committed, how many convictions have there been, and when the last conviction was. Remember, a landlord also has a duty to protect other residents from known risks, or risks that the landlord should have been able to recognize.

If the applicant is a registered sex offender, for example, there are more specific laws you'll need to research before you rent your property. You can always refuse to rent to a sex offender for that reason. They're not a protected class.

REAL ESTATE ESSENTIAL

The 1996 Megan's Law requires that a list of registered sex offenders be made available to the public. The law does not specifically require that landlords provide information on known sex offenders.

If you're choosing between two applicants, you need to be careful that you don't violate any of the state and federal discrimination laws that could apply to a protected group. We review these laws more specifically in Chapter 17, but for now, just remember the key to carefully consider why you're choosing one applicant over another and be sure you're making a fair and legal decision. Because there's a risk of discrimination lawsuits, it's good practice to keep records of all applications and rejections for at least the past 3 years.

You did it! You chose an applicant! Now you need to communicate with the person and let him or her know the good news. At this time, also review the amount of rent and security deposit due, share any specific rental policies you have, and arrange for the rental documents to be signed. If your new tenants live out of town or state, you can let them digitally sign the lease with a program such as Adobe Acrobat or let them sign the agreement and fax or email it to you.

Inheriting Tenants

It's not unusual to purchase a rental property that's currently occupied with a renter. So what happens when you inherit a tenant?

The great news is, you purchased a rental property that's currently producing income, and right now you have 100 percent occupancy.

The tricky part is, you're entering this relationship blind and had no control of the rental documents, the tenant approval process, and possibly no knowledge about where and how much the security deposit is. Prior to purchasing a rental that's currently occupied, you need to obtain a copy of all rental documents, including rental applications from the current owner.

WATCH OUT

Do not buy a rental property with a deadbeat tenant who's not paying the rent. Have the current landlord evict the tenant prior to purchasing the property.

There are three key elements to inheriting tenants: paperwork, money, and communication. Remember to obtain all rental documents from the current owner prior to purchasing the property. Also have the tenant sign a lease addendum that identifies you as the new landlord with contact and payment information. Believe it or not, it's not unusual for tenants to continue to pay rent to the old landlord. Take the extra step to be sure you get the rent you're entitled to.

Next, you need to figure out the details surrounding the tenant's security deposit and any possible prepaid rent. Money details should all be communicated and processed as part of the purchase contract through the title company processing the sale of the property. The total amount of collected deposits needs to be transferred from the old owner to you, along with any fees, like parking fees, the tenant may have paid for services not yet rendered. You also need to ask if the tenant prepaid the last month's rent and be sure you're credited this amount.

Also check if the current property owner was holding the security deposit in an interest-bearing account. If so, the tenant would be entitled to the interest his or her deposit earned. If you don't get it now, you'll have to pay it out of pocket when the tenant leaves. Remember, security deposits are regulated on a state-by-state basis, and your tenant may be entitled to his or her deposit interest, even if there were charges to the deposit.

The final step in inheriting tenants is communication. Start by introducing yourself as the new landlord. Good communication from the beginning is essential in developing strong working relationships with your tenants. Odds are pretty good the tenants have already heard the property was being sold, but you never know. It's also a good idea to get updated contact information from the tenants. This can easily be accomplished with a contact information sheet you ask them to complete. This can even be your rental application form.

Remember, tenants are also interested in learning about you and will appreciate knowing what to expect from their new landlord. Don't forget to provide all tenants with the new maintenance and contact information.

Negotiating Rent Rates

Before you listed your property for rent, you researched what to charge and set a rate that's competitive in your rental's neighborhood but also gives you a profit. Expect potential renters to ask for a lower rate.

It's possible your potential tenants ask for a rental rate reduction because, regardless of the current rental market, people often simply want to pay less. If you want to get a reasonable market rent because you've priced your property strategically to begin with, here are a few tips to help get the price you want without souring the deal:

Anticipate the negotiation: You have researched your market, you know the comps, and you have priced your property accordingly. (And yes, they probably know the comps, too.) However, be ready for them to want to negotiate, and don't get frustrated and walk away from a possible good deal. Take the time to develop a dialogue.

Give them understanding: Everyone wants to know they're being listened to and to understand what they're paying for. If someone is trying to get a lower rent rate from you, be sure they know exactly what's included in the rent—especially if other items or services like storage or parking are included. Sometimes all potential tenants need is a little understanding of all the great features they get with your property.

Develop a relationship: Explain to them that, as their landlord, you'll take good care of them and they're in good hands. Illustrate how your previous or current tenants have enjoyed the property.

> **RENTAL REMINDER**
>
> Making new tenants comfortable with you as a landlord helps them see they're not getting a run-of-the-mill property to rent, but they're getting a thoughtful landlord, too.

Offer incentives: Rather than lower your rate, you might want to offer to throw in an extra service, like a membership to the local gym or a monthly metro pass. Think outside the box. If you also own a vacation rental, offer a discount if they choose to rent it for their next vacation. Or if they want to move in next week, offer to give them the first week free if they move in this week.

Leave some wiggle room: You want to price your property as strategically as possible, but go into the process knowing everyone wants a deal. Set your rate and then cushion it with a little wiggle room. This way, you can still price yourself competitively and negotiate to make your tenants feel like they're getting a deal. A win-win for all!

Avoiding Scams and Frauds

Rental scams are an unfortunate and ugly side of the real estate industry, but scamming is commonplace these days, and tenants and landlords alike have to protect themselves. Here are some smart ways to avoid being scammed.

International: Double-check all the details when dealing with international tenants. In some parts of the world, scams are a full-time business. If it seems too good to be true, it usually is. Always ask for—and check—references.

Credit cards: Accept them. Cashier's checks and wiring schemes are all the rage these days. If possible, use credit cards for all transactions. Credit cards will more thoroughly protect both you and your tenant from fraud.

Pick up the phone: Don't just communicate with your tenants via email. Require a phone conversation before meeting a potential tenant for a property tour or talking about where to send money. It's always wise, especially when doing business through the internet, to speak directly with the person you're working with. An email exchange isn't enough. Exchange phone numbers, and be sure the person's number works and is legitimately his or hers.

Friday night fraud: Be wary of renting your property on a Friday night for a weekend move-in. People who request to move in on a Friday night usually have a very good story, may come from a reputable company, and have a perfectly good reason to move in over the weekend. Then they pay by check, which takes a few days to clear the bank, but it never does ... it just bounces all the way back. Did you know even a cashier's check can bounce these days?

Take your time, and never rush to lease a property to anyone who shows up on Friday and wants to move in over the weekend. It will save you a lot of time, money, and headaches in the long run.

The Least You Need to Know

- Choosing the right tenant is vital to your investment success.
- Do your due diligence before allowing a tenant to rent your property.
- If you have to say no to applicants, be sure they know why.
- Never discriminate against any applicant.
- If you inherit tenants, get to know them and establish your rules.
- Be aware of rental scams, and don't allow yourself to fall prey to them.

The Business Side of Rentals

You found the right property, prepared it, and found the right tenant. The contracts are signed, the tenant has moved in, and the rent is being paid on time, building your income stream. Now it's time to learn about running the day-to-day details.

Have you heard the old saying about financial success, "It's not about the money you earn, but it's about the money you don't spend"? This is especially true with rental properties, not only when it comes to managing your expenses, but also when managing potential liabilities that can cost you even more money.

A smart landlord understands that the rent you collect does not equal profit. A smart landlord also realizes that, to maximize the return on an investment, the money collected must be handled with care.

In Part 4, we help you ensure that the money keeps coming in and you're handling it with care.

CHAPTER 11

Money Management

If you're in rental real estate to make money, you'll want to read this and the next chapter. In this chapter, we cover a lot of details about money, from rent collection, to the best banking processes to have, to security deposits, and more.

All About Rent

We discussed the importance of setting the right rental rate in an earlier chapter. You analyzed your target market, market demand, and your location, among other factors, and you determined a rental rate that's competitive for your location and type of property but still nets you a nice profit.

Now it's time to start collecting rent from your tenant.

In This Chapter

- Collecting, processing, and increasing rent
- Understanding security deposits
- Late fees and other fees
- When tenants don't pay

Collecting Rent

In the good ol' days, a landlord could simply knock on your door every month to collect the rent. Although that's still a route you can take, generally that doesn't happen much anymore. So how is the rent collected today?

You have several options. Remember, this is your money, so choose what's best for you, not just what the tenant wants. And be sure your rent collection policy is in writing as part of the rental document. Now, about those options.

If you live in or have an office near the rental property, you could ask the tenant to deliver a check for the rent to you every month.

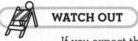

WATCH OUT

If you expect the tenant to drop the check into a mailbox, be sure it's secure and someone else doesn't walk off with your money.

Electronic transfers or bill pay is another option. The money arrives overnight and can't get lost in the mail. You may incur bank fees, so be sure to ask your bank about this before you accept this type of payment.

PayPal might work for you, too. The nice thing about PayPal is it doesn't require you to set up a merchant account. Funds are transferred quickly from one account to another for a fee of between 2.2 percent and 2.9 percent of the amount charged plus 30 cents a transaction. If you have more than one property, PayPal has different professional levels for use.

You also can accept credit card payments. Just set up a merchant account that accepts credit cards. You'll be charged a percentage of the transaction—generally 2 or 3 percent, depending on your credit history and the type of credit card you're processing. When you charge a Visa or MasterCard, it generally takes 3 to 5 days for the funds to be deposited into your account and up to 7 days for American Express.

If you can meet with your tenants every month and can swipe their credit card, Square (squareup.com) is a great solution. Or you can go to Corporate Housing by Owner (corporate housingbyowner.com) and create a fee account that will enable you to set up monthly credit card processing online.

If your tenant moved into the property in the middle of the month, it's a good idea to prorate the first month, or collect rent just for the days in the month the tenant lived there. That way, rent will always be due on the first of the month.

By collecting rent on the first of the month, it's easier to see when rent is late and easier to calculate a late fee. If you have more than one property, you can then know all your rent is due for all your properties on the same day.

When you receive the rent payment, it's a good idea to give a receipt. You can do something as simple as send the tenant a "Your rent was received on _____/_____/_____. Thank you." email as your written receipt.

This is also a great opportunity for you to communicate with the tenants about additional information that might affect them, such as building repairs or street closures.

Banking

After you've collected rent, what do you do with it? Should you deposit it into your personal checking account? No. Don't do that. There are a number of reasons this can be a bad idea.

As a new landlord, it's best to set up separate bank accounts for your rental business rather than use your personal accounts. Right now we're talking about *commingling* your personal funds and your rental funds, which only increases your financial liability if things go wrong. In the world of real estate property management, very strict laws prohibit the commingling of funds between the property manager and the property owner.

Start off smart, and set up a separate checking account and even a business credit card for your rental property to keep your rental expenses easy to track.

> **DEFINITION**
>
> **Commingling** means to mingle or mix. In property management, it could mean a property manager depositing client funds in the broker's personal or general accounts. A property manager found guilty of commingling funds may generally have his or her license suspended or revoked by the state department of real estate.

Imposing Late Fees

No matter when a lease is signed, or when the tenant moves in, you should always ask in advance that the rent be paid on the first of each month. It's a good idea to specify in your rental documents what day rent is due and what happens if the rent is late.

Rent is considered late if you don't receive it on the first. It's up to you when you start charging late fees. Landlords typically charge a late fee starting on the fifth of the month. Your rental documents should specifically state when late payments will be charged.

There are a number of ways to impose a late fee. Typically, it's a fixed fee (like $50), a percentage of the rent (like 5 percent), or a per-day fee (like $5). Whatever you decide to do, document it in your rental documents, and be fair and consistent from month to month and tenant to tenant in the way you handle the fees. Remember, the goal generally isn't just to make an extra $100 a month; the goal is to encourage the tenant to take paying the rent seriously and to ensure you have a consistent income. If you let your tenants be late one month, they'll assume you'll let them be late every month.

> **REAL ESTATE ESSENTIAL**
>
> There's a difference between when you can charge a late fee and when you can start the eviction process for nonpayment of rent. Tenants may argue they have till the tenth day of the month before you can legally charge a late fee. That's not true. You have the legal right to demand that the rent be paid on the date it's due.

Increasing Rent

Re-evaluate the rental rate on your property when a tenant moves out and before you start marketing for your next tenant. Do the same when a current tenant's lease comes up for renewal. This doesn't mean you'll get to or even necessarily want to increase the rent, but you should always have a good understanding of what market rent currently is.

Start by asking your current tenants if they plan to renew for another year. Do this at least 2 months prior to their lease expiration date. Let them know if you'll be adjusting the rental rate when you ask. If they choose to extend their lease, get the new lease signed a month before the expiration of their current lease.

You don't *have* to increase the rent on an existing tenant, and we'd advise you to carefully think about it before taking any action. Remember, a great tenant might be more valuable than an extra $100 a month.

Security Deposit Basics

Always collect a security deposit before a tenant moves into the property. Typically, this deposit is equal to 1 or 2 months' rent.

You'll hold the deposit until after the tenant moves out and you've had a chance to inspect the property. If the property is in good shape, and you don't see any damages you'll need to repair, you can return the security deposit to the tenant. If you do see damages, make the repairs using the security deposit as funds. If any is left over, you may return that to the tenant. You also can use the security deposit to cover expenses such as skipped rent.

If your tenants ask to apply the security deposit to expenses during their stay, tell them no. The deposit is there to protect you from loss, and the tenant should be held responsible for any rent or expenses incurred during their stay.

States have different deposit regulations, but generally set the maximum amount you can charge, what type of bank account you need to use to hold the deposit, who gets any interest earned, and how quickly you need to return the remaining deposit after the end of the lease.

Real estate property managers are required to hold security deposits in an escrow account. Private landlords are less regulated, but it's good business to hold the deposit in a savings account or money market account. Tenants generally assume their deposit is tucked away safe in the bank somewhere and don't realize individual property owners could legally spend their deposit, but they'd be responsible for replacing the cash when the tenant departs.

Another reason to set up a separate account for the deposit is to ensure it's not considered income on your tax return. After all, this isn't your money; you're just holding it until the tenant departs your rental property.

In the beginning, with your first rental property, just deposit it in your checking account. If you deposit it in your savings account, it'll accrue interest. You'll be required to calculate this and pay it to your tenant.

 **WATCH OUT**

> States have a number of varying laws regarding how you can hold a security deposit, what you can charge against it, and when you need to return it. Check your state laws, your local landlord association, or your housing authority for more details.

What Can You Charge?

The amount you can charge for a security deposit is limited in many states. Typically, you're allowed to enforce a security deposit equal to 1 or 2 months' rent. Sometimes the age of the tenant, whether the property is furnished, what kind of rental agreement is being used, and whether a pet is being permitted affect the amount.

So how much should you charge? Our advice is to limit your financial liability and charge as much as your state allows. The bigger the deposit you get, the more the tenant has at stake, and the better chances he or she will respect your rental property. In reality, you can charge only as much as the market can afford to pay, which is usually below the legal limit set by your state and local laws.

In addition to a security deposit, you can charge the tenant for accidental renter damage insurance (ARDI) just in case something goes wrong. (We look more at ARDI in Chapter 14.)

In situations such as areas with high tenant turnover or applicants with poor credit, or if you are concerned about a pet causing damage, you'll sleep better knowing you've collected a solid deposit. However, in areas where it's more difficult to find a tenant, you might use a lower deposit amount as a feature to entice a tenant to rent your property.

Be sure to double-check your state regulations before you charge a deposit. Don't get caught accidentally breaking the law.

Keeping or Returning It

State laws are very specific about what you can charge to a security deposit. You can't just decide to keep it; you need to provide the tenant with a detailed account of all charges.

Security deposits can be used for repairing property damage incurred on the property as a result of the tenant. The deposit can also be used to cover the cost of cleaning up a large mess or replacing items missing from the property, like a light fixture or a microwave.

You cannot charge the tenant for normal *wear and tear* on the property. Wear and tear is sometimes difficult to determine and can sometimes cause conflict with a tenant. An extreme example is if you had a tenant move out of a property after 10 years and the carpet needed to be replaced. No, you couldn't charge the tenant for damage to the carpet because it had already exceeded its life expectancy. Remember when you go to charge a security deposit that the definition of wear and tear is subject to the opinion of a court. You also cannot charge the deposit for your own time and work.

DEFINITION

Wear and tear is the gradual physical deterioration of a property resulting from general use, passage of time, and weather. Generally, a tenant must return the leased premises to the landlord in good condition, ordinary wear and tear excepted.

If you're planning to return part of or all the security deposit, it's a good idea to hold on to the money for as long as possible under your state's laws. This time enables you to really examine the property to determine exactly what needs to be fixed that might have been overlooked during previous inspections. Only when you're sure all the damage has been covered should you return the deposit.

Can You Increase a Security Deposit?

As circumstances change, a landlord might want to increase a security deposit—when, for example, a tenant brings a pet to the property.

If you're using a fixed-term lease, you cannot raise the security deposit during the term of the lease unless it's specifically allowed in the lease document. In this case, you need to wait for the lease renewal date to increase the security deposit.

If you're using a written rental agreement that's currently a month-to-month tenancy, you can increase the security deposit the same way you can increase the rent. All you need to do is give the tenant notice in writing; typically, a 30-day notice is specified. You can raise the security deposit without raising the rental rate as long as the new deposit rate does not exceed the state limitations.

> **WATCH OUT**
>
> Rent control can restrict security deposits. Check your local laws for specific details.

What About Interest?

When it comes to interest on security deposits held on behalf of a tenant, things can get complicated.

Many states require a landlord to pay interest on deposits to the tenant if the deposit earns interest while it's in the bank. State laws can also dictate how much interest must be paid, when the interest is to be paid, and what type of notifications a landlord needs to give to the tenant.

Usually, the interest rates mandated by state law are lower than the interest a bank would pay on the funds. Sometimes the landlord can earn some interest on the deposit as well. This happens when there's a difference between the bank rate and the state rate. This is what enables a landlord to collect an administration fee.

Also, it's pretty typical that the interest is paid to the tenant in one of two ways, either annually or at the end of the lease.

What Other Fees Can You Charge?

Security deposits aren't the only kind of deposits or fees you're permitted to collect from a tenant.

A growing trend is adding a specific deposit for pets who could cause additional damage to the property. Instead of refusing to rent a property to a tenant with a pet, you can ask for a special pet deposit. In addition, you can increase the monthly rent if a pet lives in the property. Then you can charge a specific pet cleaning departure fee.

When a tenant who had a pet in the property departs, always clean the property with the assumption that the next tenant is allergic to pets. This way, you get a clean property and don't miss out on the next tenant.

In a tight rental market, a potential tenant may leave a hold deposit, an amount of money deposited with the landlord that allows the tenant the first right of refusal on that property. This process allows the tenant to look around at more properties without the fear of not having a place to rent. If you accept hold deposits, be sure you clarify, in writing, which deposits are refundable and which are not.

As mentioned earlier, a landlord has the right to charge a reasonable fee as part of the application process to cover credit and background checks. The company you hire to run the checks will charge you a fee you can then pass directly to the potential tenant. One advantage of charging this fee to the applicant is that it could prevent a bad applicant from wasting your time—and his or her money. Assuming the tenant passes all the checks, you can choose to absorb this cost or even agree to refund the fee or apply it to the first month's rent.

Some fees are considered nonrefundable, such as fees for credit checks, cleaning, or pets. If a fee is nonrefundable, be sure you specifically spell this out in the rental documents to avoid any disagreements. Some states, like California, specifically prohibit landlords from charging a nonrefundable fee. Check your state for rules and regulations.

The Collection Department

Don't confuse *collections* and *evictions*. Eviction is the legal process of removing a tenant from your property; this might or might not be the result of delinquent rent. (We discuss evictions later in Chapter 13.) Here, we're looking at money and what you can do when a tenant refuses to pay rent or expenses due.

The first step is properly communicating in writing to the tenant what's due. Even in today's world of email, you'll likely get a better response from a tenant if you mail a bill stamped with a big red "Past Due" across it.

> **RENTAL REMINDER**
>
> You can buy Past Due stamps at most office supply stores. For greatest impact, print the past due invoice on a colored sheet of paper, generally yellow or pink.

If the tenant continues to be delinquent and you're unable to collect past due money, you might need to hire a collection agent.

A collection agency charges you a percentage of what it collects, but it's one way to get some of the money owed to you. In these situations, the collection agency might start by seeking a legal judgment against the tenant. When the agency receives a judgment, it's able to pursue legal remedies against the tenant, including tax liens and wage garnishment.

In addition, the collection agency takes the necessary steps to report the bad debt to the credit reporting agencies to protect future landlords from the delinquent tenant.

Another option would be to file a lawsuit in a small claims court.

Ideally, your situation won't ever come to this, but it's important to be prepared and protect yourself.

The Least You Need to Know

- You have many options when it comes to ways of collecting rent.
- Be sure your rental agreement clearly outlines when rent is due, when late payments start, and how much you charge for late rent.
- Understand your state's specific rules and regulations regarding security deposits, what you can keep it for and what you can't, and what to do about interest earned on it.
- If a tenant doesn't pay the rent, you need to have a plan of action to get what's due to you.

CHAPTER 12

More Money Management

Welcome to part two of money management. In Chapter 11, we talked about collecting rent, fees, and deposits. Now the question is, what's your profit? And what are your obligations, tax-wise, to the government? There are different ways to calculate your profit, and there are different ways the government determines the value of your property.

Our goal in this chapter is to be sure you know what questions to ask your accountant, the IRS, and your tax assessor because this can and will make you money.

All About Accounting

Keeping track of the money connected with your rental property isn't a simple task. With rent coming in, expenses going out, and deposits set aside and earning interest, there's a lot to consider.

Setting up a good accounting system is an essential element in your pursuit of rental property success. You'll want to know if you're making money on your rental property and whether you should buy another one. You'll also need to know if you're losing money on the property and whether you should think about selling it. What's more, both state and federal agencies will want to know your numbers to get their fair share via taxes.

In This Chapter

- The importance of good accounting
- Helpful accounting software
- Uncle Sam and taxes
- Understanding depreciation and deductions
- Tax assessments: what's your property worth?

Accountants

Due to the complexity of tax codes, most landlords choose to hire professionals to prepare their annual taxes. If your rental property is in another state, you'll have to complete a tax return for the state where the property is located, in addition to the state where you reside. And some states, like California, have recently introduced new requirements for out-of-state property owners. This might mean you have to pay quarterly tax installments to the state.

Tax issues related to real estate investments can be highly involved and generally change on an annual basis. When choosing an accountant, it's best to find one who regularly works with property owners and is familiar with the specifics of taxes related to real estate.

Certified public accountants (CPAs) are accounting professionals, like real estate agents, who have passed a licensing exam and met all the additional requirements specific to their state. Property managers and landlords aren't required to utilize a CPA for financial reports, but you might find a CPA more helpful when it comes to tax planning and preparing complicated tax returns.

If you're just getting started and need some help keeping track of your income and expenses, you can hire a local bookkeeper and then hire a CPA during tax season. As with all vendors, be sure to properly qualify your potential bookkeeper and ask for references.

Accounting Software

Landlords utilize three types of software: accounting, property management, and spreadsheet.

Accounting software enables you to track all your income and expenses. You also can create reports on trends over a period of time. However, accounting software generally doesn't allow you to track a lot of property and tenant details.

Property management software enables you to track all your property and tenant details. It provides features for recurring maintenance items as well. However, property management software is generally limited in the financial reporting it can do.

Spreadsheet software can be simple or complex, depending on how you set it up. With it, you can track income and expenses and produce reports. There are better programs for tracking your rental success, so use spreadsheets only as a part of your overall system.

RENTAL REMINDER

Generally, you can purchase software for your computer or subscribe to online programs for a monthly fee. You also can utilize property management smartphone apps to keep you as mobile as possible.

Taxes

The U.S. government wants to get involved with your rental property, and that's just the way it works. But until there's a flat tax system, you need to learn and understand the many ins and outs of the taxes related to your rental investment. It's all about tax planning.

The good news is that having an income property opens a whole new world of tax opportunities and deductions. To maximize these opportunities, we suggest working with a tax professional who has specific investment property experience.

If done correctly, tax deductions are one of your biggest benefits in determining the annual rental income on your investment. If done incorrectly, tax evasion can result in fines and possible jail time.

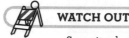 **WATCH OUT**

Security deposits are not income and are not taxable. Do not include these on your tax returns. If you keep part of a deposit after a tenant departs, declare that as income.

Schedule E Deductions

Once you've acquired your first rental property, you need to complete the Schedule E form every year and attach it to your 1040 tax return. The form is fairly simple as tax forms go and shows how much income you received on the property minus your expenses.

The great news is that you've done all the work you need to do by creating your property's profit and loss statement. We don't want you to pay more taxes than you need to, so we want to double-check that you've properly accounted for all your expenses. The following table lists standard deductions you might be able to take to reduce the taxable income on your property.

Generally, you can't deduct the value of your own work. For example, if in your day job you're a plumber, you can't deduct the value of your work. To learn more about what you can and can't deduct on your taxes, go to irs.gov.

Schedule E Deductions

Item	Amount Deducted
Advertising	
Auto and travel	
Cleaning and maintenance	
Commissions	
Insurance	
Legal and professional fees	
Management fees	
Mortgage interest paid to banks	
Other interest	
Repairs	
Supplies	
Taxes	
Utilities	
Depreciation expenses or depletion	

Depreciation

Are you having fun saving money yet? There's also a *depreciation* factor you can apply to your Schedule E to reduce the taxable income you earn on the property.

DEFINITION

Depreciation is an income tax deduction that allows a taxpayer to recover the cost or other basis of certain property. It's an annual allowance for the wear and tear, deterioration, or obsolescence of the property. Depreciation can occur even when the market value of a property increases. Only income properties can be depreciated.

Some investors purchase a property simply to take advantage of depreciation factors to reduce the amount of taxes they pay during the year. However, be aware that the amount you depreciate reduces your annual taxes, but it's added back in when you sell the property and increase your taxable capital gain.

Also be aware that only property value can be depreciated, not land value. The IRS allows you to determine what amount of the total property value is land and what's property. If your investment is a condo, for example, the land value will be low, but if your property is a private home, the land value is proportionately higher.

Check with your local property assessor to determine the separate land and building values on your property, and be sure your numbers are reasonable. In the event of an IRS audit, these numbers will be reviewed.

According to the IRS:

> You recover the cost of income-producing property through yearly tax deductions. You do this by depreciating the property—that is, by deducting some of the cost each year on your tax return. Three factors determine how much depreciation you deduct each year:
>
> * Your basis in the property
>
> * The recovery period for the property
>
> * The depreciation method used

You can't simply deduct your mortgage; principal payments; or the cost of furniture, fixtures, and equipment as an expense. You can deduct depreciation only on the part of your property used for rental purposes.

Depreciation reduces your basis for figuring gain or loss on a later sale or exchange. You may have to use IRS Form 4562 to figure and report your depreciation.

Property Tax Assessments

Most local governments charge a tax on real estate, and how much the government believes your property is worth generally differs from the current market value of the property.

Property tax is a percentage of the property value as determined by the government assessor. This determination is done every few years. Be sure you review your property evaluation to double-check that the details on your property are correct. It's not unusual to find items that are incorrect and potentially cost you higher taxes.

If you find an error, contact your assessor's office to have it corrected. For example, your property may be 2,100 square feet, but the assessment shows 2,700 square feet. In this case, you could be paying taxes on an additional 600 square feet you don't own.

The Least You Need to Know

- Hire an accountant to handle the tax-related issues you'll encounter as a rental property owner.

- Accounting software can help you keep track of your finances.

- Keeping track of your expenses can help you find valuable tax deductions.

CHAPTER 13

Renter Arguments, Evictions, and Vacancies

We'd love to tell you everything will run smoothly with your rental property at all times. But you will encounter problems along the way. You'll have bad tenants, and even your good tenants will have bad days. And eventually, your tenants will move out and you'll have to start the process of filling your property over again. None of this is a big deal if you know what to do and you're prepared in advance.

In this chapter, we help you stay in control of what's going on with your tenant. Arguments, evictions, and vacancies happen all the time, but if you plan for them and put together a plan of action for each scenario, the time and worry you spend fixing these issues when they occur will be significantly shorter. You'll have a shorter vacancy time and, if it happens, a shorter time in court dealing with an eviction. As a result, you'll get back to your main goal—making money.

In This Chapter

- Dealing with tenant arguments
- Understanding housing and building codes
- Handling evictions
- Getting help with evictions
- Preparing for your next tenant

The Hatfields and the McCoys

The best way to avoid disputes with your tenant, or between your tenants, is to establish firm ground rules and outline these rules and policies in your rental documents.

Before signing, the tenants should thoroughly read through the documents, discuss them with you, and express any concerns or questions they might have about them before they move in. When a tenant asks a question, answer it directly and as quickly as possible.

If the applicant doesn't speak English, find an interpreter to communicate the lease details. Be sure the interpreter signs the lease as proof that the document was properly communicated to the tenant.

When the questions have been answered and the lease has been signed, the tenant should get a copy for future reference. Keep the original documents filed away for your records.

Even if you clarify points in the rental documents with the new tenant, sometimes disputes still happen. Whatever it is, it's extremely important to keep a level head and not get overly emotional. You're running a business and need to make business decisions that keep your customers—your tenants—happy.

Tenant Complaints

When tenants contact you with a complaint, listen. Understand what they're saying and where they're coming from. Tenants commonly dispute whether the security deposit will be returned and how much. They also commonly dispute how much wear and tear you think they caused to the property.

> **RENTAL REMINDER**
>
> You can avoid wear-and-tear disputes by doing pre- and post-rental video inspections. Be sure the video contains a time and date stamp to verify when it was taken.

Remember that some complaints you can't solve. For example, your tenant complains about the noise outside their downtown condo, but there's nothing you can do about that. Just listen and let them know you sympathize, but you can't actually do anything to change the noise outside. Maybe you can provide them with some suggestions on how to diminish the noise, like noise-reducing draperies your tenants can hang on the wall to muffle the sound.

Other complaints you need to address immediately. Take action right away if any tenant complains about something that can cause his or her home to become unsafe. If tenants complain that a stair is broken or a railing is very loose, you must fix that immediately, before you go to bed that same night. The last thing you need is to put it off and have a tenant suffer an injury.

If you can't address the issue on your own right away, contact your maintenance person to take care of it straight away. Then have your tenant notify you when the repair has been completed and he or she is satisfied with the results.

Some tenants use complaints to take advantage. As unbelievable as it might sound, tenants might bring in a jar of bugs, release them in the rental property, and complain that the unit is infested. They might demand monetary compensation for their discomfort or they won't pay their rent until the problem is solved.

Don't let a tenant take advantage of you. In a situation like this, having documentation that the property is maintained by a pest control company will help. In some cases, it just might be in your best interest to let the tenant out of the lease and move on to a better one.

Landlord Complaints

What if the dispute is yours? What if your tenant likes to play loud music early in the morning and you receive numerous complaints from other neighbors? Or what if your tenant constantly cooks cuisine that emits odors your other tenants don't like?

You need to talk to your tenant about these complaints, but these issues might be more difficult to solve because there's not always a legal solution to back you up.

Start by discussing the issue with your tenant, and follow up the conversation with a written warning. Set specific timelines and consequences if the complaints have not been corrected. Also, know your legal rights or talk to your attorney, who can follow up with another written warning.

On issues like these, each state regulates what steps you need to follow to evict a tenant. If nothing helps, you might need to take the tenant to court if there's a legal reason you can get him or her to stop. Your main responsibility is to document all the details in writing and connect with a real estate attorney to get you through the process.

Housing and Building Code

A building code is a set of legal rules and guidelines that specify the minimum standards of how a building should be built and maintained to make it safe. Building codes generally deal with construction, electrical, and mechanical aspects of the property. If you renovate a building, and the renovation is extensive enough, you're required to obtain a building permit from the city to ensure your project adheres to the current building codes. In addition, a building inspector needs to inspect your project and give you a certificate verifying that the property meets the legal standards.

In addition, there may be other codes you need to follow, including fire and health codes. Fire codes deal with safety issues and fire prevention for the building. Health codes deal with health-related aspects of the property, such as sanitary issues.

RENTAL REMINDER

Schedule an annual property inspection with the fire marshal. He or she will complete a general inspection and test all smoke detectors. Some fire marshals have a form for you and the tenant to sign confirming that all detectors are in working order.

Code Complaints

If tenants aren't happy with how you handle a complaint, they might report you to the local housing and building code officials. These complaints typically have to do with specific living conditions, such as cracks in plaster, chipping paint, broken gutters, peeling wallpaper, a torn or missing screen, or a number of other conditions.

If a tenant files a legitimate housing-code violation against you and the official finds that the violation exists, you are given a period of time to fix the issue. Make the necessary repairs immediately, and take photos to document the completed work. If you fail to address the violation, you could face a fine or a possible prison term.

It's possible a tenant could file a claim about a building code violation that's incorrect or doesn't apply to you. The latter could be the case if your property is older and is grandfathered in on the codes. In cases like this, if a complaint is filed, you need to file an appeal to avoid paying a fine.

There are no grandfather clauses for fire codes. Your property must always be kept up-to-date on any improvements needed to meet the current fire codes.

But just because you're appealing an order from a housing official to fix a code violation, you're not exempt from making the repair. It's in your best interest to always make repairs in a timely fashion.

Retaliation Laws

Many states have laws that protect tenants who make a complaint against their landlord. These are referred to as retaliation laws and protect the tenant from any act of retaliation from a landlord in response to the tenant filing a complaint.

As a landlord, you cannot file for an eviction, remove certain services, or attempt to implement an unreasonable and significant rent increase after a tenant has complained about unsafe or illegal living conditions, filed a complaint with you or a government agency, joined or organized a tenant organization, or exercised a legal right allowed by your state or local law, such as withholding the rent for an uninhabitable unit.

Remember, more laws protect your tenant than protect you. You have to look out for yourself. That starts with getting to know your state's landlord retaliation laws.

Courtroom Battles

The best way to avoid courtroom battles with your tenant is to adhere to the guidelines in this book. Screen and select the best tenant to avoid "professional tenants." A professional tenant is someone who knows how to work the system and take advantage of select protections in the law to live rent free. Say you own a property that's a corporate rental and the company pays the rent for the employee. A professional tenant finds fault with the property to get cash back from you while the company still pays full rent.

However, sometimes you'll battle with your tenant and may, unfortunately, find yourself in court. If it's gone this far, you need to be prepared. We can't emphasize enough the importance of keeping all written communication between you and your tenants, copies of any important signed documents, and any before-and-after photos. This is where that material comes in handy. Bring this and any other useful documentation to court with you, and you'll be prepared to present a solid case.

> **WATCH OUT**
>
> In some states, tenants can sue a landlord for damages equal to *double* the amount of their rent if a code violation is not corrected within the appropriate time given by the state.

Having the right team members to help you with your rental property comes in handy here, too. By now, you should have an attorney on your team whom you trust and who is knowledgeable in real estate law and landlord-tenant disputes. If you haven't already gotten one, find one now. It's important to have someone to turn to before you go to court.

If you go to court over a dispute, be courteous at all times. Explain your side, but do not let your emotions get the best of you. Conduct yourself as the business professional you are. If you've carefully documented everything, talked to your attorney, and done your homework on the court process, you stand a better chance of winning your case.

Tenant Versus Tenant

Sometimes tenants have disputes with other tenants in the same building. Maybe one tenant dents another tenant's car in the parking lot and refuses to pay to have it fixed. Your tenants may come to you, the landlord, to find a resolution.

Most state laws restrict the amount of control and power you have in situations like these. Even if you wanted to get involved in a dispute between your tenants, you don't really have the authority. Your only course of action is to explain to your tenant that this event does not involve you and they need to take the offending tenant to court if they're unable to work out a solution.

If you have one tenant who is consistently disrupting the rest of the tenants in the building, you might be able to evict him or her on the premise of being a nuisance. (We discuss eviction specifics later in this chapter.) If any tenant action causes a safety issue to anyone else in the building, you need to address it immediately.

Grounds for Eviction

Unfortunately, there may come a time when your tenant isn't quite what you had hoped for and you want him or her to vacate the premises. However, you can't break a contract without a reason, and you can't evict a tenant without cause. You have to have a legitimate reason, something the person did—or, in some cases, didn't do—that broke the agreement the two of you had. Maybe your tenant didn't pay rent or didn't vacate the unit when the lease was up. Maybe your tenant moved in a roommate without telling you or brought a pet into a no-pet building.

How you evict depends on where you live. Most states have devised a few specific types of evictions recognized by state laws. These types of evictions also have specific procedures and requirements you need to follow so you don't end up breaking the law, too.

Nonpayment of Rent

"I'll have the rent for you next week," your tenant says. And next week goes by … and then the next … and nothing.

Nonpayment of rent is the most common reason for eviction. Each time a tenant fails to pay you rent, you lose money. To file an eviction because of nonpayment of rent, you need to produce the rental documents the tenant signed that state the due date for rent payments.

> ($) **REAL ESTATE ESSENTIAL**
>
> Some states automatically give tenants a grace period to pay rent before you can proceed with an eviction. If rent is paid in full within this grace period, you can't start an eviction. So if your rental documents state the tenant's rent is due on the first of the month and the legal grace period for your state is 10 days, your tenant legally has until the tenth of the month before you can begin the eviction process.

You can work with your tenant, too. If it's a one-time thing, and your tenant has approached you asking for an extension, it's up to you to decide if you want to give approval. Whatever you decide, document it in writing.

Lapse-of-Time

Lapse-of-time evictions, also called expiration of lease, come in a close second as the most common reason for eviction. Generally, when a lease expires, the landlord is under no obligation to renew it. This is true whether the lease is written or oral, year-to-year, or month-to-month.

In a lapse-of-time eviction, a landlord evicts the tenant on the basis that the lease or rental agreement has expired. Although a lapse-of-time eviction can be done when a lease is in the final month, landlords who give month-to-month tenancies most commonly use this type of eviction procedure.

You can make a lapse-of-time eviction without giving any other reason other than the lease is up and you want the unit back. Many landlords prefer to use this type of eviction and have month-to-month tenancies because it makes it easier to get the property back.

Breach of Lease Terms or Statutory Duties

In Chapter 5, we reviewed rental agreements and leases and the clauses you could add to them. Adding these rules ensures the tenant has an understanding of what's expected, and it gives you the legal right to take action should the tenant fail to comply with the clauses stipulated in the rental agreement you both signed.

If you believe your tenant is in violation of the lease, send a written notification to the tenant with receipt confirmation notifying him or her of the breach. Give the tenant an opportunity to fix the breach prior to starting the eviction process.

Maybe you have a nuisance clause in your lease and your tenant later caused a nuisance. As a result, in most states, you can evict due to breach of lease, which means the tenant violated a previously agreed-upon rule. However, just like the nonpayment process, states have different grace periods that allow the tenant to fix the breach before you can file an eviction notice.

Illegal Conduct or Serious Nuisance

Tenants have the right to use and occupy a rental unit as long as they don't infringe on the enjoyment of others or violate federal, state, or local laws. If they do, they may be considered a nuisance. Nuisances are commonly classified as private or public.

A private nuisance refers to an activity that does not involve physical trespass but nevertheless interferes with an individual's reasonable use or enjoyment of his or her property. A nuisance could be as simple as someone throwing loud parties every night or a tenant who continuously disturbs the neighbors, resulting in police visits to the property. In fact, the police visit often confirms that the tenant behavior is a nuisance.

A public nuisance is an activity that threatens the public health, safety, or welfare or does damage to community resources. An assault on a landlord or other tenant; use of the leased premises for gambling, prostitution, or drug sales; and other illegal conduct are all grounds for eviction. Unlike breach of lease terms or statutory duties, tenants cannot *cure an eviction* based on illegal conduct or serious nuisance, and there is no grace period before you start the eviction process.

> **DEFINITION**
>
> **Cure an eviction** (sometimes called *quit an eviction*) means to resolve or fix the issue or issues that caused the grounds for eviction.

Building Your "Bouncer Team"

At a nightclub, the bouncer is the big guy at the front door who prevents the wrong people from getting inside and muscles out any troublemakers who did get in.

In real estate, if things go bad with your tenant and you need to get him or her out of the property, you need help. Remember, time is money. The longer the wrong tenant is in your property, the longer you lose money.

Unfortunately, there's no large real estate bouncer who can toss out your tenant, but a number of professionals can save you time and money and help you get your property back. Let's call them your "bouncer team."

Your team should also include the background verification companies who help you qualify potential tenants to avoid renting to the wrong one.

We've stressed in several chapters already the importance of having and using an attorney. You'll want one who specializes in real estate law and evictions and perhaps another—if not the same one—who knows litigation. If you're fighting a tenant in court, hire a qualified attorney with eviction experience to help you, especially if this is your first time. After you have a good understanding of how the eviction process works, you might feel comfortable enough to handle the process on your own.

In some states, you can hire an eviction company that, for a flat fee, handles some or all of the eviction process for you. Such companies can prepare and serve the notice of eviction, file and serve the summons and complaint, process the preclaim judgment, submit the trial appearance fee, complete the court paperwork, show up in court so you don't have to, meet the marshal for the physical eviction, write the security disposition letter, prepare the damage paperwork, and even deal with small claims filing if necessary.

A collection agency is another member of your bouncer team. After an eviction is complete, odds are, your former tenant still owes you some money for rent or damages. As part of the eviction process, the court issues a money judgment or a document stating the amount your former tenant owns you. If you're unable to collect the money by sending the tenant a few reminders, you can hire a collection agency. A collection agency charges up to 50 percent of what it collects, so you won't get all your money back, but you do get some. What's more, your former tenant's credit history is updated to reflect his or her bad payment history with you to protect his or her next landlord from the same problem.

What about the police? Dial 911 only in an emergency situation. If your tenant is suffering a heart attack, if a tenant poses a potential threat or presents a danger to other tenants or to you, or if there's another potentially dangerous situation on your property, call the police.

However, if you need help with an eviction (the police or a marshal can physically remove a tenant from a property if they refuse to leave), find a firearm on your property, or believe illegal activities may be occurring in your property, call your local nonemergency number. In many areas, the number is 311, but look up the number for your area to be sure, and add it to your phone contacts.

You should also visit your local police station and let them know you're a new landlord. Ask for information on emergency preparedness and any other information they may have.

Tenants have been known to contact the police with a complaint against a landlord. If this happens to you, don't get upset. Remember, the first responsibility of an official is to inspect the situation, ask questions, and document their findings. Their job does not include taking sides.

The Eviction Process

It takes only a few hours of work and a relatively small amount of money to properly interview and screen a prospective tenant, but the time and cost to conduct an eviction, or *unlawful detainer*, can be huge.

> **DEFINITION**
>
> **Unlawful detainer** is another way of saying eviction, or the removal of a tenant from a rental unit.

Landlord-tenant laws differ in every state. Because of the complexity of the laws, we won't cover all the details of all the laws here. Rather, we look at the general process. Be sure you get a copy of the landlord-tenant act for your state so you know how it works.

Before you get started, you need to clearly identify who you're evicting and why. If you're evicting a tenant because he or she has an illegal roommate, you must identify the roommate as part of the eviction process. In some states, regardless of how a tenant obtained occupancy of the property, the law requires you to go through the legal eviction process if the person is living in the property.

The eviction process actually starts when the tenant breaks a provision, lease, or rental agreement, or when you're unable to resolve the dispute, you want the tenant out of the property, and the tenant refuses to leave.

There are six steps in the eviction process:

1. Notice to quit

2. Summons and complaint

3. Appearance in court

4. Answer to complaint

5. Trial

6. Judgment and execution

Notice to Quit

Your first task is to serve the tenant a notice he or she must vacate the property. This notice has different names, but the most common is "notice to quit" or "notice to cure." You must serve the notice to quit to the tenant in a specific manner as dictated by your state.

On the notice to quit, you should include the names of the tenant(s), the address of the property, and the reason the notice is being posted. Depending on your state, other stipulations might apply. Maybe the notice must be served by an impartial person, such as a law enforcement official or a sheriff. Some states allow the notice to be handed in person to a tenant in the household who is over a certain age. Other states allow the notice to be mailed.

The notice should give the tenants details on the amount of time they have to resolve the problem, or it can tell the tenants they must vacate the property by a certain date as prescribed by law. You can obtain state specific forms on the internet, from the court, or from your attorney.

The good news is that many tenants take this notice seriously and resolve the item that caused the notice in the first place. If you've served the tenant a notice to quit because the rent is past due, often the tenant will pay the rent owed during the allotted time. In this case, you must accept the rent and cancel the notice to quit. If the tenant tries to pay *after* the grace period, do not accept any partial payments, or you'll have to void the eviction process and start over with a new notice to quit.

WATCH OUT

If tenants are evicted and they leave behind some of their property, some states require that these belongings be stored in a professional bonded and secured storage facility. Typically this cost is the landlord's responsibility. Check your state laws before you toss their stuff in the trash.

Summons and Complaint

The next step of eviction begins after the "fix" date listed in the notice to quit, or the date by which the tenant must resolve the issues that caused the notice. This could also be the date given to vacate the property. This step is generally referred to as the "summons and complaint" of the suit you're bringing against the tenant.

This summons, which is served on the tenant, includes the name and address of the plaintiff (you and the property) and identifies the tenant as the defendant. The summons and complaint explains the reason for the action and stipulates a specific period of time, usually known as an "answer date" to respond to the complaint. How the summons is delivered to the tenant depends on the rules of the state in which your property is located.

In addition to serving the summons to the tenant, you need to file it with the court. It must be filed prior to the answer date on the summons so the court is ready to proceed.

What happens next is specific to each state. In some states, a court date is set. In others, the date is already dictated by law. In yet other states, the clerk sets the court date. Some courts hear housing-specific cases on a set schedule, such as a certain day of the week. You need to know how your courts work to ensure your eviction process goes as smoothly as possible. Remember, time is money. In addition, each state dictates the documents required from both you and your tenant.

Whatever your state's procedures, the outcome is the same: a court date is set and both you and your tenant(s) need to be in court on the date and time set by the court to hear the case.

Appearance in Court

This is your chance to tell your story and document your case. To do that, you must bring with you all the proof you have to make your case. For example, bring pictures of damage, original records of payments made by the tenant, and, of course, the signed lease or rental agreement. If necessary, you'll be asked to bring a certified copy of your property deed to prove you own the property.

If you have a witness, bring that person along, too. If the witness is employed and can't get time off work, you might need to subpoena the person to require his or her appearance in court. You can obtain the needed subpoena documents from the court.

Answer to Complaint

The defendant, your tenant, is always given the opportunity, either in writing or in person, to specifically answer your complaint.

If the tenant fails to appear in court on the scheduled day of the hearing, you can request that the court grant you a default judgment for failure to appear. Basically, this means the judge rules in your favor just because the tenant didn't show up.

A tenant could request a continuance to another date if he or she is unable to appear in court on the scheduled day. Depending on the reason and the attitude of the court, the court may or may not assign a new court date.

You may ask for a continuance, too. If you fail to appear in court, the eviction process is ended and you then have to start over.

Trial

Like everything else, the trial process varies from state to state. Here's a basic idea of how a trial works:

Your case is called by the court clerk to determine whether you're ready to go to trial. When you hear your name called, respond that you are in the court, and be prepared to proceed. Depending on your state or the court you're in, the next step could vary. In some courts, you're assigned to a mediator or a housing specialist who speaks with both you and the tenant and tries to arrange a settlement both of you can agree upon. If an agreement is reached in this manner, it's frequently called a "stipulated judgment."

In some courts, you won't see a housing specialist but instead appear in front of a judge who listens to both sides of the argument and makes the decision. The judge might make a decision on the spot, or he or she might reserve the decision for a later date and mail the decision to you and the tenant.

If the tenant fails to meet a provision of the stipulation agreement, you can file a judgment for failure to comply with the court. The court signs the judgment or assigns a court date to hear the motion.

If you find yourself back in court, the process starts over, with you and the tenant sitting down with the housing specialist, a judge, or a commissioner of the court so a new agreement between you and the tenant can be made. The next step is up to the court. It could continue to give the tenant another chance or give you judgment for execution.

Judgment and Execution

If the judge rules in your favor—or a judgment is granted to the plaintiff—the eviction process is almost over.

You'll receive a written execution from the court to remove the tenant from the dwelling. At this point, depending on your state, you might have another waiting period between the date of judgment and the date you can apply for an *execution*. This is generally 5 days.

DEFINITION

An **execution** is a judicial process whereby the court directs a police officer to seize a property from the tenant—to physically remove the person from your rental.

When you have the execution from the court, give it to a local law-enforcement official recognized by the court to carry out the physical eviction of the tenant from the property. This official notifies the tenant and the court of the date and time the tenant and his or her belongings will be removed from your rental property.

At that set date and time, the official goes to the property and escorts the tenant from the property. Often the official also makes an inventory of what's being removed.

When the property is empty, the official turns over the property to you. Before you do anything else, change the locks.

Creating a Property Turnover Plan

Think of your turnover plan as a mini business plan that walks you through the steps you need to take to get your rental property from one tenant to the next as quickly as possible while ensuring it's still properly maintained. By planning ahead—whether your property becomes vacant expectedly or unexpectedly—you'll know what to do and won't waste any time trying to remember what you did before. Remember, one of the key elements in the formula for being a successful landlord is time, and your turnover plan helps you maximize your time.

When your property is occupied by a paying tenant, consider it in the green zone (green = money). As soon as your tenant gives you notice to vacate or you receive an execution date from the court, think of your property as in the red zone (you're not making any money). Your turnover plan should start as soon as your property enters the red zone. Don't make the mistake of starting your turnover plan after the property is vacant. That's too late. You want as little vacancy as possible. When one tenant moves out, you should have another ready to move right in.

Cleaning: Your turnover plan should include a list of cleaning tasks you need to have done after your tenant leaves, along with the contact information for the cleaning company you use. You want the property as presentable as possible to find the best next tenant.

Have the carpets cleaned because that's typically the first thing a potential tenant notices. Also be sure any additional repairs are completed before you start showing the unit. Do not wait to schedule vendors until the property is vacant. Schedule them as soon as you know the unit will be empty. Those days of waiting could cost you rental income.

Upgrades: Schedule a general upgrade every time your property is vacant. When a tenant gives you notice, schedule a time to walk through the property and identify items that need to be fixed or upgraded.

> **REAL ESTATE ESSENTIAL**
>
> Part of your turnover plan should include measurements of each room and all the windows. This enables you to get quotes for new carpeting or blinds as quickly as possible without having to enter the property or wait for the tenant to depart.

By getting into a routine of upgrading, you avoid walking into a property years from now that needs massive upgrades and sits vacant in the meantime because nobody wants to live there.

Marketing: Again, your goal is to plan ahead. When your tenant gives you notice to vacate, start marketing your property to new potential tenants immediately. Follow the same steps you took when you first marketed your property (go back to Chapter 9 and review or create your marketing plan). Be sure to update any websites or internet property listings you have as well.

In addition to your specific marketing plan, reevaluate the market and your rental rates and see if it makes sense to raise your rates. You might uncover new and interesting places to market your property, and the rental reviews might prove you can raise your rate even more than you thought you could.

The Least You Need to Know

- Even if your tenant reads and understands the policies, clauses, and rules in the rental agreement, arguments and disputes can and do still happen.
- Documentation, in writing and in photographs, is the key to succeeding when any disputes arise.
- Have a "bouncer team" comprised of an attorney, a collection agency, and maybe even the police in place to help you with disputes and evictions.
- It's important that you know and follow the rules of eviction in your state.
- As soon as you know your current tenant is leaving, clean, upgrade, and market your property for new tenants.

CHAPTER 14

The Importance of Insurance

Insurance can be a complicated aspect of the rental property business to understand. On one hand, it's something every landlord must have. No mortgage lender lends money to purchase a property without the property being insured. It's so important that once you have insurance, some lenders require your insurance carrier to notify them if the insurance policy is adjusted or terminated.

On the other hand, insurance is something you hope you never to have to use because if you do, it means something happened to your property—a fire or a flood maybe—that damaged or destroyed your property.

Regardless, the bottom line is that you do need insurance, and the right insurance, to protect your property.

In This Chapter

- Why you must have insurance
- What kind of insurance do you need?
- Setting your deductible
- Understanding adjustments

Yes, You Do Need Insurance

It's worth repeating: you need insurance on your rental property. When it comes to buying insurance, you should shop around for it the way you'd shop for a car. Compare prices and try to get the best deal.

All insurance policies and companies are different, and you should customize your policy to cover both your needs and the needs of your rental property. Your coverage and how much it will cost you depend on various factors, including the size and type of your property, when it was built, what you use it for, and where it's located. If your rental is in an area close to water or a flood plain, for example, you need to purchase flood insurance.

There are also different types of insurance—title, loss of rent, and liability, among others (more on these later)—you might need. These further determine how much you'll be covered and will have to budget for insurance.

> **RENTAL REMINDER**
>
> You can bundle your insurance policies for your primary residence and your rental property to save money. So instead of buying separate policies, you can bundle them into one, which is usually less expensive.

If you own a condominium, don't assume the building's insurance policy covers the inside of your property. Generally, if the building is lost, such as in a fire, the building's insurance pays to rebuild the building, but it doesn't pay for anything inside your walls.

If you're renting your property furnished, tell your insurance agent. Generally, you can get additional coverage for the items inside your property for only $100 to $200 per year. This is an easy and relatively inexpensive way to protect your investment.

Types of Insurance

Different types of insurance are available for residential properties, including the following:

- Homeowner's insurance
- Landlord's insurance
- Replacement-cost insurance
- Cash-value insurance
- Mortgage insurance

- Title insurance

- Liability insurance

- Specific loss insurance

- Loss-of-rent insurance

- Renter's insurance

- Accidental rental damage insurance (ARDI)

Understanding what's available helps you ask the right questions to make the best decision for you and your property.

Homeowner's Insurance

A homeowner's insurance policy covers your personal home, your possessions, and people in your property. Generally, a standard homeowner's insurance policy protects the following:

- The physical structure of your home

- Other structures on your property (storage sheds, pools, boathouses, and such)

- Your personal property and belongings inside your home, up to specified limits

- Your liability or legal responsibility for any injuries incurred on your property

- Additional living expenses if a fire or other disaster that's covered under the insurance policy leaves you temporarily unable to live in your home

Often, for an additional fee, you can select optional homeowner's insurance coverage, such as these types:

- Higher limits of liability for property damage or bodily injury

- Replacement cost for personal property

- Protection for valuables (jewelry, watches, furs, and other items)

- Additional coverage for electronics or computer equipment

When you purchase a property, you purchase a homeowner's policy. However, before your first tenant arrives, change the policy to a *landlord's* insurance policy. Failure to make this change and notify your insurance provider that you're renting the property could result in cancellation of your policy.

Landlord's Insurance

Just like homeowner's insurance, this policy covers both the building and the contents. It also can cover your rental property from financial losses. For example, if you're unable to rent the property due to damage sustained in a fire, you can submit a claim to recover that lost rent.

Replacement-Cost Insurance

In the event of a disaster, your building is a total loss, a replacement-cost policy gives you the money it would take to replace your building at current costs.

Cash-Value Insurance

A cash-value policy is a little different from the replacement-cost policy. In a cash-value policy, if you insure a building you bought for $100,000 and it burns down, the insurance company sends out an appraiser to determine the current market value for your building.

If the building appraises for less than $100,000, you receive the appraisal amount.

Mortgage Insurance

Mortgage insurance protects the lender in case you default on your loan. Depending on your financial situation and how much earnest money you put toward your rental property purchase, lenders might require mortgage insurance. This is especially true if you have less than 20 percent equity in the building.

Mortgage insurance isn't a policy you can request. You get it only if the mortgage insurance requires it because it protects them, not you.

Title Insurance

Title insurance is important when you buy a property. It protects you against problems with your claim of ownership. Like mortgage insurance, it's your lender that requires this insurance.

Title insurance guarantees that the title to a parcel of property is clear of any claims or *liens,* that the title is properly in the name of the title owner, and that the owner has the right to sell or otherwise transfer the property to someone else.

> **DEFINITION**
>
> A **lien** is a claim one person has on a property belonging to another as security for a debt or obligation.

If there's an issue with the title, the insurance company pays damages to the new title holder or secured lender, or it takes steps to correct a problem that's discovered later, such as an incorrect boundary line.

Liability Insurance

Liability insurance protects you from claims of liability connected to your rental property. This coverage is extremely important because it covers your legal costs if you're sued in a personal injury lawsuit.

Landlords are especially vulnerable of lawsuits because tenants can and will blame you for anything that goes wrong, from them falling down the stairs because one was loose to them being scalded because the water heater made the water in the kitchen sink too hot.

In addition to personal injury coverage, your liability insurance should cover claims of libel, slander, discrimination, invasion of privacy, and unlawful eviction.

The good news is that liability covers the costs of both the money awarded to an injured party and the costs associated with your legal defense. Never, *ever* rent a property without liability insurance!

Specific Loss Insurance

Fires, hurricanes, floods, and tornadoes can damage or destroy your property. You might be surprised to learn the damage may or may not be partially or completely covered by your main insurance policy, depending on your policy. What additional insurance you need depends on your property's location. If you live in a designated flood zone, you need flood insurance.

Specific loss insurance covers the cost of replacement, reconstruction, or repair beyond what's covered by your standard property insurance policy. Policies cover damage to the building, and they might also cover damage to nearby structures, personal property, and expenses associated with not being able to live in or use the property when it's damaged.

 REAL ESTATE ESSENTIAL

Insurance premiums increase based on how much coverage you have and where your property is located. Insurance companies even determine your premiums based on whether your neighborhood is considered a high-crime area. Frequently, an insurance company requires properties located in distressed areas to be inspected on a regular basis to ensure that the property continues to be free from defects that could translate into potential losses. Remember, insurance companies are for-profit businesses. They plan to pay out less than they receive from you in premiums.

Loss-of-Rent Insurance

Loss-of-rent insurance covers you if you are unable to rent your property. But this isn't just for when you can't find a renter. Instead, it's for more serious situations. For example, say your rental property is damaged so severely from a flood that it's uninhabitable. As a result, you cannot collect rent because the tenant cannot live there until the property is repaired.

Some landlord's insurance policies automatically include loss-of-rent coverage. Other policies require you to purchase this coverage separately.

Renter's Insurance

Your property's insurance policy doesn't cover your tenant's possessions or cover them in cases of liability. It's a good idea to ask your tenants to get renter's insurance and provide a copy of the policy to you.

Renter's insurance provides coverage for a tenant's belongings against loss due to damages from fire, water, or theft. It covers losses such as repair and replacement of property that's damaged or stolen from places away from home, such as in a hotel room or a parked car. Additional living expenses, such as corporate housing, incurred because the tenant had to leave the rental property due to damages are also covered. Finally, renter's insurance covers liability claims made directly against tenants because of their negligence.

> **WATCH OUT**
>
> If your tenant files a loss complaint against his or her renter's policy and the insurance company finds you negligent and at fault for the loss, the insurance company may be able to sue you for the money they paid the tenant.

Accidental Rental Damage Insurance

The insurance industry isn't static. It continues to evolve and add new and different products all the time to help protect us. Accidental rental damage insurance (ARDI) is the perfect example of this.

ARDI covers damage your renters cause to your rental property. For example, say the tenant turned on the bathtub and got distracted by a phone call. The bathtub overflowed and caused extensive water damage. ARDI should cover this.

Typically, ARDI maximum is set around $3,000. Unlike renter's insurance, which the tenant purchases to protect his or her own belongings, ARDI protects you from damage the tenant accidentally causes to your property.

Some landlords like to collect a cash security deposit and have the tenant purchase ARDI. Other landlords accept the ARDI in place of an actual cash deposit.

These policies are simple to purchase and cost less than $200 a year. They're available through sites like Corporate Housing by Owner (corporatehousingbyowner.com).

The Insurance Process

Typically, when something happens to your property, you contact your insurance company and they tell you to submit a *claim* so you can receive funds to replace or repair your property. Essentially, the claim is an official request for payment as per the terms of your policy. These days, you can fill out an insurance claim online. Before submitting a claim, properly document— both in writing and by taking photos—all the details.

> **DEFINITION**
>
> A **claim** is a report you file with your insurance company when something happens. This officially notifies them of the damages you want them to cover.

Here's how to file an insurance claim:

1. Check out the damage and assess the situation. Be sure your property is secure and that anyone who might be injured receives medical attention.

2. If necessary, call the police.

3. Document everything you know about the situation by taking photos and writing notes.

4. When you know everything is safe and you've documented the situation, call your insurance agent as quickly as possible to let him or her know what happened.

5. Complete an insurance claim form.

Stay in communication with your agent, the adjuster (more on adjusters coming up), and the insurance company to follow the progress of your claim.

Typically, an adjuster will come check out the damage and write up a report, and you'll receive word on whether your insurance company will cover the cost of the damage and how much it will pay. If it will, there are two ways to process the payment. One way is for you to pay for the repairs and the insurance company then sends you a check for the total repairs minus your deductible. Another option is that the insurance company pays the entire repair bill, and you send them a check for your deductible.

Before you call your agent, however, you really need to ask yourself if you should submit a claim. Keep in mind that if you have excessive and repetitive claims, you might be at risk of being dropped by your carrier or having your rates increased significantly. Before submitting an official claim, call and talk through your situation with your insurance professional. He or she can give you the pros and cons of submitting the claim.

Deductibles

An insurance *deductible* is the amount of money you have to pay toward a claim before your insurance kicks in and your insurance company pays the balance.

When you purchase an insurance policy, you set the deductible you'll be responsible for paying. Typically it's $100, $200, or more. The higher the deductible you're willing to pay, the lower your *premium* is for the insurance policy.

> **DEFINITION**
>
> A **deductible** is the amount you pay out of pocket before the insurance company begins to pay for damages. A **premium** is the financial cost of an insurance policy, paid either as a lump sum or in installments during the period covered by the policy.

Choose a deductible that works for you financially and allows you to take care of any claim you might have. If you choose a $1,000 deductible, for example, but you don't have $1,000 to cover it, you may have a problem getting your claim paid and repairs done.

Adjustments

When you submit a claim, an adjuster reviews your property, the claim, and your policy. If the loss is connected to the physical property, the adjuster takes into account the age of the material used at the time of the loss. If, for example, you just put on a new roof and a few months later a hail storm destroys it, the insurance company should pay for a new roof.

However, if you have a 30-year-old roof on your building and hail damages it, the adjuster will look at the life of the roof before approving or denying your claim. If the life of the roof is supposed to be only 15 years, the adjuster will deny your claim and your insurance company then won't pay for a new roof because it's older than its useful life.

If you're halfway through the life expectancy of the roof, the adjuster will note this and your insurance company will pay for half (total cost – depreciation) of the replacement cost minus your deductible.

Payments

A property insurance policy names you as the policy holder and any lender as an additionally insured. This means that, in the event of a loss, the insurance company cuts a check for the loss, and it requires both your signature and the signature of someone of authority from the lending company before you can cash it.

Say your property burns down, and the insurance company pays $100,000 to cover the loss. You have a mortgage for $75,000, so the lender would be entitled to $75,000 before you can cash the $100,000 check. You then receive the balance. This protects the lender from you just taking the $100,000 and not fixing the property they have a lien on.

RENTAL REMINDER

Review your insurance policy on an annual basis. If the value of your rental property has increased, increase your insurance coverage, too. And if you improve a property with upgrades, such as a fire-prevention system, let your insurance company know. Certain upgrades could lower your premiums.

The smart landlord learns to appreciate insurance and isn't afraid to file a claim when necessary.

The Least You Need to Know

- You absolutely need property insurance to cover you in case of loss or damage.
- Shop around for the best prices and insurance packages.
- If you're in a flood zone, you should buy flood insurance.
- Notify your insurance company if you complete upgrades that improve your building, and see if they qualify for a premium discount.

CHAPTER 15

Building Your Business

You've made it this far, so you should be feeling confident and prepared to succeed as a landlord. But do you want to take being a landlord to the next level? Do you want more properties? Do you want to make investment real estate your full-time job?

If real estate is your passion and you have an entrepreneurial spirit to own a business, this chapter could help you turn that dream into a reality.

Owning Your Own Business

Do you want to own your own rental property business? Owning a business takes a lot of hard work and is very different from investing in real estate. Most people don't appreciate how much time they must dedicate to getting a business off the ground and profitable. Are you ready for the extra push it will take?

In This Chapter

* Going into business
* Determining your audience
* Building your business plan
* Understanding financing and insurance
* Keeping current

The Small Business Administration (SBA) suggests you ask yourself these questions before embarking on entrepreneurship:

Do you have the physical and emotional stamina to run a business? Business ownership can be exciting, but it's also a lot of work. Can you face six or seven 12-hour workdays every week?

How do you plan and organize? Research indicates that poor planning is responsible for most business failures. Good organization of financials, inventory, schedules, and production can help you avoid many pitfalls.

Is your drive strong enough? Running a business can wear you down emotionally. Some business owners quickly burn out from having to carry all the responsibility for the success of their business themselves. Strong motivation helps you survive slowdowns and burnout.

> **REAL ESTATE ESSENTIAL**
>
> The first few years of starting a business can be hard on family life. It's important for family members to know what to expect and for you to be able to trust that they'll support you during this time. You might experience financial difficulties until the business becomes profitable, which could take a while, and you might have to adjust to a lower standard of living or put family assets at risk in the short term.

If you answered "yes" to these questions, you might be ready to give entrepreneurship a try. The next question is, do you go solo, bring in a partner, or purchase a franchise?

Going Solo

Do you like the idea of being solely in charge of the business? If so, you might want to be a sole proprietor. In this case, you own the unincorporated business by yourself.

There are pros and cons to a solo gig. One of the pros is the tax advantages, such as the ability to deduct your business losses. However, going it alone leaves you completely liable for any debts you may incur or lawsuits that may be filed, even against your employees. For instance, if an employee completes a maintenance job that damages another unit, the owner of the damaged unit could sue you for damages and come after your personal assets.

Working with a Partner

If you won't want to own the business by yourself, you could share the fun, work, and pay by going into partnership with someone else. A partner can reduce some of the stress of starting a new business. Each of you can take certain responsibilities, for example, and cover each other on days off.

You can also partner with someone who has access to financial resources or may be skilled in an area you're not. If you have marketing experience, you could team up with someone who has accounting experience.

If you go into business with someone, document all the details of responsibility between the two of you. Don't just go into it because it sounds fun. Complete a background and credit check on any potential partner, just like you would a potential tenant. Also, spend some time with your potential partner talking about goals and visions for the new company before signing on the dotted line. Be sure you're both moving in the same direction.

Buying a Franchise

If you don't want to start your business from scratch, purchasing an already established *franchise* system might be a better option for you.

> **DEFINITION**
>
> A **franchise** is an already established business that allows you to use its brand and name recognition and also provides support and training on a proven business model.

When you own a franchise, you're still the boss of your franchise, but you have a proven system and a team of support you can turn to for help with advertising, marketing, training, personal training, and finances.

Real Estate Brokerages

If your business is just going to be about your own real estate rental properties, you don't need a real estate license. However, if your plan includes taking care of rental properties you own as well as those someone else owns, then the rules and laws change significantly.

If you plan to manage property that doesn't belong to you, you need to be a licensed real estate agent and may even need to own a real estate brokerage to be in compliance with your state's real estate laws. Most states require you to have a real estate license for at least 2 years before you can have your own real estate brokerage. (In Texas you must be a real estate agent for *10 years* prior to having your own brokerage!) Before you quit your day job, understand how your state's real estate laws affect your plan.

Even if you don't plan to start your real estate property management business now, getting your real estate license is a good idea if your goal is to be an active real estate investor. To get your real estate license, you need to take real estate classes and then a real estate exam. When you pass your state exam, you need to find an established real estate broker you can work with for the required time before you start your own brokerage.

If you choose to start your own brokerage firm, you need to take additional real estate classes and a longer, more extensive state real estate exam.

Choosing a Target Market

Even before you start your business, determine who your audience is. If, for example, you've created a property management niche for yourself, like specializing in managing corporate housing, who are your customers? Are you going to target urban property owners, business districts, or university or hospital areas? You don't want to invest in a business that doesn't serve a need or make money.

Let's say you decide to create a property management business that caters only to senior housing, but no properties are zoned as senior housing in the geographic area you plan to serve. In this case, you need to find out who you want your customers to be and if there is a need for your services in that area. Then you can target your business accordingly.

Other possible focuses could be student housing, housing focused on health-care professionals, mobile home parks, single-family homes, multiunit apartment buildings, vacation rentals, or commercial real estate.

Creating Your Business Plan

Every business should have a plan. A solid *business plan* can help you manage your rental property business better and is essential if you need financing from a lender or partner.

> **DEFINITION**
>
> A **business plan** is a strategy that precisely defines your business, identifies your goals, and illustrates your income potential. Its basic components include a balance sheet, an income statement, and a cash flow projection. A well-thought-out business plan helps you allocate resources properly, handle unforeseen complications, and make the right decisions.

Gwen Moran, co-author of *The Complete Idiot's Guide to Business Plans Plus,* says your plan should answer five key questions:

- What is your business?

- Who is working your business?

- Why is your business better than someone else's?

- Where will you find customers?

- How much money will your business need?

Let's look at each of these questions in a bit more detail.

What Is Your Business?

Your business plan should reflect a solid understanding of current market conditions and how your product or service is better than what's already out there.

Industry analysis is essential, whether you're operating within a particular geographic region or a specific industry. Do your homework by reading trade journals and tapping into research from key industry associations, including the local Small Business Development Center or a nearby chapter of the Service Corps of Retired Executives.

Who Is Working Your Business?

Having the right people working on and in your business is essential. Include in your business plan the bios and key talents for each partner, if you have partners, along with all employees, professional advisers, and consultants you intend to employ.

It's important to have proper staffing projections so you can better understand the investments you need to make in appropriate personnel.

Why Is Your Business Better?

Your business should always have a unique selling proposition. Customers and clients need a reason to choose to work with you and your rental property business rather than someone else's. Are you the upscale property manager who provides the best service in the area, for example?

Knowing your place in the market is essential to helping you evaluate everything from your competition to your profit margins. Lenders and investors will want to see that you understand where your business fits into the competitive landscape, too.

Where Will You Find Customers?

Customers are essential to a business's success. You need a sufficient supply of customers to survive. In your business plan, define your key potential customers as clearly as possible. Who are your primary and secondary markets, or who else can you serve? How many of them are there? How will you find them and reach them to market and sell?

If you can't answer these questions, you don't have a viable business.

How Much Money Will Your Business Need?

From investing in properties, to making upgrades and repairs, to simply buying office equipment, running a property management business can take on many forms and have many expenses. You need to have a good handle on how much money is essential for starting, running, and growing your business. Work with your financial adviser or accountant to prepare proper financial benchmarks.

Once you've completed your business plan, don't just leave it on the shelf. A successful business owner reviews and revises his or her business plan on a quarterly basis.

> **RENTAL REMINDER**
>
> You need an employee identification number (EIN) or a federal tax identification number to identify your business. If you're starting as a sole proprietor, you can use your Social Security number at first. However, many sole proprietors still elect to use an EIN because it reduces the chances of identity theft, and banks often require one to open a business account.

Know Your Competition

Before you start your own business, you should know something about your competition. Who are they? How long have they been in business? What services do they offer? Take time to research the other property management companies in the area. Talk to the tenants, too.

Considering commercial real estate management? Visit office buildings and talk to the tenants. Are they happy with the building management? What do they like and dislike about the management company? What services would they want that they don't currently have?

Armed with this information, you can think about how your company will stand out from your competition.

Establishing a Client Base

Of course, a property management company needs properties to manage, but where do you find them? If you've already established yourself in rental properties, start spreading the word. Let your contacts know what you're doing so they can refer business to you.

If you're just starting out, you're going to have to prove yourself. Be ready to answer tough questions, especially, "Why should we trust you with our property?" Answer this question honestly and professionally. Focus on your strengths. Do you have a marketing background that helps you bring in the tenants? Are you experienced in building maintenance? Have you been a condo association president? Let them know about your personal rental property experience.

It would be a good idea to have a few professional references from past tenants, vendors, or businesspeople you have worked with as well.

Financing Options

Some businesses can be started on a shoestring budget. If you're planning on managing a small property someone else owns, for example, your business requires less start-up capital (money) than if you're planning on buying a large apartment building.

Regardless of your budget, where is your money coming from to start your business? Here are some financing options available to you:

Fund it yourself: You can use your personal savings. This is called self-funding.

Borrow it: Borrowing money from a bank, family member, creditor, or other entity is another option for getting your business off the ground.

Use equity capital: Equity capital is money raised by a business in exchange for a share of ownership in the company. In other words, they pay you cash and they get a stake in your business through stock.

Contact the SBA: The SBA provides a number of financial assistance programs for small businesses. Visit sba.gov to evaluate your eligibility.

REAL ESTATE ESSENTIAL

Remember, the first few years of getting a business off the ground can be trying, both emotionally and financially. If you're seeing a profit right away, don't jump to spending it right away. Instead, work efficiently for at least an entire calendar cycle to ensure the stability of your business before you spend extra cash on anything but essentials.

Necessary Licenses

As mentioned earlier, you might need a real estate broker's license to manage or sell other people's real estate. You also might need business licenses for your location.

Your state or local governments have a division of local licenses or a department of economic development that can tell you exactly what you need to know about business licenses.

Don't forget about tax licenses. If you plan on purchasing anything, even as small as a lightbulb, and reselling it at an increased rate through your business, you need a sales tax license.

In addition, you might need a lodging tax license if you're renting properties for shorter terms that require you to process a lodging tax on the rental amount.

Insuring Your Business

Business insurances are just like home and car insurance. They protect you just in case your business is sued or something happens to your property.

Here are some types of business insurance you might need:

Property insurance: This insures against loss or damage to your office or property.

Casualty insurance: This covers loss in case of an accident.

Liability insurance: This insures you if you're sued for negligence.

Workers' compensation: This protects your employees should they get hurt on the job.

Health insurance: This provides health care for you and your employees.

Life and disability insurance: This protects the business in case of the untimely death of you or a partner.

You may need additional policies, such as commercial auto insurance and business interruption (or continuity) insurance. Business interruption insurance covers your loss of income if your business suffers a disaster while it's closed because of a disaster or is in the process of being rebuilt after it. This policy covers the profits you would have made if you'd been open.

> **WATCH OUT**
>
> When you're a manager of someone else's property, it's a good idea for them to name your company as an additional insured on their policy. (This can be done at no additional cost.) This protects you from liability without you having to get additional insurance on the properties you just manage and don't own. You can stipulate this as a requirement in your property management agreement.

Setting Up and Running Your Office

If you're like many new property management business owners, oftentimes you're the book-keeper, office manager, leasing staff, mail clerk, receptionist, property inspector, cleaner, and broker, all in one. If you're lucky, you might have a parent, a sibling, or a college buddy helping you out when you need an extra hand. It can seem overwhelming, but remember that you're also the president and CEO, and you can tell yourself what to do.

Being in business for yourself means you need to run your operation smoothly and consistently. As it grows, so will your need for better organization and efficiency. If you're just starting out, your business might just be you, your laptop, and your kitchen table. However, as you acquire more rental properties, you'll acquire more and more work, more and more details to organize and track, more money coming in from your tenants paying rent, and money going out as you pay your bills. Investing in the right tools and people grows your business and maximizes your investment.

Before you start, you'll need supplies. Visit your local office supply store and buy the essentials, such as a stapler, pens, file folders, and a desk to put them all on. You'll need a computer, too.

For tax purposes, you don't need to have separate personal and professional computers, desks, or other equipment just yet. It's fine to keep it simple and use what you have in the beginning. What matters in the end is how you do your taxes and what you can deduct as a business expense. Before you get too busy running your business, take time to meet with both your tax accountant and your financial planner to ensure that how you run your business will make you as successful as possible and maximize your profitability.

Your next big investment after a computer should be a key-cutting machine, which could cost you around $1,000. If cutting unit keys isn't done properly, it can be a huge waste of your time. If you don't buy a key machine, you'll waste valuable time running around and waiting to get keys cut and hoping the person doing it knows how to do it right. Buy the key machine now, as well as a locked storage case to house all your property keys.

RENTAL REMINDER

Never get caught without a key. Create a second secure key storage box where you can lock away the original master key for all your properties.

Today everyone has a cellphone, but you don't want to use your personal phone for business. Set up a separate digital business phone number instead. As long has you have an internet connection, you never need to pay for a phone line. In addition, some other great features are available on digital phone lines. For example, you can set up the system to email you a digital recording of any message you receive.

You don't need a fax machine, but you do need a printer that can also scan and photocopy. Any document that may have been traditionally sent via fax can be easily scanned into a PDF format and either emailed or faxed.

Note that not all printers are the same, and one cost you'll incur is the toner. Shop around and compare the cost of replacement toners to determine what printer you want to buy. Some stores, such as Staples, offer a credit if you return your toner cartridges to the store. It's an incentive to keep recycling them.

Pick up a paper shredder, too. You'll need it to safely shred unwanted documents containing personal and financial information.

If you're managing more than one property, it's easy for details to get lost unless you back them up on a computer system. Several types of management and landlord software programs are available that enable you to track data and documents, rent, bills, and property data. A good property management software program includes these items plus a check ledger, multiple accounts, and account report capabilities. See Appendix B for some of the more popular programs.

Software can cost from a few dollars a month to thousands, so research multiple products and compare features that would be best for you.

Stay Updated

It's important to stay connected with the real estate industry to ensure you're up-to-date on changing laws, rules, and trends in residential property management.

Publications

One easy way to stay current is to subscribe to—and read—real estate trade publications. If you don't want a physical, paper subscription, you can opt for digital versions.

We recommend you subscribe to publications such as *Professional Real Estate Investors Magazine* and *Multi-Housing News*. Check out *The Cooperator*, too.

> **RENTAL REMINDER**
>
> You also can set up alerts in your web browser to stay on top of news. An alert is a name, term, or phrase you can ask your browser to watch for and send you an email anytime that term is used on a website, on a blog, or in a news item. If you set up an alert for "changes in San Francisco rent control laws," for example, and your local newspaper writes about it, you'll find out without having to read every newspaper and blog.

Trade Organizations and Associations

Another great way to get focused industry information is to look into joining national and local trade organizations, such as Building Owners and Managers Association (BOMA), the Institute of Real Estate Management (IREM), the National Association of Residential Property Managers (NARPM), and the National Property Management Association (NPMA). If you have a real estate license, also consider membership in your local real estate board and National Association of Realtors.

As you develop as a landlord, and maybe even as a full-time property manager, these organizations support you with vendors, continuing education opportunities, best practices, lobbying, and even topic-specific white papers.

BOMA and NARPM hold local chapter meetings for members. Property managers, service providers, and vendors attend. The IREM offers online, home-study, and classroom courses on hundreds of real estate–specific topics. The NPMA offers local courses, too.

Also check your state and local trade associations. In New York, for example, the New York Association of Realty Manager offers courses specific not just to the industry, but also to New York City. Trade organizations provide networking and leadership opportunities for you through committees and boards, educational courses, and discounts on goods and services offered through the organization or affiliates.

Chambers of Commerce

A great way to learn more about business and develop a larger community support system is through your local Chamber of Commerce or business development organizations.

A Chamber of Commerce advocates for local businesses and even offers conferences, educational classes and workshops, and social opportunities for you to connect with other members. You can improve your business skills, meet other associates, and promote and market your business.

Continuing Education and Conferences

Looking for conferences in your area? Check with the trade organizations you belong to, your local Chamber of Commerce, or websites such as AllConferences.com. Numerous additional degrees and certification programs are available to you.

Don't attend a conference without having an idea of what you want out of it, though. Some people attend conferences to get away from the day-to-day routine of work, develop new business strategies, or socialize with peers or potential customers. Other conferences are more specific about meeting vendors, learning new skills, and networking.

The Least You Need to Know

- If you're ready to expand your rental property business, it's time to start a business plan.

- Know who your competition is, and be sure you offer more services or a greater product than they do.

- It's essential that you determine whether there's a market for your service before you set up shop.

- Stay up on industry information by reading trade journals and joining trade organizations.

- Become part of your local business community by joining your local Chamber of Commerce or other business organizations.

CHAPTER 16

Rules, Laws, and Fair Housing

As a new landlord, you might be feeling like you need a law degree to understand all the legalese you're now required to know. There are bylaws, proprietary leases, and homeowner rules, and there are federal, local, and state laws, such as the Americans with Disabilities Act, Fair Housing Act, Equal Credit Opportunity Act, and much more.

You have a fantastic home for rent in a great neighborhood, with lots of families, and in the right school district. When you're searching for an applicant, can you say "yes" to the Caucasian family but "no" to another family because they are not Caucasian? Can you say "no" to the two men who want to rent the house? Can you advertise the house as a family house? Can you advertise the property for one occupant or for adults only?

In This Chapter

- Avoiding discrimination
- Renting to those with disabilities
- Following your state and local laws
- Terrorism, rentals, and discrimination
- Penalties for breaking fair housing laws

These are types of questions you're faced with as you work to advertise and rent your property. If you don't know the laws relating to rental properties, you could be breaking them without even realizing it.

You don't need a law degree, but you do need a thorough understanding of these laws to manage your property. Violating these laws can result in serious consequences, including hefty financial penalties.

The good news is, you don't need to head to an expensive law school to figure all this out. In this chapter, we simplify the laws you need to know.

Discrimination Laws

Federal, state, and local laws forbid various types of *discrimination*. The most common types of discrimination prohibited by federal laws are against race and disability. Most states also have discrimination laws, although some aren't quite as comprehensive as the federal laws. In some cases, though, the state law surpasses federal guidelines to address something not covered by the federal laws, such as discrimination based on sexual orientation.

> **DEFINITION**
>
> **Discrimination** is the unfair treatment of a person or group on the basis of prejudice.

No matter how well intentioned you might be, discrimination is illegal. The key to avoiding discrimination accusations is to carefully consider why you're choosing one applicant over another and be sure you're making a fair and legal decision.

The Fair Housing Act

The main federal law you need to know is Title VIII of the Civil Rights Act of 1968, known as the Fair Housing Act (FHA). Amended in 1988, it prohibits discrimination in the sale, rental, and financing of dwellings and in other housing-related transactions. The 1988 amendment added two categories: individuals with physical and mental disabilities, and families with children under the age of 18.

The FHA covers a lot more than just racial discrimination. It also means you can't reject an applicant because you don't want young children or an unmarried couple living in your property. Specifically, the FHA protects the following categories from discrimination:

- Race and color

- Religion

- National origin

- Handicap or disability

- Age

- Familiar status, including families with children under the age of 18 and pregnant women

- Gender

Fair housing laws apply to any person with the right to sell, rent, lease, or manage residential housing. It covers any transaction related to housing—including advertising, inquiring, showing, selling, renting, leasing, pricing, evicting, misrepresenting availability or asking price, or failing to communicate an offer. The law declares that every individual has a basic civil right to secure decent housing in accordance with the individual's right to pay and without discrimination.

Frequently, discrimination violations occur when a landlord advertises a rental property. Even a well-intentioned landlord can violate the law if he doesn't word his advertisements correctly. For example, your property is located in a Latino neighborhood. You advertise the property only in Spanish and offer leases only in Spanish. You think you're appealing to potential Spanish-speaking residents, but you're actually discriminating against possible English-speaking tenants. In most states, English is the only language you can solely use in an advertisement and in rental documents that does not violate fair housing laws.

Also, a landlord cannot advertise for a tenant from a specific religion or a person born in a specific country—or limit potential tenants to U.S. citizens.

RENTAL REMINDER

Go to the U.S. Citizen and Immigration Services website (uscis.gov) to find out how you can legally verify an applicant's citizenship or immigration status.

Also avoid offering discounts for potential tenants from a specific club, such as the local men's club. Remember, you cannot single out one group of people based on their origin.

What does this mean to you? It means you need to be very careful when rejecting a potential tenant. If you're suspected of discrimination, you could face an expensive lawsuit and a sizable fine. The FHA law applies to all types of housing—public and private—including single-family homes, apartments, condominiums, mobile homes, and other dwellings.

As a landlord, your interactions are also covered by the Fair Housing Act. As a landlord you must not:

- Advertise or make a statement that violates any of the protected classes.

- Falsely deny the availability of a rental property—basically telling someone the property is no longer available if that's not true.

- Make stricter polices based on the characteristics of a certain tenant. For example, you can't add more background checks on one tenant over another simply based on what they look like.

- Provide different services or repairs to one tenant over another.

- Refuse to rent to members of certain groups or religions.

- Set different terms, conditions, or privileges for rental of a dwelling unit, such as requiring larger deposits of some tenants or adopting an inconsistent policy of responding to late rent payments, before or while it's rented.

- Terminate a lease for discriminatory reasons. You can't evict someone because they joined a new church or started dating someone from a different race.

Occupancy Standards

No, you cannot refuse to rent to a family with children. Unless your property or neighborhood is zoned for tenants who are 55 and older, you do not have the right to refuse to rent to a family with children.

You also cannot set unreasonable limits as to the number of occupants who can occupy a property. For example, if you're renting a four-bedroom house, you can't say only two tenants can live there.

Limiting who can live in the property and how many people can live there can be viewed as a form of discrimination. Occupancy limits are actually set by state and local building, housing, and health codes and are based on your property's square footage, number of bedrooms, and number of bathrooms. It is best to follow these guidelines.

The U.S. Department of Housing and Urban Development has issued a statement confirming its adoption of the policy that an occupancy standard of two persons per bedroom is considered reasonable under the Fair Housing Act. As of this writing, 32 states have adopted the general two-per-bedroom standard.

WATCH OUT

Check for your city's specific occupancy laws. They may vary from state to state.

Federal Law Exemptions

The FHA law does include some exemptions:

- Owner-occupied buildings with four or fewer rental units

- Single-family housing units rented without discriminatory advertising and without the help of a real estate broker

- Housing operated by certain types of religious organizations and private clubs that limit occupancy to their own members

- Housing reserved exclusively for senior citizens in which certain qualifications must be met

Be alert that just because federal law allows for these exemptions doesn't necessarily mean these exemptions exist in your state. Always double-check your current local laws.

State Laws

In addition to federal laws, state and city laws protect certain groups of people. The most prominently protected categories are described as sexual orientation and gender identity.

Check your specific state's laws for fair housing, civil rights, and human rights.

Understanding Disabilities

The U.S. Department of Housing and Urban Development (HUD) defines a person with a disability as "any person who has a physical or mental impairment that substantially limits one or more major life activities; has a record of such impairment; or is regarded as having such impairment." Major life activities include walking, talking, hearing, seeing, breathing, learning, performing manual tasks, and caring for oneself.

In general, a physical or mental impairment includes hearing, mobility, and visual impairments; chronic alcoholism; chronic mental illness; autoimmune deficiency syndrome (AIDS) and AIDS-related complex; or mental disabilities that substantially limit one or more major life activities.

HUD goes on to better describe what is expected from you, the landlord:

> It is unlawful for a housing provider to refuse to rent or sell to a person simply because of a disability. A housing provider may not impose different application or qualification criteria, rental fees or sales prices, and rental or sales terms or conditions than those required of or provided to persons who are not disabled. For example: A housing provider may not refuse to rent to an otherwise qualified individual with a mental disability because s/he is uncomfortable with the individual's disability. Such an act would violate the Fair Housing Act because it denies a person housing solely on the basis of their disability.

The law requires landlords to make reasonable accommodations for persons with disabilities. A reasonable accommodation is a change in rules, policies, practices, or services so a person with a disability has an equal opportunity to use and enjoy a dwelling unit or common space.

Reasonable Modifications

You also must do everything possible to assist tenants with disabilities, but you're not required to make changes that would fundamentally alter your rental or create an undue financial and administrative burden. Reasonable accommodations may be necessary at all stages of the housing process, including application and tenancy, or to prevent eviction. For example, you can make a reasonable accommodation for a tenant with impaired mobility by giving the tenant a reserved parking space in front of his or her rental unit, even though all parking is unreserved.

"Reasonable modifications" can be just as confusing as "general wear and tear." The definition isn't very specific. Basically, a reasonable modification is a structural modification made to allow someone who has a disability the full enjoyment of the housing and related facilities. The law requires you, the landlord, to make reasonable modifications that accommodate disabled tenants, but it does not always specify what those reasonable modifications are.

The law also requires you to allow persons with disabilities to make reasonable modifications themselves. If you rent to a person with a disability, you must permit him or her to install a ramp into the building, lower the entry threshold of a unit, or install grab bars in a bathroom.

Even if a tenant is only temporarily disabled—say someone just had back surgery and needs a ramp to get in and out of the building—you must accommodate him or her. Reasonable modifications are usually made at the resident's expense, but resources are available to help fund these modifications.

RENTAL REMINDER

To learn more about FHA laws, visit FairHousingFirst.org, an initiative sponsored by HUD designed to promote compliance with FHA design and construction requirements. The program includes a training curriculum, toll-free information line, and website that provides technical guidance.

Section 504 of the Rehabilitation Act of 1973

When it comes to housing and other basic necessities, many disabled residents receive federal funding or live in federally funded buildings. In 1973, to foster economic independence and prohibit discrimination against the disabled, Section 504 of the Rehabilitation Act was passed. This act states that you cannot discriminate against any disabled tenant who receives federal funds and who requires reasonable accommodations.

According to HUD:

> Section 504 provides that no qualified individual with a disability should, only by reason of his or her disability, be excluded from the participation in, be denied the benefits of, or be subjected to discrimination under any program or activity receiving Federal financial assistance.

If you're buying an apartment building with four or more units, or if you're renovating one, you need to pay attention to the following accommodations:

- Accessible entrance on an accessible route

- Accessible public and common areas

- Usable doors

- Accessible route into and through the dwelling unit

- Accessible light switches, electrical outlets, thermostats, and environmental controls

- Usable kitchens and bathrooms

- Reinforced walls in bathrooms

Americans with Disabilities Act

The Americans with Disability Act (ADA) of 1990 is known as the first comprehensive civil rights law for people with disabilities. The ADA prohibits discrimination against people with disabilities in employment (Title I), public services (Title II), public accommodations (Title III), and telecommunications (Title IV). The act was later amended in 2008, making changes to the definition of disability and the understanding of major life activities.

In addition to the federal laws, some states have laws that enhance the power of the ADA. For example, California's Unruh Act provides that a violation of the ADA constitutes actionable discrimination and cause for a lawsuit.

ADA lawsuits are a fairly recent phenomenon, while disagreements between landlords and tenants over responsibility for repairs have persisted for centuries. To learn more, visit ada.gov.

Addicts

Federal fair housing laws also extend protection to recovering alcoholics who are actively and regularly participating in a medically based treatment or an Alcoholics Anonymous program.

In addition, former drug addicts, including anyone with prior convictions for illegal drug use, but not for drug dealing or manufacturing, are protected under discrimination laws.

 **WATCH OUT**

Landlords cannot ask tenants whether they have disabilities or addictions. A landlord's potential tenant questions and actions must treat every tenant the same.

State and Local Laws

Most of the time, state and local antidiscrimination laws mirror the federal laws, making it illegal to discriminate. However, state and local laws often are more detailed and sometimes forbid other types of discrimination not covered by the federal guidelines.

The following sections profile some common antidiscrimination laws some states and localities have adopted.

Uniform Residential Landlord and Tenant Act

The Uniform Residential Landlord and Tenant Act (URLTA) is an example of a law governing residential landlord and tenant interactions, created in 1972 by the National Conference of Commissioners on Uniform State Laws in the United States.

There are three general purposes for URLTA:

- To update the law pertaining to rental of dwelling units and the rights and obligations of landlords and tenants

- To support and encourage landlords and tenants to maintain and upgrade the quality of their housing

- To simplify laws and make them consistent on a state-by-state basis

> **REAL ESTATE ESSENTIAL**
>
> In 1972, the Uniform Law Commission (ULC) adopted the Uniform Residential Landlord and Tenant Act (URLTA). Besides being enacted in 20 states, it provided an impetus for the widespread adoption of the implied warranty of habitability and laws restricting retaliatory eviction.

As a general matter, the law standardizes and simplifies the eviction process, requires the tenant to pay rent into court while an eviction has been started and is being contested, limits the amount of any security deposits, provides for prompt repayment of security deposits, requires certain minimal conditions of habitability, and imposes penalties for breach of provisions. Several states have already adopted URLTA.

Residential Lead-Based Paint Hazard Reduction Act

This law, passed in 1992, requires that potential renters of any housing that was built before 1978 receive certain information about lead and lead hazards in the residence prior to renting. It also provides the opportunity for an independent lead inspection for you, the buyer.

If your building was built before 1978, you must give your tenants an EPA-approved pamphlet on identifying and controlling lead-based paint hazards called "Protect Your Family from Lead in Your Home." It's also available in other formats and languages.

In addition, you must supply any known information concerning lead-based paint or lead-based paint hazards pertaining to the building. For multiunit buildings, this includes records and reports concerning common areas and other units if that information is available.

Finally, you must attach a lead disclosure to the lease, or insert language in the lease, that includes a "Lead Warning Statement" and confirms that you have complied with all notification requirements.

> **REAL ESTATE ESSENTIAL**
>
> Most private housing, public housing, federally owned housing, and housing receiving federal assistance are affected by this rule. Landlords must retain a copy of the lead-based paint disclosures for no less than 3 years from the start of the leasing period.

Megan's Law

Passed in 1996, the federal version of Megan's Law requires that a list of registered sex offenders be made available to the public. In addition, some states have their own Megan's Law. The state versions require law enforcement to actively notify the public of the presence of registered sex offenders.

Landlords are not required to provide information on known sex offenders to potential tenants, but you can avoid possible liability by including resources for these lists.

As a rule, most landlords want to screen out tenants with criminal records, particularly convictions for violent crimes or crimes against children. Checking a prospective tenant's credit report is one way to find out about a person's criminal history.

Self-reporting is another. Rental applications typically ask whether the prospective tenant has ever been convicted of a crime and, if so, to provide details.

Running an investigative report—a background report about a person's character, general reputation, personal characteristics, or mode-of-living—is another option, but it's a less common way of discovering any criminal history.

Terrorism

Whether we like it or not, the fear of terrorism continues to impact the way Americans live, travel, and work. But regardless of the threat of terrorism, you cannot stop abiding by all the fair housing laws. Every individual's civil rights remain the same.

However, there's some general information you should know and procedures you can set up just in case you're faced with a tenant you suspect might be participating in acts of terrorism or if your property is damaged by an act of terrorism.

Patriot Act

On October 26, 2001, the United and Strengthening America by Providing Appropriate Tools Required to Intercept and Obstruct Terrorism Act, or USA PATRIOT Act, was signed into law. This act updated and strengthened laws governing the investigation and prosecution of terrorism within the parameters of the Constitution and our national commitment to the protection of civil rights and civil liberties.

To help protect U.S. citizens against future attacks, the government adopted specific provisions of the Patriot Act. The Patriot Act created new guidelines that affect nearly every industry, and an extension is likely to continue to impact how real estate professionals conduct business.

In short, the Patriot Act imposes detailed record-keeping and reporting requirements on certain individuals and businesses to help the government identify suspicious activity and to prevent money laundering and financing for terrorism.

It's worth your time to learn and understand these requirements and the ways in which you can comply with these regulations.

Investigating Tenants

Your duty as a landlord starts by thoroughly investigating potential tenants prior to renting to them. Landlords can use the rules issued by the U.S. Treasury Department's Office of Foreign Assets Control (OFAC) that identify specially designated nationals, including known or suspected terrorists, international narcotics traffickers, persons who threaten international stabilization efforts, and other suspect individuals and entities.

Property owners, landlords, real estate settlement agents, and title insurers are prohibited from leasing property to these specially designated nationals unless previously authorized. The OFAC rules subject these individuals to economic sanctions and freezing of assets.

To comply with OFAC regulations, review the specially designated nationals list at treas.gov/ofac to determine whether any parties in the transaction are listed by name. If necessary, you also can utilize a private search service like the services found at TransUnion SmartMove (mysmartmove.com) to find out more.

If you find a potential match, contact OFAC's Compliance Program Division for further guidance.

Be Prepared

To be prepared, you should follow a few important steps:

Review leases and purchase agreements: An increasing number of these include clauses that require tenants to state that they're not a specially designated national or part of a terrorist organization and that they never have been indicted, convicted, or detained on charges involving money laundering. If this wording isn't already in your rental documents, add it.

Prepare an action plan: Be prepared if you encounter problems in transactions or are subject to governmental investigations. This includes procedures for communicating with authorities, complying with subpoenas, retaining records, and complying with federal and state laws.

Consider security measures: Assess the costs and benefits of security measures such as video surveillance and neighborhood watch programs. In addition, develop an emergency evacuation plan, and investigate terrorism insurance.

Stay informed: As the threat of terrorism continues, be aware of your duties to comply with the Patriot Act's regulations. Making use of legal counsel, industry resources, and policy groups to help understand these obligations is essential because the rules often change or are reinterpreted.

Terrorism Insurance

Before September 11, 2001, commercial insurers provided terrorism coverage without extra costs in general insurance policies. In 2002, however, that changed, and terrorism insurance became very expensive or wasn't available in policies.

After September 11, the insurance world changed "as insurers realized the extent of possible terrorism losses," according to a recent report from the Congressional Research Service.

It's estimated that financial losses from the September 11 terrorist attacks were approximately $32.5 billion ($40 billion in current dollars)—the largest amount ever recorded for a non-natural disaster. Congress responded by passing the Terrorism Risk Insurance Act (TRIA) in 2002. As a result, insured losses are covered by private insurers that are then reinsured by the federal government. In other words, if a terrorist attack occurs, the federal government shares some of the loss with private insurers. The amount covered depends on the size of the loss.

> **REAL ESTATE ESSENTIAL**
>
> TRIA brought "much needed capacity back to the market at a critical time," according to the Insurance Information Institute.

So now terrorism insurance is offered separately with its own price that depends on current risk levels. According to the Congressional Research Service report, the initial price of terrorism coverage was high when the insurance was first introduced, but it has declined in the last decade.

Penalties

If you violate federal or state discrimination laws, you can face stiff penalties. In California, for instance, there's a minimum fine of $4,000 for each violation, not including damages and legal costs.

Discrimination complaints filed with the HUD are investigated by the Office of Fair Housing and Equal Opportunity (FHEO). HUD tries to reach an agreement between you and your tenant, but if the complaint is not successfully resolved, the FHEO determines whether reasonable cause exists that a discriminatory housing practice has occurred.

If they believe you may have discriminated against your applicant or tenant, a hearing is scheduled before a HUD administrative law judge. You and the tenant have the right to move the matter to a federal court. If you choose a federal court, the Department of Justice takes over HUD's role as counsel, and the matter proceeds as a civil action.

If HUD determines that your state or local agency has the same fair housing powers as HUD, HUD refers your complaint to that agency for investigation and notifies you of the referral. That agency begins work on your complaint within 30 days, or HUD takes it back.

If, after investigating a complaint, HUD finds reasonable cause to believe discrimination has occurred, it informs you and your case is heard in an administrative hearing within 120 days, unless you or the respondent want the case to be heard in federal district court.

> **REAL ESTATE ESSENTIAL**
>
> If you're found guilty of discrimination, you could face several possible penalties. You might be required to rent the property to the aggrieved person, for starters. You also might be required to pay the tenant's attorney fees.

You also might have to pay actual monetary damages. This amount may reflect the cost of the tenant to find another property, the additional rent the person has to pay elsewhere, and damages that would reflect the humiliation and distress they suffered.

You might be required to pay punitive damages, too, meaning extra money paid as punishment for outlandish and intentional discrimination. Fines can easily be $25,000 and higher for continued and outlandish discrimination.

In addition, you have to pay a penalty to the federal government. The maximum penalties are $16,000 for a first violation and $65,000 for a third violation within 7 years. Many states have comparable penalties that would be assessed in addition to the federal fines.

The Least You Need to Know

- You don't need to be a lawyer, but you do need to be familiar with several important laws that you must not break.
- You cannot discriminate against any potential applicants.
- You must make reasonable accommodations for a disabled tenant when requested, but the tenant must pay for it.
- Regardless of terrorism concerns, you must still abide by the fair housing laws.
- Failure to abide by laws can cost you a ton of money in penalties.

Hiring a Property Manager

One thing we can guarantee is that life is unpredictable, and as a result, how you run your rental properties will change as time goes on.

When you started, it was just you managing your first property. You might have had a day job and managed your property on the side while you earned profit. Now, as you purchase more properties, you might still want to keep your day job and have someone else help you manage the property. Or maybe you're managing the property, but you want to tap into a property manager's expertise to help you get higher rents. Or maybe you relocated to a different city and need someone to landlord in your absence. These are all reasons why you might need to hire a property management company to support you.

In this chapter, we focus on what you need to know to decide whether to hire a property management company, how to find the right one, and what you can expect when you do.

Why Hire a Property Manager?

As you progress as a real estate investor, you need to know about, and have access to, the right property management company. In fact, even if you don't use them all the time, it's smart to use property managers from time to time. When you get to the point that you have multiple properties to take care of, property managers can back you up, make you more money, and handle issues you don't have the time or knowledge to deal with.

As you've learned throughout this book, good property management goes beyond just collecting rent. It includes everything from getting the property consistently rented to qualifying tenants and dealing with issues when something goes wrong. It's nice to have someone else who can help with all that.

There are four key reasons you should hire a property manager:

- Time

- Market knowledge

- Laws

- Tenants

More Time for You

Your most valuable personal asset is the 24 hours you have in every day. Even though new technologies enable you to get more done, there are still only 24 hours in a day in which to work, eat, sleep, spend time with your family, and so on. By hiring a property manager to manage some of or all your details, you'll get some of your time back.

Just think—you won't need to advertise, answer calls, qualify tenants, complete paperwork, collect rents, handle maintenance, inspect the property, or handle any of the details yourself. Instead, while another property manager handles them, you can make more financial gains by managing your money instead of managing details connected to your rental.

Current Market Knowledge

A knowledgeable property management company evaluates market conditions every day so that information is available when they need to rent their next property. Remember when you completed your market research to establish the rental rate on your property? How long ago was that? Have you updated that market research every month since, or are you going to start from scratch when your property becomes available to rent again?

A property management company won't start from scratch because that information is what it lives and breathes every day. It knows what the savvy tenant is looking for and suggests specific property upgrades that get you higher rents.

> **REAL ESTATE ESSENTIAL**
>
> Property managers have the knowledge to get you volume discounts on services and products they can pass on to you.

Current Law Knowledge

If you regularly read, watch, or listen to the news, you may notice that state and federal legislature, as well as court systems, are frequently adding and changing laws that affect you as a landlord. Regulations, rental laws, and tax laws can make you money or cost you money if you don't know about and understand them.

Property managers watch real estate trends and belong to trade organizations that subscribe to extensive legislature-monitoring systems. This monitoring enables them to learn about new laws being passed. As a result, they become active in lobbying to prevent new laws from getting passed that could negatively affect an investor's ability to make money on a rental.

Tenant Connections and Knowledge

Property managers have personal connections within the community that enable them to find potential tenants. For example, one manager might have a long-standing relationship with the human resources director of a local Fortune 500 company. Every time this company hires a new executive, he or she is given a relocation package that includes neighborhood orientation tours and contact information for this property management company. As a result, these executives may never even look for a rental property on the open market.

In addition to having access to tenants, the fact that the property manager regularly qualifies tenants means he or she has a streamlined application process and has a heads-up on the newest tenant frauds. These systems protect you from renting to a wrong tenant. Other services such as electronic rent collections can get your rent collected sooner.

Full-service property managers do everything possible to provide you with a hassle-free investment when it comes to tenants.

> **REAL ESTATE ESSENTIAL**
>
> A superintendent is not the same as a property manager. A superintendent is someone you hire to work for you, either as an employee or as an independent contractor to do minor repairs. A superintendent does not need to be licensed as long as he or she stays within the scope of minor repairs. A superintendent does not handle any money or rent the property.

Finding the Right Company

Each property management company approaches management very differently. One company could be automated with online reporting, accounting, and communication technologies. And another can be old school and do everything through the mail. You need to decide which setup works best for you.

In general, property managers offer the following services:

- Tenant advertising
- Property touring
- Applicant screening
- Lease processing
- Rent collection
- Account receivables
- Maintenance
- Emergencies
- Policy enforcement
- Accounting
- Tenant departures
- Property turnover
- Leasing and management fees

Let's take a closer look at a few of these so you understand what you're getting.

A Note on Maintenance

There are three aspects of maintenance and how property management companies charge you for it:

- An hourly rate

- A markup on outside vendors

- A markup on materials used

All these fees should be properly itemized in your property management agreement so be sure there's no confusion. For example, if your property needs a bathroom upgrade, the manager provides the general oversight of the project, picks new fixtures, and paints the room, but he or she might hire a specific vendor to tile the floor.

If the contract stated $32 an hour for labor plus a 25 percent markup for all the work done by an employee of the property management company, you'd be charged $32 an hour. For the fixtures and the services provided by the outside vendor, you'd be charged cost plus 25 percent. If the bill came to $1,000, you'd see $1,250 on your monthly statement.

When hiring a property management company, ask how they handle different maintenance requests. If they don't have anyone on staff who does basic property maintenance, you could be paying too much for minor repairs.

> **REAL ESTATE ESSENTIAL**
>
> Property management fees are usually a percentage of the rental rate, a leasing bonus, and specific fees associated with repairs or tasks. Property managers legally cannot meet with other managers to set the rates that apply to the entire market. However, all real estate fees follow the same pattern. A standard property management rate is between 10 and 50 percent of the rent collected. Longer-term unfurnished rentals are charged the lowest fees, while vacation rentals that turn over every few days are charged the highest management fees. Monthly corporate housing management companies fall somewhere in the middle.

A Note on Accounting

Accounting is all about the money, and because your goal is to make money, don't skip over understanding how a property management company handles your money.

Know how they collect rent, what to do if they can't collect, and when they pay it to you. Know where they bank and how they handle *escrow accounts*. Know what accounting statements they send to you and when.

> **DEFINITION**
>
> An **escrow account** is an account in which money is held in trust until a transaction is completed. For example, the property manager collects rent from the tenant that's then due to you. The property manager is required by law to hold your money in escrow until he or she pay it to you.

Will you get a monthly statement or an annual statement, or will you log in to their online management program and get real-time accounting statements? How will they report your rental income to the IRS, and when can you expect your annual 1099 tax statement from them?

A Few More Questions to Ask

Before you sign any property management agreement, ask for references from other property owners in their system.

Then ask other important questions, such as these:

- How long have you been a property manager?

- What type of property management do you specialize in?

- How long have you had a real estate license and in what state(s)?

- Do you have any professional designations?

- What organizations do you belong to and why?

- Do you have examples of other properties similar to mine you've been successful with?

- What are your fees?

- How does your management program work? Do you have that in writing?

You're asking for a lot of details, but when finding the right property manager, it's worth it. You'll realize the truth to this when you start to have more time, money, and quality renters. Property management isn't rocket science, but there many details to keep track of, so having the right manager with knowledge and experience gets you the results you expect and deserve from your investment.

What About a Resident Manager?

You can choose not to go with a full-service property management company and instead have a tenant take on the role of resident manager. This often is done as a trade with the tenant, who receives a lower rental rate and a set fee for their service.

A resident manager can handle a wide range of tasks, from basic maintenance needs to leasing. Before hiring a resident manager, be sure they're qualified and understand what their duties are. Work out some details, too:

- Is the manager responsible for selecting tenants, collecting rents, making repairs, or hiring and firing vendors?

- How much will the manager get paid? What will the rent reduction be?

- Is the job part time or full time?

Licensing

No special license is required for you to buy and rent your own property. However, a license is required if you plan to manage property for someone else. The same is true for a manager you want to take care of your property. Before you hire a manager, be sure the company or individual is licensed in your state through the Secretary of State and holds the correct real estate licensing required by your state's Department of Real Estate and any applicable tax licenses. The state license is called a real-estate brokers license.

REAL ESTATE ESSENTIAL

A property manager doesn't need to be a member of the Board of Realtors.

If the property management firm has leasing agents who quote rates on your property and execute a lease agreement, these individuals need to have the required real estate licenses. Someone employed by the property management company who does not have a real estate license can give a property tour to a prospective tenant and hand out a flyer with the rates on it, but this person cannot discuss rates or lease details with the prospective tenant.

Most states require that anyone engaging in property management have a real estate broker's license. This can be confusing because many state real estate statutes don't mention property management. However, they describe activities that are typically undertaken by property managers as activities that require a real estate broker license.

Property management is described by the following activities:

- Advertises the availability of rental property

- Prepares or discuss a property management agreement with an owner

- Negotiates leases or lease terms

- Shows a rental property

- Drives or accompanies a potential renter to a rental property

- Collects rents

As always, there are exceptions. Individual states regulate real estate activities, and they're not uniform in their treatment of property management. Some states don't even require a real estate license to engage in property management, and other states allow property managers to work under a property management license rather than a broker's license. The vast majority of states, however, require a property manager who is engaging in renting and leasing activities to have a real estate broker's license or be a real estate salesperson working for a real estate broker.

Most states also require that a property manager take additional continuing education courses every few years to stay licensed, certified, and current. Maintaining a real estate license can take some time. Check with your state to find out exactly what courses are needed and what your property manager needs to take.

When looking for a property manager, you'll likely come across some designations. Here's what they stand for:

Certified Property Manager (CPM): A CPM is a personal designation available to members of the National Association of Realtors (NAR) who specialize in property management and have met the strict requirements in the areas of education, examination, management planning, ethics, and experience.

Accredited Resident Manager (ARM) for individuals and **Accredited Management Organization (AMO)** for businesses: These are professional designations for a person trained to manage residential properties earned by fulfilling the requirements of the Institute of Real Estate Management (IREM), an affiliate of the National Association of Realtors.

Certified Manager of Community Associations (CMCA): This designation from the National Board of Certification of Community Association Managers (NBC-CAM) signifies that a manager has passed a national exam and met the requirements for managing condominium, cooperative, and homeowner's associations.

Residential Management Professional (RPM) or Master Property Manager (MPM): These designations from the National Association of Residential Property Managers (NARPM) are for individuals to certify proficiency in property management and specific experience.

Certified Residential Property Management Company (CRPMC): This designation, also from NARPM, is awarded to professional property management companies that demonstrate a high standard in both procedures and customer service.

Certified Corporate Housing Professional (CCHP): This designation from the Corporate Housing Providers Association (CHPA) exemplifies competence and professionalism in the corporate housing industry and has practical application and operational knowledge in operations, financial management, and sales and marketing.

These accreditations are offered by the Building Owners and Managers Institute International (BOMI):

Real Property Administrator (RPA): This designation is earned through a strict program focused on budgeting, accounting, real estate investment, finance, environmental health and safety issues, law and risk management, design, operation, maintenance of building systems, and ethics.

Facilities Management Administrator (FMA): This designation is for those responsible for ensuring that a facility runs smoothly by creating a safe and productive workplace (for a company) and by taking care of tenant issues such as comfort, safety, daily operations, and maintenance (for rental properties).

Systems Maintenance Administrator (SMA): This designation is for a person in charge of a team of technicians who run the day-to-day operation of a building. SMAs learn how to streamline the operations of a building and manage energy-efficient, environmentally sound, and cost-effective building systems.

Systems Maintenance Technician (SMT): This designation is for a person who maintains major building systems such as heating, refrigeration, electricity, and plumbing. SMTs learn about the technologies and trends in the maintenance industry and are able to maximize the efficiency and safety of building systems. Trained SMTs possess a broad spectrum of the overall mechanical requirements of the commercial real estate industry.

Setting Expectations

A good property management company works with you to set and communicate your goals and objectives for your property. Your goals could be, for example, increased profits, lower vacancies, lower tenant delinquencies, happier tenants and lower turnover, positive tenant relations, quality and appropriate property improvements, and fewer complaints and repairs.

> **REAL ESTATE ESSENTIAL**
>
> If a property manager is not meeting your goals or is otherwise not working out, you can fire him or her in accordance to the management contract you have. If you have a fixed-term management contract, you might need to pay a fee or wait until the current tenant departs before removing your property from the management program. However, you can terminate a contract any time for just cause. If the manager performs poorly, does not follow instructions, violates the law, or endangers and threatens the safety of the tenants, you may release him or her from the contract.

Your agreement with the property manager can include several duties.

The property manager assumes the management and operations of the property. To begin, the manager should thoroughly inspect the property to gauge the present condition and recommend changes to you. After getting your approval, the property manager then gets started making the necessary improvements.

The property manager also makes reasonable efforts to lease the property, and he or she is responsible for all negotiations with prospective tenants. The property manager also has the right to execute and enter into, on your behalf, leases and rentals of the property, as well as lease extensions and renewals.

The property manager will use good faith, due diligence, and all reasonable efforts to achieve the highest rental income for you, consistent with managing the property in the long term. Accordingly, the manager can set rental rates, deposit requirements, and discounts, and otherwise manage the business aspects of the rental. The property manager also deposits all rent into an escrow account until he or she pays you.

He or she also provides or coordinates all managerial and housekeeping services for the property.

Specifying duties gets you only so far. The key is to never assume the property manager does certain tasks, such as tenant checks, and similar matters. Instead, always ask these questions:

- Will you pay my mortgage?

- Will you annually inspect my furnace?

- Will you change the air filter in my furnace?

- Will you check my insurance policy or ask about a warranty prior to repairing an expensive item?

These types of questions save you money and frustration so you don't get caught with a large repair bill that should have been covered by an extended warranty.

Just as you developed a checklist of priorities prior to purchasing the right rental property, you need to understand what makes a qualified property management company and how to find the right match for you.

Many great property managers are out there, but don't just assume anyone with a real estate license is the best person to manage your rental property. Do some research, interview candidates, and be comfortable with the manager you choose.

The Least You Need to Know

- If you purchase multiple properties, consider hiring a property manager to help you take care of them.

- A property manager handles everyday tasks of running a property so you can focus on the bigger picture—making money.

- Do your due diligence when hiring a property manager: ask questions, get references, and check out his or her background.

- Outline duties and responsibilities in a contract between you and your property management company.

- If your property management company fails to complete its responsibilities, release it from the contract and find a better company.

Glossary

accredited management organization (AMO)   A property management firm that has received credentials from the Institute of Real Estate Management.

accredited resident manager (ARM)   A certification awarded to those who meet the standards set by the Institute of Real Estate Management for residential real estate management professionals.

adjustable rate mortgage (ARM)   A mortgage with an interest rate that's periodically adjusted.

agent   *See* real estate agent.

amenity   A feature that increases attractiveness or value, especially of a piece of real estate or a geographic location.

annual percentage rate (APR)   The interest rate for a whole year (annualized), rather than just a monthly fee/rate, as applied on a loan, mortgage loan, credit card, and so on.

apartment   A room or a group of related rooms, among similar sets in one building, designed for use as a dwelling.

applicant   A person who applies for or requests something. For the purposes of this book, we refer to an applicant as someone applying to rent a property.

background check   The process of looking up and compiling criminal records, commercial records, and financial records of an individual or an organization.

broker   *See* real estate broker.

budget   An estimate, often itemized, of expected income and expenses for a given period in the future.

building code   A set of rules that specify the minimum acceptable level of safety for constructed objects such as buildings.

business plan   A strategy that precisely defines your business, identifies your goals, and illustrates your income potential. Its basic components include a balance sheet, an income statement, and a cash flow projection.

bylaw   A standing rule governing the regulation of a corporation's or society's internal affairs.

capitalization rate   The ratio between the net operating income produced by an asset and its capital cost (the original price paid to buy the asset).

certified corporate housing professional (CCHP)   A designation from the Corporate Housing Providers Association that exemplifies competence and professionalism in the corporate housing industry and indicates that the recipient has practical application and operational knowledge in operations, financial management, sales, and marketing.

certified manager of community associations (CMCA)   A designation from the National Board of Certification of Community Association Managers that signifies a manager has passed a national exam and met the requirements for managing condominiums, cooperatives, and homeowner's associations.

certified property manager (CPM)   A personal designation available to members of the National Association of Realtors who specialize in property management and have met strict requirements in the areas of education, examination, management, plan, ethics, and experience.

certified residential property management company (CRPMC)   A designation from the National Association of Residential Property Managers awarded to professional property management companies that demonstrate a high standard in both procedures and customer service.

claim   A report filed with your insurance company when something happens, such as a fire, and you officially notify them of the damages you want them to cover.

clause   A distinct article or provision in a contract, treaty, will, or other formal or legal written document.

commingling   To mingle or mix. In property management, it could mean a property manager depositing client funds in the broker's personal or general accounts. A property manager found guilty of commingling funds may generally have his or her license suspended or revoked by the state department of real estate.

condominium   A multiunit building, office building, or residential building in which the units are individually owned, and each owner receives a recordable deed to the individual unit purchased, including the right to sell, mortgage, and other actions.

contract   An agreement between two or more parties for doing or not doing something specified for a value, as in a rental lease or real estate purchase agreement.

cooperative ownership (co-op)   In this situation, you buy shares in the corporation (partnership or trust), but you do not specifically own your own apartment unit. Basically, you're a stockholder in the building. Co-ops generally limit how you can rent your property and may not produce the highest financial returns.

corporation   An association of individuals, created by law or under authority of law, having a continuous existence independent of the existences of its members, with powers and liabilities distinct from those of its members.

covenants, conditions, and restrictions (CC&R)   Restrictions on the use of a property. Generally, CC&Rs are established and maintained through a homeowner's association.

cure an eviction   To resolve or fix the issue or issues that caused the grounds for eviction. Also called *quit an eviction*.

deductible   The amount you pay out-of-pocket before your insurance company begins to pay for damages. Typically, the higher your deductible, the lower your premium payment.

denial   A refusal. For the purposes of this book, we refer to denial as a refusal to rent housing. Rental denial must adhere to the federal and state Fair Housing Laws.

depreciation   An income tax deduction that allows a taxpayer to recover the cost or other basis of certain property. It's an annual allowance for the wear and tear, deterioration, or obsolescence of the property.

disaster   A calamitous event, especially one occurring suddenly and causing great loss of life, damage, or hardship, such as a flood, airplane crash, or business failure.

disclosure   To make known, reveal, or uncover. In real estate, property owners are required by law to disclose certain property defects.

discrimination   The unfair treatment of a person or group on the basis of prejudice.

down payment   An initial amount paid at the time of purchase, such as with installment buying and time sales.

duplex   A building, generally under one ownership, containing two side-by-side units with individual entrances occupied by two unique parties.

Equal Credit Opportunity Act (ECOA)   A U.S. law enacted in 1974 that says anyone extending credit cannot discriminate based on protected identifiers like race, sex, and age.

equity   The amount of value a property owner possesses as determined by the fair market value of the property minus the amount owed on a mortgage.

escrow account   An account in which money is held in trust until a transaction is completed. For example, a property manager collects rent from a tenant that's then due to the property owner. By law, the property manager is required to hold the money in escrow until he or she pays it to the property owner. Property managers also use escrow accounts to hold security deposits on behalf of tenants.

eviction   To expel a person, especially a tenant, from land or a building, by legal process, as for nonpayment of rent.

execution   A judicial process whereby the court directs a police officer to seize a property from a tenant.

facilities management administrator (FMA)   A designation for those responsible for ensuring that a facility runs smoothly by creating a safe and productive workplace (for a company) and by taking care of tenant issues such as comfort, safety, daily operations, and maintenance (for rental properties).

Fair Housing Act   A U.S. law passed in 1968 that prohibits discrimination based on race, color, sex, national origin, or religion.

Federal Housing Administration (FHA)   Part of the U.S. Department of Housing and Urban Development, the FHA provides residential mortgage insurance on qualified loans.

flat   A condominium that's generally an older, single-residential property that's been subdivided into condominium units with one unit per floor. This term is more often used in European countries.

flip   There are two kinds of flip in real estate. When purchasing a property, *flip* means to buy, fix up, and sell a property for a profit within a short period of time. In reference to rentals, *flip* means to clean, inspect, and prepare the property for the next tenant's arrival.

franchise   An already-established business that allows you to use its brand and name recognition and also provides support and training on its proven business model.

furnish   For the purposes of this book, to supply a house, room, or structure with necessary furniture, carpets, appliances, and so on.

gross income multiplier (GIM)   A rough measure of the value of an investment property obtained by dividing the property's sale price by its gross annual rental income.

gross rent multiplier (GRM)   The ratio of the price of a real estate investment to its annual rental income before expenses.

homeowner's association (HOA)   A regulatory body established to govern a building or community. HOAs are generally run by a professional management company and governed by an elected group of homeowners.

homeowner's insurance   A type of property insurance that covers a private residence, and the homeowner's possessions, against loss, damage, or accident. Also referred to as hazard insurance.

housing code   A set of minimum standards set by local regulators that specify standards for both construction and maintenance of residential properties.

incentive   Something that incites or tends to incite to action or greater effort, as a reward offered for increased productivity.

insurance premium   The premium paid by the insured party to the insurer.

investment   The spending of money or capital to gain profitable returns, as interest, income, or appreciation in value.

investor   Someone who puts money to use, by purchase or expenditure, in something offering potential profitable returns, as interest, income, or appreciation in value.

landlord   A person or organization that owns and leases out homes or other real estate properties. *See also* lessor.

lease   A contract renting land, buildings, or real estate, to another; a contract or instrument conveying property to another for a specified period or for a period determinable at the will of either lessor or lessee in consideration of rent or other compensation.

lessee   The person to whom property is rented or leased. In residential leasing, he or she is often referred to as the *tenant*.

lessor   The person who rents or leases property to another. In residential leasing, he or she is often referred to as the *landlord*.

liability insurance   Insurance that protects an individual or entity (the insured) from the risks of liabilities imposed by lawsuits and similar claims.

libel   Anything that's defamatory or that maliciously or damagingly misrepresents.

lien   A claim one person has on a property belonging to another as security for a debt or obligation.

maintenance   Care or upkeep, as of property.

master property manager (MPM)   A designation from the National Association of Residential Property Managers for individuals to certify proficiency in property management and specific experience.

Megan's Law   U.S. laws that require sex offenders to register with local law enforcement agencies, notifying them where they live.

mortgage   A conveyance of an interest in property as security for the repayment of money borrowed.

mortgage insurance   An insurance policy on a mortgaged property that protects the lender in case of default by the borrower. Also know as a mortgage guaranty.

Multiple Listing Service (MLS)   A real estate database. Traditionally, such a system was available only to real estate agents, but today, they're open to the public via the internet. The systems vary from one area to another. In some, rental properties are included, while others might list only for-sale properties.

multiunit building   An apartment building that houses several apartments. The building is owned as an entire complex. Individual units are not independently owned as in a condominium building.

National Association of Residential Property Managers (NARPM)   An association of real estate professionals who manage residential properties.

notice to quit   The notice given by a landlord or owner to a tenant either to leave the premises (quit) by a certain date, usually 30 days, or to pay overdue rent or correct some other default.

occupancy   The state of being filled; for the purposes of this book, it means a rental property is being lived in.

premium   The financial cost of an insurance policy, paid either as a lump sum or in installments during the period covered by the policy.

profit   The monetary surplus left to a producer or employer after deducting wages, rent, cost of raw materials, and other expenses.

property   Something a person owns; the possession or possessions of a particular owner.

property inspection   The process of examining and documenting the condition of a property, generally connected to the purchase or lease of the property.

property manager   A person or firm charged with managing a commercial or residential property.

proprietary lease   A type of lease agreement in which a person gets stock in a cooperative.

quit an eviction   To resolve or fix the issue or issues that caused the grounds for eviction. Also called *cure an eviction.*

rate   The amount of a charge or payment with reference to some basis of calculation.

real estate   Property, especially land.

real estate agent   A licensed individual who represents a client in a real estate transaction to buy, sell, or lease real estate in exchange for a commission. An agent must hang his or her real estate license with a real estate broker.

real estate broker   In most states, a broker holds a higher-level license than a real estate agent and is licensed to hire real estate agents to work under his or her supervision. Also called a *real estate agent.*

real property administrator (RPA)   A designation from the National Association of Residential Property Managers for individuals to certify proficiency in property management and specific experience. The designation is earned through a strict program focused on budgeting, accounting, real estate investment, finance, environmental health and safety issues, law and risk management, design, operation, maintenance of building systems, and ethics.

Realtor   A person who works in the real estate business, is a member of the National Association of Realtors, and abides by its code of ethics.

rent   A payment made periodically by a tenant to a landlord in return for the use of land, a building, an apartment, an office, or other property.

rent control   Laws or ordinances that set price controls on the renting of residential housing.

rental agreement   A document that lays out key terms and policies regarding roommates, pets, and other issues related to renting a property.

replacement cost insurance   A type of insurance that covers the replacement cost of an item versus the actual cash value of the item.

Residential Management Professional (RPM)   A property management certification offered by the National Association of Residential Property Managers to licensed real estate agents who meet specific criteria, including years of experience, educational courses, and ethical standards. The agents must be specifically recommended.

revenue   The amount of income received. For the purposes of this book, it's the total amount of rent collected.

security deposit   An amount of money paid in advance on a rental property to protect the property owner in the event of default or property damage.

single-family residence   A self-standing residential property under single ownership designed to be inhabited by one family.

slander   A malicious, false, or defamatory statement or report.

square foot   A unit of area measurement equal to a square measuring 1 foot on each side; 0.0929 square meters. Used in this book to describe the interior dimensions of real property.

staging   To temporarily furnish a property with furniture and a few decorative accessories to give a potential renter a better idea of how the property would look when they move in.

summons   An authoritative command, message, or signal by which one is requested to appear, as in a court summons.

superintendent   A person who oversees or directs some work, enterprise, establishment, organization, district, or other business entity. In multiunit residential buildings, this is the onsite person who oversees building management.

systems maintenance administrator (SMA)   A designation for a person in charge of a team of technicians who run the day-to-day operation of a building. SMAs learn how to streamline the operations of a building and manage energy-efficient, environmentally sound, and cost-effective building systems.

systems maintenance technician (SMT)   A designation for a person who maintains major building systems such as heating, refrigeration, electrical, and plumbing. SMTs learn about the technologies and trends in the maintenance industry and are able to maximize the efficiency and safety of building systems. Trained SMTs possess a broad spectrum of the overall mechanical requirements of the commercial real estate industry.

tenant   A person or group that rents and occupies land, a house, an office, or the like from someone else for a set period of time in exchange for a rental payment. *See also* lessee.

tenants in common (TIC)   A building with multiple units and multiple owners. Each owner has an undivided interest in the whole property.

timeshare   A shared form of property ownership generally in vacation condominium properties. The owner has title only to a portion of time.

title insurance   A form of indemnity insurance predominantly found in the United States that insures against financial loss from defects in title to real property.

townhouse   A type of residential real estate that can be individually owned, has individual entrances, is connected side by side to other private residences through a common side wall, and is also part of a larger community association. Also known as a row house.

triplex   A building, generally under one ownership, containing three side-by-side units with individual entrances occupied by three unique parties.

trust   A relationship whereby property is held by one party for the benefit of another.

turnover   The rate at which you gain and lose properties to vacancy.

Uniform Residential Landlord and Tenant Act (URLTA)   A U.S. law that defines the rights and obligations in the landlord/tenant relationship. Also known as the Landlord Tenant Act.

unlawful detainer   A legal action to evict a tenant that involves properly terminating the tenancy before going to court and seeking possession of the property. It's another process for eviction, or a removal of a tenant from a rental unit. Also known as an eviction lawsuit.

vacancy rate   The percentage of all rental units unoccupied or not rented for a given period of time.

vacant   An unoccupied space.

wear and tear   The gradual physical deterioration of a property resulting from general use, passage of time, and weather. Generally, a tenant must return the leased premises to the landlord in good condition, ordinary wear and tear excepted.

Resources

In this appendix, we share some resources we hope you'll find useful, such as books and magazines to further your knowledge, professional real estate associations, and lots more information to help you stay up-to-date and successful in your investment property adventure.

Residential Property Management Software

As you grow your investment portfolio by purchasing additional properties, and as your rent starts to increase, you'll probably find it difficult to keep track of your property and tenant details without a good software system. Digital software is available online, or on the "cloud," to help you. You pay a monthly fee to use the software, based on the number of properties you have in the system. The online version is regularly backed up, always up-to-date, and protected by security firewalls to prevent viruses and hackers from accessing or corrupting your data.

Property management software has four basic elements:

- Property details and management
- Tenant details and management
- General accounting and reporting
- Property marketing

When evaluating which software is best for you, think about what features you need most because some software is stronger in some areas than others. Also, if you use other software programs, be sure you can download from those programs and use the data in your property management program. For example, if you keep your numbers in QuickBooks, will you be able to download your data directly into QuickBooks, or do you need to export them into an Excel spreadsheet and then upload them into QuickBooks? Or are the accounting reports and details in the property management software complete enough for your needs?

Many rental owners and managers use the following software products. Listing them here doesn't mean we endorse the products, but we feel key features of each can help you become a successful landlord.

These are just a few of the products available. Compare the features and cost structures of the software to determine which is right for you.

Aaxsys
aaxsys.com

Buildium
buildium.com

The Landlord Report/Pro
mdansby.com

PROMAS Property Management Solutions
promas.com

The Property Manager
softwareforlandlords.com

PropertyBoss
propertyboss.com

Propertyware
propertyware.com

Rent Manager
rentmanager.com

RenTec
rentecdirect.com

T-ReX Global
trexglobal.com

Turnover Manager
turnovermanager.com

Yardi
yardi.com

National Real Estate Organizations

Joining a national real estate organization is invaluable to achieving real estate investor success. The right organization keeps you informed on new trends in the industry, tracks pending legislation that could positively and negatively affect your progress, connects you with valuable vendors, and provides educational activities and networking events. Organizations are only as good as the time you choose to participate in them—either in person or by reading their information—so join only if you plan to take advantage of what they have to offer.

American Apartment Owners Association
american-apartment-owners-association.org

Building Owners and Managers Association International
www.boma.org

Building Owners and Managers Institute
bomi.org

Institute of Real Estate Management
irem.org

National Apartment Association
naahq.org

National Association of Home Builders
nahb.org

National Association of Realtors
realtor.org

National Association of Residential Property Managers
narpm.org

National Multi Housing Council
nmhc.org

Books

Following are some other books that can help you achieve your real estate success.

Abudi, Gina, and Brandon Toropov. *The Complete Idiot's Guide to Best Practices for Small Business.* Indianapolis: Alpha Books, 2011.

Corcoran, Barbara. *Shark Tales: How I Turned $1,000 into a Billion Dollar Business.* New York: Portfolio Trade, 2011.

Dempsey, Bobbi, and Todd Beitler. *The Complete Idiot's Guide to Buying Foreclosures, Second Edition.* Indianapolis: Alpha Books, 2008.

Fishman, Stephen, JD. *Every Landlord's Tax Deduction Guide.* Berkeley: Nolo Press, 2012.

Grensing-Pophal, Lin, MA, SPHR, PCM. *The Complete Idiot's Guide to Strategic Planning.* Indianapolis: Alpha Books, 2011.

Moran, Gwen, and Sue Johnson. *The Complete Idiot's Guide to Business Plans Plus.* Indianapolis: Alpha Books, 2011.

Richmond, Peter. *The Complete Idiot's Guide to Buying a Home.* Indianapolis: Alpha Books, 2010.

Rosen, Keith, MCC. *The Complete Idiot's Guide to Closing the Sale.* Indianapolis: Alpha Books, 2007.

Smith, Kimberly. *The Corporate Housing Handbook.* Denver: CreateSpace Publishing, 2013.

Magazines and Other Publications

Multihousing Professional
multihousingpro.com

National Real Estate Investor
nreionline.com

Personal Real Estate Investor Magazine
personalrealestateinvestormag.com

Realty411 Magazine
realty411guide.com

UNITS Magazine
naahq.org/read/units-magazine

Real Estate Educational Forums

BiggerPockets
biggerpockets.com

Real Estate Investor (REI) Expo
reiexpo.com

Real Estate Websites

Realtor
realtor.com

Trulia
trulia.com

Zillow
zillow.com

Additional Resources

Federal Trade Commission Complaint Assistant
ftccomplaintassistant.gov

Find Property Owner
findpropertyowner.com

Internet Crime Complaint Center
ic3.gov

Sample Documents

The documents and forms in this appendix give you a general overview of the paperwork that can help manage your rental properties more efficiently and effectively.

Remember, specific laws vary from state to state, and you should either purchase documents specific to your state or have your documents reviewed by an attorney in your state.

Tenant Communication Forms

Throughout this book, we have discussed how important good communication is to a successful rental experience. The more you can do to plan ahead and have policies and procedures in place, the more successful landlord you will be. The following sample documents can help you effectively communicate with your potential, current, and past tenants.

Acceptance Letter

The acceptance letter is to notify an applicant of approved rental. Use it to inform a new tenant of important information such as address, rent amount, and important local services and providers.

(NAME OF SENDER)
(COMPLETE ADDRESS)
(PHONE NUMBER)
(EMAIL)

Date: _____/_____/_____

(NAME OF RECEIVER)
(COMPLETE ADDRESS)
(PHONE NUMBER)
(EMAIL)

Dear Mr./Ms./Mrs. (LAST NAME),

I am writing this letter of acceptance in reference to the property located at _____. I would like to thank you for your application and hereby accept it. Please note the monthly rent will be $_____, the security deposit will be $_____, and the proposed move-in date will be _____/_____/_____. I will be connecting with you shortly to set up a time for us to review your rental documents. If you have any questions, please feel free to contact me at _____.

(SIGNATURE)
(NAME)

Departure Confirmation

This is the written document you return to the tenant upon receiving his or her departure notice confirming the departure date and reiterating your departure guidelines.

> (NAME OF SENDER)
> (COMPLETE ADDRESS)
> (PHONE NUMBER)
> (EMAIL)
>
> Date: _____/_____/_____
>
> (NAME OF RECEIVER)
> (COMPLETE ADDRESS)
> (PHONE NUMBER)
> (EMAIL)
>
> Dear Mr./Ms./Mrs. (LAST NAME),
>
> I am writing this letter as confirmation of your departure from the property located at _____ on the date of _____/_____/_____.
>
> I would like to thank you for your tenancy and hereby accept your departure notice. Please note you will need to vacate the property by the stated time of _____ on the stated departure date. In accordance to the state laws, your security deposit will be reviewed and returned to you by the following date. _____/_____/_____. If you have any questions, please feel free to contact me at _____.
>
> (SIGNATURE)
> (NAME)

Departure Notice

On a month-to-month tenancy, the departure notice alerts the landlord as to the tenant's specific date of departure. This is generally referred to as a "30-day notice" because that's the length of time the tenant is responsible for the rent from the time he or she gives notice.

(NAME OF SENDER)
(COMPLETE ADDRESS)
(PHONE NUMBER)
(EMAIL)

Date: _____/_____/_____

(NAME OF RECEIVER)
(COMPLETE ADDRESS)
(PHONE NUMBER)
(EMAIL)

Dear Mr./Ms./Mrs. (LAST NAME),

I am writing this letter to confirm my departure from the property located at
_____.

In accordance with the terms of our lease agreement, I am hereby giving 30 days written notice of termination of my lease on the above-mentioned property.

My departure date will be: _____/_____/_____.

The date given above is a definite date to vacate, and no change in the move-out date will be made without the written approval of the landlord.

Tenant forwarding address: _____ (needed for deposit refund).

Rent due through end of notice: $ _____.

(SIGNATURE)
(NAME)

Emergency Contact Numbers

Post a list of emergency contact numbers in the property. Include essential agencies such as police and fire departments.

Police: _____

Fire department: _____

Hospital: _____

Emergency care: _____

Poison control: _____

Animal control: _____

Landlord: _____

Maintenance emergency: _____

Homeowner's association: _____

Key Distribution Record

Keep track of the specific keys you give the tenant. If access cards or garage openers are distributed, be sure to also track the brand name, serial number, and possible access code for easy replacement.

Tenant name: _____

Date issued: _____/_____/_____   Date returned: _____/_____/_____

Unit key:

    Number issued: _____   Number returned: _____

Building key:

    Number issued: _____   Number returned: _____

Building access:

    Number issued: _____   Number returned: _____

Reference information:

_____

Mailbox key:

    Number issued: _____   Number returned: _____

Storage key:

    Number issued: _____   Number returned: _____

Parking access:

    Number issued: _____   Number returned: _____

Reference information:

_____

Other:

_____

_____

Maintenance Request

Use this document so tenants can let you know something in the unit may need to be repaired.

Tenant name: _____

Property address: _____

Date: _____/_____/_____

Maintenance issue:

_____

_____

_____ Yes, I authorize the landlord or necessary maintenance vendor to enter the property to repair the issues.

Comments:

_____

_____

_____   _____/_____/_____

Tenant Signature   Date

Move-In/Move-Out Checklist

Give tenants this move-in/move-out checklist as they move in so they can notify you quickly if something needs to be repaired. This also gives you signed confirmation of the condition of the unit and items therein that you can reference later if you find any damage after the tenant moves out but before you return the security deposit. This should be filled out within 24 hours of arrival and departure.

Move-In/Move-Out Unit Inventory and Condition

	Arrival Condition	Departure Condition	Estimated Repair Cost
General			
Lights (working)			
Windows, window tracks, blinds, screens (clean, working)			
Smoke detector (present, working)			
Entrance door (deadbolt/lock working)			
All walls (clean, free of large marks and scratches)			
A/C, heat (working)			
Carpet in good/clean condition throughout?			
Kitchen			
Floor, countertops, faucet, drains, disposal (clean, working)			
Cupboards, drawers (clean, working)			
Bathrooms			
Tub, toilet, sink (clean)			
Floors, countertops (clean)			
Faucet, drains (clean, working)			
Shower curtain (clean, with liner)			
Medicine cabinet (clean, clear)			

	Arrival Condition	Departure Condition	Estimated Repair Cost
Other			
Patio/balcony (clean, free of trash)			
Doors (locked)			
Garage (if applicable)			

Inspection results accepted: _____

Resident: _____

Date: _____/_____/_____

Notice of Denial

Use this notice to inform a prospective tenant his or her rental application has been denied based on credit report or other information. The notice lists principal reasons for credit denial or other action taken concerning credit. It also includes a statement informing the applicant of his or her rights according to the Fair Credit Reporting Act to dispute the accuracy of any information the consumer reporting agency reported.

(NAME OF SENDER)
(COMPLETE ADDRESS)
(PHONE NUMBER)
(EMAIL)

Date: _____/_____/_____

(NAME OF RECEIVER)
(COMPLETE ADDRESS)
(PHONE NUMBER)
(EMAIL)

Dear Mr./Ms./Mrs. (LAST NAME),

I am writing this letter of denial in reference to the property located at

_____.

Regretfully, your application to rent the above-described premises was not approved for one or more of the following reasons:

( ) Incomplete application, inaccurate or false information, or unable to verify information provided by the applicant.

( ) Insufficient income or debt-to-income ratio to meet qualifying standard.

( ) Information was received from a person or company other than a consumer reporting agency. Under Section 315(b) of the Fair Credit Reporting Act, you have a right to make a written request to me within 60 days of receiving this letter for a disclosure of the nature of this information.

( ) Adverse history of damage to other rental properties or references regarding relations with neighbors.

( ) Information was received from (NAME, ADDRESS, TELEPHONE NUMBER OF PROVIDER). (NAME OF PROVIDER) did not make the decision to take this adverse action and is unable to provide the specific reasons why the adverse action was taken. Under federal law, you have a right to obtain a free copy of a report by making demand on the provider within 60 days of your receipt of this letter. You also have a right to dispute with the provider the accuracy or completeness of any consumer report furnished by them.

During the 60-day period that starts now, you have the right to receive a free copy of your consumer report from the consumer reporting agency marked above. You may have additional rights under the credit reporting or consumer protection laws of your state. Contact your state or local consumer protection agency or a state Attorney General's office.

(SIGNATURE)
(NAME)

Notice of Returned Check

Notify a tenant of a returned check with this form. The notice outlines the details of the return, including information such as check number, date, and amount. It also outlines any resulting charges or fees.

(NAME OF SENDER)
(COMPLETE ADDRESS)
(PHONE NUMBER)
(EMAIL)

Date: _____/_____/_____

(NAME OF RECEIVER)
(COMPLETE ADDRESS)
(PHONE NUMBER)
(EMAIL)

Dear Mr./Ms./Mrs. (LAST NAME),

I am writing this letter to notify you that your check number _____, dated: _____/_____/_____ in the amount of $_____, did not clear the bank. Resubmit this payment immediately to cover your rent and avoid further charges.

Per your rental agreement, the agreed-upon charge for nonsufficient funds (NSF) is $_____.

Please pay the amount of the check, plus the $_____ NSF fee to cover the bank service charge for returned checks, immediately. If you fail to provide these funds, I may consider this nonpayment of rent and take further action.

I appreciate your tenancy, and if you have any questions, please feel free to contact me.

(SIGNATURE)
(NAME)

Potential Renter Inquiry

As soon as you get a call or an email from a potential tenant, fill out this form, which contains questions to ask and information to gather when you speak to the prospective tenant. You can keep this information manually or use a software program to manage your rental requests. This information helps track your marketing success and may also be a good source for marketing the next time your property is available.

Date: _____/_____/_____

Source: _____

Name: _____

Phone: _____

Email: _____

Unit size requested: _____

Number of adults: _____

Number of children: _____

Desired rental rate: $_____

Arrival date: _____/_____/_____

Requested area: _____

Car: Yes/No

Type: _____

Pets: cat/dog/other: _____

Weight: _____

Smoking: Yes/No

Comments:

_____

_____

Reasonable Accommodation Request Form

When a potential tenant requests additional accommodations due to a disability, have him or her fill out this request form.

(NAME OF SENDER)
(COMPLETE ADDRESS)
(PHONE NUMBER)
(EMAIL)

Date: _____/_____/_____

(NAME OF RECEIVER)
(COMPLETE ADDRESS)
(PHONE NUMBER)
(EMAIL)

Dear Mr./Ms./Mrs. (LAST NAME),

I am writing this letter to notify you that I qualify as an individual with a disability as defined by federal and state fair housing laws.

You have a policy that prohibits animals in your building located at _____ _____. Because of my disability, that policy would restrict my ability to use and enjoy an apartment in that building.

In accordance with my rights under federal and state fair housing laws I am requesting that you make an accommodation of your animal policy and allow me to have a

_____.

Please respond in writing, within 10 working days, to my request for the above accommodation.

Thank you for your attention to this matter.

(SIGNATURE)
(NAME)

Tenant Emergency Procedures

In the event of an emergency, you'll need procedures in place for medical emergencies, fire procedures, severe weather, bomb threats, and other situations that may be specific to your property or your geographical area. These instructions will be property specific, so check with your local police and fire department for guidelines specific to your area.

(NAME OF SENDER)
(COMPLETE ADDRESS)
(PHONE NUMBER)
(EMAIL)

Date: _____/_____/_____

(NAME OF RECEIVER)
(COMPLETE ADDRESS)
(PHONE NUMBER)
(EMAIL)

Dear Mr./Ms./Mrs. (LAST NAME),

While you are living at _____, your safety is our highest concern. We don't foresee any security issues, but we want to be sure you have as much information as possible to ensure your safety.

Emergency numbers:

_____

_____

Property evacuation procedures:

_____

_____

Fire escape:

_____

_____

Smoke detectors:

_____

_____

Carbon monoxide detectors:

_____

_____

Water shut-off:

_____

_____

Electrical circuit breaker box:

_____

_____

Property contact information:

_____

_____

Insurance information:

_____

_____

Warning Notice

Use this form to notify a tenant when he or she is in violation of their rental agreement, may be causing property damage, has unauthorized pets, or has gotten noise type complaints.

(NAME OF SENDER)
(COMPLETE ADDRESS)
(PHONE NUMBER)
(EMAIL)

Date: _____/_____/_____

(NAME OF RECEIVER)
(COMPLETE ADDRESS)
(PHONE NUMBER)
(EMAIL)

Dear Mr./Ms./Mrs. (LAST NAME),

I am writing this letter as an official warning in reference to your actions.

The nature of the complaint:

_____

_____

Failure to correct these actions will result in the following:

_____

_____

I appreciate your tenancy, and if you have any questions, please feel free to contact me.

(SIGNATURE)
(NAME)

Leasing Documents

When dealing with tenants, there's basic good communication (covered in the preceding section) and then there are the legal documents that are state specific, generally require an attorney to review, and need to hold up in a court of law. Leases are legally binding documents, but other areas, such as deposits or evictions, also fall into the leasing documents category. The following sample documents give you a general overview of what to expect. Either purchase documents specific to your state or have a real estate attorney review any legally binding documents you plan to use when leasing your rental property.

Three-Day Pay Rent or Quit Notice

A three-day notice to pay rent or quit is issued when a tenant has overdue rent. The notice is drafted with the full names of the tenant, the location of the rented premises, and the landlord's location and name. It's the first step in evicting tenants.

> (NAME OF SENDER)
> (COMPLETE ADDRESS)
> (PHONE NUMBER)
> (EMAIL)
>
> Date: _____/_____/_____
>
> (NAME OF RECEIVER)
> (COMPLETE ADDRESS)
> (PHONE NUMBER)
> (EMAIL)
>
> Dear Mr./Ms./Mrs. (LAST NAME),
>
> Property address: _____
>
> PLEASE TAKE NOTICE that the rent is now due and payable on the above-described property which you currently occupy.
>
> You are hereby required to pay rent in FULL within three (3) days or to remove yourself from and deliver possession of the above-described premises, or legal proceedings will be instituted against you to recover possession of said premises, to declare the forfeiture of the Lease or Rental Agreement under which you occupy said premises and to recover rents, together with $_____ punitive damages, with court costs and attorney's fees, according to the terms of your Lease or Rental agreement.
>
>
> (SIGNATURE)
> (NAME)

PROOF OF SERVICE

I, the undersigned, being at least 18 years of age, declare under penalty of perjury that I served the above notice, of which this is a true copy, on the above-mentioned tenant(s) in possession in the manner(s) indicated below:

On _____, 20 _____, I handed the notice to the tenants.

On _____, 20 _____, after attempting personal service, I handed the notice to a person of suitable age and discretion at the tenant's residence/business and mailed a copy to the tenant's residence by first-class mail, postage prepaid.

On _____, 20 _____, after attempting service in both manners indicated above, I posted the notice on a conspicuous place at the tenant's residence and mailed a copy to tenants residence by first-class mail, postage prepaid.

Executed on _____, 20 _____, at the city of _____, county of _____, state of _____.

Served by: _____

Five-Day Demand Notice

Use this form to take the first step toward collecting late rent. Inform and remind tenants of their lease default, and offer a contact number to call should they have any questions or concerns.

(NAME OF SENDER)
(COMPLETE ADDRESS)
(PHONE NUMBER)
(EMAIL)

Date: _____/_____/_____

(NAME OF RECEIVER)
(COMPLETE ADDRESS)
(PHONE NUMBER)
(EMAIL)

Dear Mr./Ms./Mrs. (LAST NAME),

Property address: _____

PLEASE TAKE NOTICE that the rent is now due and payable on the above-described property which you currently occupy.

You are hereby notified that if you fail to pay your rent in the amount of $_____ in full on or before _____/_____/_____, your tenancy will be terminated. If the rent is paid in full, your rental agreement will remain in effect. If the rent is not paid in full on or before _____/_____/_____, you must vacate the premises and surrender possession or legal eviction action will be started.

(SIGNATURE)
(NAME)

PROOF OF SERVICE

I, the undersigned, being at least 18 years of age, declare under penalty of perjury that I served the above notice, of which this is a true copy, on the above-mentioned tenant(s) in possession in the manner(s) indicated below:

On _____, 20 _____, I handed the notice to the tenants.

On _____, 20 _____, after attempting personal service, I handed the notice to a person of suitable age and discretion at the tenant's residence/business and mailed a copy to the tenant's residence by first-class mail, postage prepaid.

On _____, 20 _____, after attempting service in both manners indicated above, I posted the notice on a conspicuous place at the tenant's residence and mailed a copy to the tenant's residence by first-class mail, postage prepaid.

Executed on _____, 20 _____, at the city of _____, county of _____, state of _____.

Served by: _____

Deposit Itemized Deductions

Use this form to inventory specific detailed repairs, additional cleaning required, or missing items that were deducted from the tenant's security deposit.

(NAME OF SENDER)
(COMPLETE ADDRESS)
(PHONE NUMBER)
(EMAIL)

Date: _____/_____/_____

(NAME OF RECEIVER)
(COMPLETE ADDRESS)
(PHONE NUMBER)
(EMAIL)

Property address: _____

Please be advised that you vacated the property on: _____/_____/_____.

Security deposit received:
$_____

Date received: _____/_____/_____

Interest earned on deposit: $_____

Total amount: $_____

List of damaged property with amount deducted:

_____ $_____

_____ $_____

Total $_____

Cleaning expenses:

_____ $_____

_____ $_____

Total $_____

Total amount deducted from security deposit: $_____

Amount to be returned to tenant: $_____

My signature below states that I have sent this notice to the above tenant.

(SIGNATURE)
(NAME)

Deposit Receipt

Always provide your tenants with written confirmation of the deposit you accept for their rental.

Date: _____/_____/_____

Tenant name: _____

Property address: _____

Security deposit received: $_____

Date received: _____/_____/_____

My signature below states that I have received the above deposit from the tenant.

(SIGNATURE)

Release of the Security Deposit is Subject to the Following Provisions:

- Full term of lease has expired.

- Thirty days WRITTEN notice given.

- No damage to property and/or carpet beyond normal wear and tear.

- Entire property must be clean.

- No scratches or holes in walls.

- No unpaid balances.

- All keys returned.

- Forwarding address must be provided.

- All belongings must be removed.

Eviction Notice

This form specifies the terms and time frame for an eviction and is delivered based on state requirements to the tenant.

Date: _____/_____/_____

Tenant name: _____

Property address: _____

Rent amount due: $_____

Additional reasons:

_____

_____

You are required to vacate and surrender possession of the premises to the undersigned on or before the following:

Date: _____/_____/_____

Time: _____

If you do not agree with this eviction notice, you have the right to legal advice and may contact a lawyer at any time.

If you fail to vacate the premises by the above date, the undersigned may commence eviction proceedings against you and/or exercise other available rights and remedies under the law.

(SIGNATURE)
(NAME)

PROOF OF SERVICE

I, the undersigned, being at least 18 years of age, declare under penalty of perjury that I served the above notice, of which this is a true copy, on the above-mentioned tenant(s) in possession in the manner(s) indicated below:

On _____, 20 _____, I handed the notice to the tenants.

On _____, 20 _____, after attempting personal service, I handed the notice to a person of suitable age and discretion at the tenant's residence/business and mailed a copy to the tenant's residence by first-class mail, postage prepaid.

On _____, 20 _____, after attempting service in both manners indicated above, I posted the notice on a conspicuous place at the tenant's residence and mailed a copy to the tenant's residence by first-class mail, postage prepaid.

Executed on _____, 20 _____, at the city of _____, county of _____, state of _____.

Served by: _____

Lease/Rental Agreement

A written agreement that gives your tenants the right to use your rental property and also specifies the terms under which they may utilize the property.

Tenant Information

Name(s): _____

Address: _____

Phone: _____

Email: _____

Occupant(s): _____

Automobile (make/model/license #): _____

Rental Information

Arrival date: _____

Departure date: _____ (30-day written notice is required)

Extensions possible:

_____

Deposit: $_____ (required to reserve unit; see below)

Rate monthly: $_____ (first month's rent payable in advance)

Pets: cat/dog/other: _____

Weight: _____

Property Information

Property address: _____

Parking: _____

Unit size: _____

Bedroom(s): _____

Bathroom(s): _____

Number of smoke detectors in the property: _____

Rental Payments

First month's rent is due prior to arrival. Rent is then due on the first of each month. Late fee of 5 percent (5%) of invoice plus $5 a day.

Security Deposit/Credit Card Authorizations

Security Deposit or Accidental Rental Damage Insurance Program: For your convenience, you have the option of choosing to pay a security deposit or purchasing the Accidental Rental Damage Insurance (please choose one by initialing by the option of your choice):

_____ Security Deposit/Credit Card Authorizations

A deposit of $1,000 and a valid credit card are required. The undersigned as the owner of the credit card does hereby fully authorize Landlord to charge against the designated credit card account all charges due and owing from this rental agreement at the option of Landlord. Qualified corporations must sign a letter of responsibility. Security Deposits shall be returned to the Tenant, or written accounting made for any portion retained, listing the exact reasons for the retention (missing items/damages, rents, late fees, unit charges, departure fees, excess utilities, phone charges, other charges due under this agreement and interest as due), together with the balance of the Security Deposit within sixty (60) days after departure.

OR

_____ Accidental Rental Damage Insurance Program

You have the option of purchasing the Accidental Rental Damage Insurance Program for a nonrefundable fee of $_____ for _____ days of coverage. This optional deposit waiver covers you for any accidental and pet damage (if disclosed on this lease) up to $3,000. It does not cover any intentional, willful damage or gross negligence. Any damages to the property MUST be reported to the office before check-out. This insurance is nonrefundable but recommended.

Cancellation Policy

NO REFUNDS for early departure or nonarrival.

Key Pick-Up and Drop-Off

Key arrangements should be made with your leasing agent. There is a $50 charge for each missing key or access card.

Partial Month Calculation

All rents are billed on a monthly basis. If your stay starts or ends creating a partial month, the daily rate will be calculated as follows: monthly rate divided by 30 days.

Departure Notification/Extensions

A written 30-day departure notice must be received for all stays.

Holdover

If written notice by either party is not given at least 30 days prior to the termination of the lease, a new month-to month tenancy shall be created subject to the same terms and conditions of this Lease at a monthly rate of $_____ per month, unless otherwise agreed by the parties in writing. Such month-to-month tenancy shall be terminable on thirty (30) days written notice by either party or on longer notice if required by law.

Departure

Tenant is to leave the property clean upon departure. (Failure to do so will result in additional charges.)

Checkout Procedure

Lock all doors upon departure. Make key drop-off arrangements with your agent. Failure to depart by 11:00 A.M. shall result in an additional day of rent. Landlord is not responsible for items or mail left behind.

Parking

Not all units have parking, and space is very specific for each property. Information should be obtained from your reservation agent, and additional charges may be incurred for parking. Landlord is not responsible for stolen or damaged vehicles. Your vehicle may be towed if not parked in designated parking space. Any parking cards, garage openers, etc. not returned to Landlord will result in an additional charge ranging from $50 to $175, depending on the specific garage.

Rules and Regulations

Tenant shall comply with the specific covenants, conditions, and restrictions applicable to the rental property and/or condominium association. Violation may result in fines or eviction.

Occupying Tenants

Landlord must know the names of each person occupying this unit. Tenant info may be given to the building management.

Pets

For each pet, there is a $500 pet security deposit and a $300 nonrefundable fee. Undisclosed pets will result in a minimum $500 fee.

Smoking in Unit

All units are absolutely nonsmoking. Deposits may be forfeited and a minimum $1,500 fee assessed if tenant smokes inside the unit.

Emergencies

24-hour maintenance emergency service is available by calling _____.

Utilities

Lessee will pay for:

_____ Cable	_____ Gas	_____ Sewer
_____ Electricity	_____ Internet	_____ Telephone
_____ Garbage	_____ Oil	_____ Water

Agreements

Lessee agrees to the following:

- Make no repairs to the property without the consent of the lessor.

- Repair, at their cost, all damage made to the property, including glass, heat, air-conditioning, electrical, plumbing, and hot water.

- Keep sidewalks, steps, and parking areas free and clear of ice, snow, and other debris.

- Keep grass cut and hedges trimmed adjacent to the property.

- Allow the lessor to access the property for purpose of inspection, to show the property to prospective tenants or buyers, and to make repairs.

- Allow the lessor to enter the property in case of emergency without the lessee's permission.

- Obtain renter's insurance.

- Upon lease termination, leave the property in good condition and free of all personal items and debris.

- Leave in the property any fixture added to the property.

- Abide by all federal, state, local, and building codes, laws, and rules.

- Not allow animals without the lessor's written permission.

- Not assign or sell this lease without the lessor's written permission.

- Not park anything other than a primary vehicle in the provided parking space.

- Pay $_____ for any check returned as NSF from the bank.

Homeowner's Association

This lease is subject to the terms of the Association Documents. A copy of the Association's rules are provided to the lessee with the lease.

Indemnification

Tenant shall neither hold, nor attempt to hold, Landlord, Landlord's agents, contractors, or employees liable for any injury, damage, claims, or loss to person or property occasioned by any accident, conditions, or casualty to, upon, or about the property, including but not limited to defective wiring, the breaking or stopping of the plumbing or sewage upon the Property, unless such accident, condition, or casualty is directly caused by intentional or reckless acts or omission of Landlord. Notwithstanding any duty Landlord may have hereunder to repair or maintain the Property, in the event that the improvements upon the Property are damaged by the negligent, reckless, or intentional act or omission of the tenant or any licensees, invitees, or co-tenants, Tenant shall bear the full cost of such repair or replacement. Tenant shall hold Landlord, Landlord's agents, and their respective successors and assigns harmless and indemnified from all injury, loss, claims, or damage to any person or property while on the Property or any other part of the Property, which is occasioned by an act or omission of the Tenant, Tenant's licensees, invitees, or co-tenants. Landlord is not responsible for any damage or destruction to the Tenant's personal property. Tenant shall obtain renter's insurance at the Tenant's sole discretion and expense.

Default

If the Tenant shall be in arrears in the payment of any installment of Rent, any Additional Payments or charges due in this agreement, or any portion thereof, or in default of any other covenants or agreements set forth in this lease ("Default") and the Default remains uncorrected for a period of three (3) days after Landlord has given written notice, then Landlord may, at Landlord's option, undertake any of the following remedies without limitation:

a. declare the Term of the Agreement ended;

b. terminate the Tenant's right to possession of the Property and reenter and repossess the Property pursuant to other relief to which Landlord is entitled;

c. pursue Landlord's lien remedies;

d. pursue breach of contract remedies; and/or

e. pursue any and all available remedies in law or equity. In the event possession is terminated by reason of a Default prior to expiration of the Term, the Tenant shall be responsible for the Rent and Additional Payments and Charges occurring for the remainder of the Term, subject to Landlord's duty to mitigate such damages.

Pursuant to applicable law [13-40-104 (d.5), (e5), and 13-40-107.5, C.R.S.] which is incorporated by this reference, in the event repeated or substantial Default(s) under the Lease occur, Landlord may terminate Tenant's possession upon a written Notice to Quit, without a right to cure. Upon such termination, Landlord shall have available any and all of the above-listed remedies.

Attorneys'/Collection Fees

In the event of any default or breach of this lease agreement or for defense of unwarranted claims, the nonbreaching party shall be entitled to recover all costs and expenses, including a reasonable sum for attorney fees expended or incurred by reason of any default or breach of any of the terms of this Agreement or defense of unwarranted claim, whether or not suit is filed. The parties agree that venue for any dispute shall be proper in the county in which the premises are located, the parties waive any right to jury trial, and Resident hereby grants to landlord authorization to obtain information from credit reporting agencies for the purposes of locating the resident. Any outstanding amounts owed by the Resident shall bear interest at the rate of eighteen percent (18%) per annum from when due.

Reserved Rights

Absent written instructions on the contrary, resident hereby grants Landlord authorization to enter the unit under the following conditions: (a) To make necessary or agreed-upon repairs, cleaning, alteration, or improvements following resident's request or a 24-hour notice given by Landlord; or (b) Emergency situations.

Use

Tenant shall use and occupy the Property only as a private residence with a maximum occupancy as set forth on page 1 of this lease and shall not use the property for any purpose prohibited by the applicable laws of the United States or the State of _____, or of the ordinances of the city or town in which the property is located, or the Homeowner's Association rules in which the property is located. Tenant shall not permit any portion of the Property to be used in a manner that may endanger the person or property of Landlord, co-tenants, or any person living on or near the Property. The Tenant shall keep all portions of the Property in clean and habitable condition and will not make any alterations or additions to the Property without Landlord's written approval.

Miscellaneous

A. This rental agreement is subordinate in all respects to the rights of any recorded liens and/or encumbrances. The tenant shall subordinate to the interests of any new mortgage loan for the Property or encumbrances.

B. Survival or Representations, Warranties, and Agreements. All the representations, warranties, covenants, promises, and agreements of the parties contained in this Agreement (or in any document delivered or to be delivered pursuant to this Agreement or in connection with the Closing) shall survive the execution, acknowledgment, sealing, and delivery of this Agreement, the closing, and the consummation of the transactions contemplated hereby.

C. Entire Agreement. This Agreement constitutes the full, entire, and integrated agreement between the parties hereto with respect to the subject matter hereof and supersedes all prior negotiations, correspondence, understandings, and agreements among the parties hereto respecting the subject matter hereof.

D. Assignability. This Agreement shall not be assignable by any party without prior written consent of Landlord.

E. Binding Effect; Benefit. This Agreement shall inure to the benefit of and be binding upon the parties hereto and their respective heirs, personal and legal representatives, guardians, successors, and, in the case or Purchaser, its permitted assigns. Nothing in this Agreement, express or implied, is intended to confer upon any other Person any rights, remedies, obligations, or liabilities.

F. Enforcement. Any provision of this Agreement which is held by a court of competent jurisdiction to be prohibited or unenforceable shall be ineffective to the extent of such prohibition or unenforceability without invalidating or rendering unenforceable the remaining provisions of this Agreement.

G. Amendment. No provision of this Agreement may be amended, waived, or otherwise modified without the prior written consent of all of the parties hereto. No action taken pursuant to this Agreement, including any investigation by or on behalf of any party, shall be deemed to constitute a waiver by the party taking such action of compliance with any representation, warranty, covenant, or agreement herein contained. The waiver by any party hereto of a breach of any provision or condition contained in this Agreement shall not operate or be construed as a waiver of any subsequent breach or of any other conditions hereof.

H. Section Heading. The section and other headings contained in this Agreement are for reference purposes only and shall not affect the meaning or interpretation of this Agreement.

I. Counterparts. This Agreement may be executed in any number of counterparts, each of whom shall be deemed to be an original and all or which together shall be deemed to be on and the same instrument.

J. Applicable Law. This Agreement is made and entered into, and shall be governed by and construed in accordance with, the laws of the State of _____.

K. Further Assurances. Tenant agrees to execute, acknowledge, seal, and deliver, after the date hereof, without additional consideration, such further assurances, instruments and documents, and to take such further actions, as Landlord may request in order to fulfill the intent of this Agreement and the transactions contemplated hereby.

L. No Sublease. Tenant shall not sublet any part of the property nor assign this rental agreement, or any interest therein, without the written consent of Landlord.

M. Brokerage disclosure to Tenant. The Broker, Landlord, and Tenant referenced above have NOT entered into a tenant agency agreement. The Broker is the Landlord's Agent, and the Tenant is a customer. A customer is a party to a real estate transaction with whom the broker has no brokerage relationship because such party has not engaged or employed the broker, either as the party's agent or as the party's transaction-broker.

_____   ____/____/____

Tenant Signature   Date

_____   ____/____/____

Landlord Signature   Date

Lease Addition or Amendment

Use this form to amend or add to the original lease if you and the tenant agree to new or revised terms during the lease, such as the addition of a roommate or a pet.

Tenant name: _____

Property address: _____

Lease date: _____/_____/_____

Terms:

_____

_____

_____   _____/_____/_____
Tenant Signature   Date

_____   _____/_____/_____
Landlord Signature   Date

Lease Renewal

Use this lease renewal agreement when a tenant's lease is about to expire to allow the tenant to continue to live in the property for a specific period of time. If a lease renewal is not signed, the tenant rolls over to a month-to-month tenancy situation.

Date: _____/_____/_____

Tenant name: _____

Property address: _____

Lease date: _____/_____/_____

This document is to serve as an addition to the lease referenced above.

Terms:

_____

_____

_____   _____/_____/_____
Tenant Signature   Date

_____   _____/_____/_____
Landlord Signature   Date

Lease Termination

If you choose not to give the tenant the option to renew his or her lease, this letter gives your tenant the official notice the lease will not be able to be renewed.

Date: _____/_____/_____

Tenant name: _____

Property address: _____

Lease date: _____/_____/_____

This notice is to alert you that the lease referenced above is set to terminate on _____/_____/_____ and that you will not be offered an option to re-lease the above-referenced property.

_____   _____/_____/_____

Landlord Signature   Date

Letter of Responsibility

You'll see this letter from a corporation on behalf of its employee if it is taking responsibility for the rent and potential damage of your rental.

Date: _____/_____/_____

Landlord: _____

Company name: _____

Property address: _____

Tenant name: _____

Lease date: _____/_____/_____

Our company, _____, will be responsible for the payment of rent, departure fee, and additional fees incurred in connection to the lease referenced above. This agreement shall remain in effect for the duration of occupancy of our employee(s). In addition, we will be responsible for the payment, if applicable, of excessive cleaning or damage above wear in connection to the rental property listed below.

Complex: _____

Property address: _____

Arrival date: _____/_____/_____

Departure date: _____/_____/_____

Monthly rent: $_____

Deposit: $_____

Departure fees: $_____

Name of occupant(s): _____

_____ will be named as the responsible party on the rental of the above-listed property and will make all rental payments. Upon lease execution, Tenant will be invoiced the first month's rent. Each subsequent monthly rent will be invoiced in advance and is due on the first of each month and is late on the fifth of each month.

Company Leasing Unit will be responsible for the payment of additional fees billed to the unit:

Company Leasing Unit will accept responsibility for any undue damage beyond normal wear and tear.

AGREED TO AND ACCEPTED:

_____   _____/_____/_____
Company Signature   Date

_____   _____/_____/_____
Landlord Signature   Date

Rental Rate Change Notice

Notify residents that their total monthly rent, including amenities, will be increased with this rental rate change notice. The document should include fields to input the new monthly rent, anticipated 6-month lease renewal rate, and anticipated 12-month lease renewal rate.

Date: _____/_____/_____

Tenant name: _____

Property address: _____

Lease date: _____/_____/_____

This notice is to alert you that the lease referenced above is set to terminate on _____/_____/_____ and that the new rental rate, should you choose to extend, will be $_____ per month for _____ (period of time for extension).

_____   _____/_____/_____

Landlord Signature   Date

Permission to Enter Notice

Unless in an emergency, it's essential to get written authorization from your tenant prior to entering the rental property. The Permission to Enter (PTE) notice can also be utilized if the tenant has requested maintenance or if you need to enter the property for general maintenance or to show the property to the next potential tenant.

Date: _____/_____/_____

Tenant name: _____

Property address: _____

Lease date: _____/_____/_____

You are hereby given notice that your landlord/agent will be entering your rental unit on _____/_____/_____ between the times of _____ and _____.

OR

I authorize Landlord or qualified vendors to enter the property referenced above on _____/_____/_____ between the times of _____ and _____.

The purpose for entering is as follows:

_____

_____

_____   _____/_____/_____
Tenant Signature   Date

_____   _____/_____/_____
Landlord Signature   Date

Pet Agreement

Agree to pets in writing. This agreement documents the conditions under which tenants may have pets and details any deposits or fees per animal.

Date: _____/_____/_____

Tenant name: _____

Property address: _____

Lease date: _____/_____/_____

This document is to serve as an addition to the lease referenced above.

The following pet is authorized in the rental property:

_____

The following additional terms are added to the lease:

_____

_____

The new rental rate will be: $_____

The additional security deposit will be: $_____

_____   _____/_____/_____
Tenant Signature   Date

_____   _____/_____/_____
Landlord Signature   Date

Property Management Agreement

Should you decide to put your rental property into a property management company's management program, you'll receive this agreement.

THIS AGREEMENT made and entered into by and between:

_____

_____

Recitals:

a. Owner holds title and is the owner of the following described real property:
_____, here referred to as the property.

b. Property Manager is in the business of operating and managing real estate similar to the above-described property. Property Manager may also be referred to in this agreement as Agent.

c. Owner desires to engage the services of Property Manager, a professional rental management company, in order to obtain the best rental revenue and the highest-quality management services, and Property Manager desires to provide such services on the following terms and conditions.

Employment of Property Manager

1.1. Property Manager shall act as the exclusive agent of Owner to manage, lease, operate, and maintain the property.

1.2. This agreement shall be for a term of 12 months commencing on
_____/_____/_____.

1.3. If this Agreement has not been terminated in accordance with the provisions below relating to termination, it shall automatically renew for an additional 1-year term at the end of the initial term and at the end of each succeeding renewal term.

1.4. Owner is returned _____% of the adjusted gross rents with Property Manager credited with _____% of the adjusted gross rents. Owner's return will be prorated based on actual number of days contracted to tenant. Adjusted gross rents shall mean gross rents less applicable taxes, referral fees, maid service fees, and other direct costs of booking the unit.

Agent Duties

2.1. On assuming the management and operation of the property, Property Manager shall thoroughly inspect the property. This inspection shall contain the opinion of Property Manager concerning the present condition and recommended changes. After conferring with Owner and obtaining approval to make any necessary improvements, Property Manager shall undertake completion of the improvements. Missing inventory items will be automatically placed in the unit and charged to the owner's account.

2.2. Property Manager shall make reasonable efforts to lease the property and shall be responsible for all negotiations with prospective tenants. Property Manager shall also have the right to execute and enter into, on behalf of Owner, lease and rental tenancies of the property. Property Manager may negotiate all extensions and renewals of such tenancies and leases.

2.3. Rental Agent shall use good faith, due diligence, and all reasonable efforts to achieve the highest rental income for Owner, consistent with caring for and preserving the Property in the long term. Accordingly, Rental Agent shall have the sole authority to set rental rates, deposit requirements, and discounts, and otherwise manage the business aspects of the rental activities.

2.4. Rental Agent shall deposit all rental receipts in a trust account complying with the rules and regulations of the State Commission until monthly disbursements are made.

2.5. Rental Agent shall provide all managerial and housekeeping services for the Property.

Owner's Duties

3.1. To keep the Property in "first class" structural condition, furnished in a manner acceptable to Rental Agent, and maintain any grounds under the exclusive control of the Owner in a manner reasonably determined by Rental Agent to exhibit the Property's highest potential.

3.2. Owner agrees to provide:

_____

_____

3.3. Owner agrees to provide the following utility expenses, at Owner's expense:

_____

_____

3.4. Owner shall timely pay all costs associated with ownership of the Property, including, but not limited to, debt service, owner association assessments and membership fees, and charges for access to onsite or subdivision amenities.

3.5. Owner agrees to pay Rental Agent for a thorough seasonal clean which shall include a professional carpet cleaning and touch-up painting. Charges incurred by the property from work done by subcontractors may be disbursed on Owner's behalf by Rental Agent and collected from Owner's account.

3.6. Owner agrees not to enter the property, or to permit any person to enter the property, without the prior approval of Property Manager during any period of time covered by this agreement.

Advertising and Promotion

4.1. Rental Agent shall advertise vacancies by reasonable means, such as featuring unit on the web or displaying in office windows.

4.2. Rental Agent shall, at its sole expense, design, compose, produce, and distribute all printed promotional materials and advertising. Rental Agent shall plan, organize, and implement all marketing activities deemed reasonable and/or necessary by Rental Agent.

4.3. Rental Agent's primary marketing is through direct relationships with corporations, relocation companies, and other corporate housing agencies.

Maintenance, Repairs, and Operations

5.1. Property Manager shall use its best efforts to keep the property maintained. In this regard, Property Manager shall use its best skills and efforts to serve the tenant of the property and shall purchase necessary supplies, make contracts for, or otherwise furnish electricity, gas, fuel, water, telephone, window cleaning, refuse disposal, pest control, and any other utilities or services required for the operation of the property. Property Manager shall make or cause to be made and supervise necessary repairs and alterations to the property.

5.2. Maintenance caused by negligence will be charged to the tenant; however, in all events, Owner shall be responsible to Property Manager for all such maintenance if uncollectible from tenant. The cost of all maintenance, repairs, and operations shall be deducted from any revenues delivered to Owner.

5.3. In the event that an appliance (such as a refrigerator) or fixture (such as a hot water heater) shall fail, Rental Agent shall immediately attempt to contact Owner and make arrangements for the immediate repair or replacement of the failed item. In the event Rental Agent is unable to timely communicate with Owner, Rental Agent shall be authorized to make the repair or replacement on Owner's behalf and at Owner's expense whenever Rental Agent determines that those costs would be less than the potential loss of rental revenue the Property would suffer if the guests vacated or had to be moved to another property.

5.4. In-house maintenance labor fees: $_____

5.5. Subcontracted maintenance, contracted out on Owner's behalf, is passed on to the Owner with a _____% markup.

Reimbursements

6.1. Costs resulting from this agreement, except for those costs expressly assumed by Property Manager, shall be charged to Owner. To the extent there are insufficient funds available from revenues received from the operation of the property, the Owner shall reimburse Property Manager for such costs within 15 days after demand for such reimbursement.

Government Regulations

7.1. Property Manager shall manage the property in full compliance with all laws and regulations of any federal, state, county, or municipal authority having jurisdiction over the property.

Insurance

8.1. Owner shall maintain, at Owner's expense, comprehensive general liability insurance, including coverage for premises, operations, and contractual liability with limits of not less than $500,000 per occurrence.

8.2. It is recommended that Owner carry either individually or through their HOA fire and casualty insurance covering all structures, "Loss of Rents" coverage, and damage to personal property coverage.

8.3. Owner shall name Property Manager as an additional insured and provide Property Manager with certificates of insurance from time to time to evidence that such insurance remains in effect over the term of this agreement.

Collection of Income; Institution of Legal Action

9.1. Property Manager shall use its best efforts to collect promptly all rents/other income issuing from the property when such amounts become due. It is understood that Property Manager does not guarantee the collection of rents.

9.2. In the event a tenant fails or refuses to pay any sum due for the rental use of the Property or for damage to the Property, Rental Agent shall use good faith and due diligence to collect such funds from the guest's deposits, open credit cards, or other means reasonably available, including drafting and issuance of demand letters and/or the conduct of negotiations with the tenant.

9.3. Property Manager shall, in the name of Owner, execute and serve such notices and demands on delinquent tenants as Property Manager may deem necessary or proper. Property Manager, in the name of Owner, shall process collection reports against a delinquent tenant or the property of a delinquent tenant as may be necessary to enforce the collection of rent or other sums due from the tenant, to enforce any covenants or conditions of any lease or rental agreement, and to recover possession of any part of the property.

Bank Accounts

10.1. Property Manager shall deposit (either directly or in a depositary bank for transmittal) all revenues from the property into the general property management trust account of Property Manager, here referred to as the trust account. Property Manager shall not commingle any of the above-described revenues with any funds or other property of Property Manager. From the revenues deposited in the trust account, Property Manager shall pay all items with respect to the property for which payment is provided in this agreement, including the compensation of Property Manager and the reimbursements due to Property Manager. After such payments, Property Manager shall remit any balance of monthly revenues to Owner concurrently with the delivery of the monthly report referred to in this agreement.

Records and Reports

11.1. Property Manager shall maintain books, accounts, and records reflecting all revenues and all expenditures incurred in connection with the management and operation of the property.

11.2. Property Manager shall furnish to Owner, no later than the end of the next succeeding month, a detailed statement of all revenues and expenditures for each preceding month, a summary of all concessions, and rental concessions.

11.3. Within thirty (30) days after the end of each calendar year, Property Manager shall prepare and deliver to Owner a statement of revenues received and expenditures incurred and paid during the calendar year that result from operations of the property.

Additional Duties and Rights of Property Manager

12.1. In addition to the foregoing, Property Manager shall perform all services that are necessary and proper for the operation and management of the property and shall report to Owner promptly any conditions concerning the property that, in the opinion of Property Manager, require the attention of Owner.

12.2. Property Manager shall use reasonable diligent efforts to correct problems as they may occur. However, Property Manager makes no representation that Property Manager is capable of providing repairs in all circumstances, and Owner agrees that Property Manager shall not be responsible for any loss of rental income or for damages to the Unit from circumstances not discovered by Property Manager or for Property Manager's failure to make repairs.

12.3. Property Manager shall be under no obligation to advance any of its funds to pay any expense, tax, or charge on behalf of Owner.

Termination and Renewal

13.1. At the termination of this agreement, it shall be renewed automatically on an annual basis.

Sale of Property/Access

14.1. Nothing herein shall be interpreted to relieve Owner from the obligation to honor all binding reservations made by Rental Agent.

14.2. Owner shall notify Property Manager in writing of any possible sale or listing for sale of the property as soon as such sale is negotiated.

IN CASE OF ANY DISPUTE REGARDING ANY TERMS OR PERFORMANCE OF THE TERMS OF THIS AGREEMENT, THE DISPUTE SHALL BE SUBJECT TO BINDING ARBITRATION IN ACCORDANCE WITH THE RULES AND REGULATIONS THEN EXISTING UNDER THE AMERICAN ARBITRATION ASSOCIATION IN THE CITY OF _____, STATE OF

_____.

Should either party bring suit to enforce any of the terms of this agreement, the prevailing party shall be entitled to recover court costs and reasonable attorney fees.

This agreement may not be modified unless such modification is in writing and signed by both parties to this agreement.

IN WITNESS WHEREOF, the parties have executed this agreement.

_____   _____/_____/_____

Property Owner Signature   Date

_____   _____/_____/_____

Property Manager Signature   Date

Rental Application/Background and Credit Check Application

Before accepting a prospective applicant, conduct a background investigation. This form authorizes and records background information such as a prospect's residential and credit histories. Information collected on the form includes reference checks, previous resident addresses, and credit or income verification.

Date: _____/_____/_____

Tenant name: _____

Home phone: _____

Cell phone: _____

Email: _____

Social Security number: _____

Date of birth: _____/_____/_____

Driver's license number and state: _____

Co-tenant name: _____

Home phone: _____

Cell phone: _____

Email: _____

Social Security number: _____

Date of birth: _____/_____/_____

Driver's license number and state: _____

Current address: _____

How long at this address? _____

If less than 3 years at current address, list previous addresses:

_____

_____

_____

Other states you have lived?

_____

_____

Current monthly rent: $_____

Current employer: _____

Salary: $_____

Supervisor's name: _____

Phone: _____

Additional income:

_____

_____

Current landlord's name: _____

Phone: _____

Previous landlord's name: _____

Phone: _____

Have you ever been convicted of a crime? Yes/No

If yes, give date(s) of arrest and state of police department:

_____

_____

Nature of the crime:

_____

Closest relative (name, address, phone, email, relationship):

_____

_____

List pets and descriptions:

_____

_____

Credit card information: _____

Name of bank: _____

Address: _____

Phone: _____

Checking account number: _____

Major credit card type: _____

Account number: _____

Expiration date: _____/_____/_____

A nonrefundable fee of $_____ per person is required to process this application. Landlord will approve or decline the credit application within 72 hours.

- I authorize Landlord to use my Social Security number to check my credit report for rental purposes only.

- I certify that the information given on this application is true and correct.

- I hereby authorize, without reservation, any and all corporations; former employers; credit agencies; educational institutions; law enforcement agencies; city, state, and county courts; military services and persons to release information they may have about me to Landlord or background check company. This releases the aforesaid parties from any liability and responsibility for collecting the above information. I further acknowledge that a telephonic facsimile shall be as valid as the original.

_____   _____/_____/_____

Applicant's Signature   Date

Property Forms

You can't afford *not* to take care of this huge financial investment. You just spent hundreds of thousands of dollars to purchase this rental property, and you expect to pull in rental income for a long time to come. The following documents can help. These don't need to be reviewed by an attorney, and they're not state specific. Look at these documents as general ideas, and then update the details to cover all the important aspects of your specific rental property.

Appliance Tracking Sheet

Before you rent your property, make a complete list of all the appliances, including the make, model, serial number, warranty information, year purchased, and general condition. Update this list between each renter. These details will streamline maintenance issues and make filing an insurance claim a lot easier.

Date: _____/_____/_____

Appliance	Make	Model	Serial Number	Warranty	Year Purchased	General Condition
Dishwasher						
Dryer						
Furnace/ HVAC						
Garage door opener						
Garbage disposal						
Microwave						
Oven/stove top						
Refrigerator						
Thermostat						
Washer						
Water heater						

Cleaning Checklist

Use this checklist, or one you adapt specific to your property, to log the cleaning information of the interior and exterior of your property. Give this list to any outside cleaning company you may hire to clean the property between tenants.

Date: _____/_____/_____

Area/Item	Completed	Notes
Kitchen		
Stove		
Refrigerator		
Sink		
Dishwasher		
Cupboards		
Floor		
Walls		
Baseboards		
Fixtures		
Bathroom(s)		
Showers/bathtubs		
Sinks		
Toilets		
Cupboards		
Floors		
Walls		
Baseboards		
Fixtures		
Vents		

Area/Item	Completed	Notes
Living Room/Bedrooms		
Floors		
Walls		
Baseboards		
Fixtures		
Vents		
General		
Fireplace		
Garage		
Porch		
Front door		
Fixtures		
Yard		
Washer/dryer		
Windows		

Maintenance Checklist and Record

Use this checklist, or one you adapt specific to your property, to log the routine maintenance items of the interior and exterior of your property. Keep a history of a unit's repairs and services with a maintenance record. This form can be used to record the date and description of work, as well as any remarks or comments remaining

Date: _____/_____/_____

Area/Item	Completed	Notes
Mechanical		
Heater		
Air conditioner		
Water heater		
Appliances		
Dishwasher		
Refrigerator		
Garbage disposer		
Washer/dryer		
Plumbing		
Sinks		
Toilets		
Water softener		
Sump pump		
Pipes		
General		
Fireplace		
Lightbulbs		
Air vents		
Windows/window wells		
Roof		
Walls		
Flooring		
Sprinklers		

Work Order

Use this form to indicate what maintenance work is to be done, when it should be completed, and who will do the work. After completing the work order form, you can use it as the maintenance record of the response to the service request or to charge the tenant for the work done.

Tenant name: _____

Property address: _____

Date: _____/_____/_____

Issue(s):

_____

_____

Work done:

_____

_____

Materials

Quantity	Material(s)	Cost per Item	Total
Total material cost			

Labor

Employee	Date	Time In	Time Out	Total Time	Cost
Total labor cost					
Total work order					

Index

D

E

F

J-K

L

Q-R

U

V

W-X-Y-Z